PUPIL AND TEACHER

An Introduction to Educational Psychology

22774

710 050677-0

PUPIL AND TEACHER

An Introduction to
Educational Psychology

by

JAMES MAXWELL, M.A., B.Ed.

Principal Lecturer in Psychology
Moray House College of Education, Edinburgh

GEORGE G. HARRAP & CO. LTD
London · Toronto · Wellington · Sydney

First published in Great Britain 1969
by GEORGE G. HARRAP & CO. LTD
182 High Holborn, London, W.C.1

SBN 245 59692 5

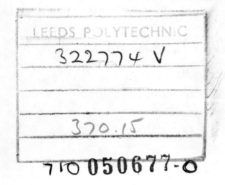

Composed in Monotype Times Roman and printed by J. W. Arrowsmith Ltd.,
Bristol 3.
Made in Great Britain

Preface

According to the astronomers, the universe is expanding rapidly. Something similar has been happening in psychology during the last fifty years. Different branches of the study are developing so rapidly that any connections between them are being lost. It is no longer possible to write a book on psychology based on a coherent body of doctrine and covering all branches of the subject.

Psychology has much to offer to the teacher, both as a source of knowledge about children's behaviour and as a way of thinking about children. If the diversity of contemporary psychology is becoming more than a professional psychologist can encompass, still less can the practising teacher be expected to keep himself well informed and able to distinguish between what is new and what is valid. This book aims at relating some of these diverse developments in psychology to teaching practice. The core of the book is the classroom rather than a system of psychological doctrine.

There are many whose assistance in the writing of this book should be acknowledged. It owes much to discussions with my colleagues in the Psychology Department of Moray House: Dr J. H. Duthie (now of Stirling University), Miss M. M. Cowe, Dr J. R. Calder, Mr K. Hignett, Mr H. S. McNair, and Dr W. D. S. Stewart, and in particular to Mr J. W. Coulthard, who read the draft manuscript, and whose pertinent comments proved very helpful. Less directly, but still substantially, students training as teachers have contributed much, as have practising teachers with whom the various topics have been discussed from time to time.

Finally, thanks are due to the writers and their publishers who have permitted their material to be quoted in the text.

J. M.

Contents

Learning

Learning is the very substance of education, and we would expect that the extensive research and theorizing by psychologists on the processes of learning would help the teacher engaged in educating children. In fact, the amount of information of immediate value to the teacher is disappointingly small. As Bugelski says (*The Psychology of Learning*, p. 452), "There is a great gap between the laboratory and the classroom. Nothing is gained by ignoring the gap." Another psychologist, Meredith, has likened education to cookery. A knowledge of colloid chemistry may help the cook to avoid disasters, but the skill needed to make a good omelet is not wholly dependent on a knowledge of chemistry.

How the Teacher's and the Psychologist's Approach to Learning differ

Why, then, has the work of the psychologists not had greater application in education? It is not that psychologists are more interested in rats than in children, or that they regard education as irrelevant to learning. It is rather that teachers and psychologists have different immediate aims, that they are asking themselves different questions about learning, and are therefore seeking different answers and using different methods to find these answers. The ultimate aim of both is probably much the same, to find ways to help children to learn in the most effective and satisfying way; but they approach that ultimate aim by different routes.

The teacher is concerned with the selection of the kinds of behaviour a pupil is required to learn. It may be specific, such as the learning of a list of irregular verbs, or the method of solving simultaneous equations. Or it may be more general, in the construction of a curriculum in English or geography. He is also concerned with the learning of acceptable forms of behaviour, punctuality, neatness, orderliness in school, and more generally with the kinds of behaviour described as truthfulness, consideration for others, and the like. And since selection invariably involves rejection, the teacher is concerned that the pupil does not learn forms of behaviour considered as undesirable. Much of education is directed to the prevention of learning the wrong answer, the bad habit, the unacceptable behaviour. To the psychologist as such, who is engaged in the study of learning, many of the teacher's distinctions are not very relevant. If the process of learning is the same, it is not of great concern to the psychologist whether the list of verbs is in French or Latin. So too with the learning of habits. If the ways in which a child learns bad habits are the same as those in which he learns good habits, the psychologist, though he may socially disapprove, cannot make a distinction in terms of learning processes. What the psychologist is interested in is how pupils learn behaviour which they also have learned is wrong, and so should not be learned. If the psychologist can establish the conditions under which children readily acquire undesirable habits, he has also learned something which may help him to understand how children may learn desirable habits.

The teacher is also concerned about the methods of presenting the material to a class of children. He seeks the most effective and interesting presentation, but too seldom examines objectively and critically how effective his chosen methods are, in comparison with others. The special contribution of the psychologist is not to endorse one method rather than another, but rather to investigate, by objective assessment of the changes in children's behaviour, what are the likely consequences of the use of such a method by a certain kind of teacher, with certain kinds of pupils. For example, the psychologist may find that pupils learning to read by methods based on a sight, or 'look and say', approach may become faster silent readers than a matched group of pupils who learn by a mainly phonic approach, but that the latter group are better and more expressive readers aloud. Or he may find that the use of the initial teaching alphabet material results in the good readers becoming even better, but does not appear to have any advantage over traditional orthography for those pupils who find difficulty in learning to read. At this point the teacher must decide which method is most appropriate for his educational aims; the psychologist proceeds to make further and more detailed investigations into what differences there are between the two ways of learning.

It often happens that the psychologist is unable to give the teacher any information. The teacher may be under educational pressure to introduce mathematical concepts into the primary school curriculum, and has to adopt some method of presentation. The psychologist cannot reach any conclusion without evidence, and until the behaviour of children who have been presented with such concepts can be studied by the psychologist, he can reach no clear conclusion. In such a situation, there can be a wide gap between psychological investigation and classroom practice. The best the psychologist can do is to reach a very provisional opinion based on other studies of learning and development in children. In this particular instance, the psychologist would tend to have serious doubts about the ability of primary school children to learn a mathematical mode of thought, but his first response would be to seek further objective evidence rather than make recommendations about either content or method. The teacher, on the other hand, has to decide what to do, and may be under pressure to adopt changes before the psychologist has had time enough to collect adequate evidence about the effects of reforms on the pupil's later learning and behaviour.

Another concern of the teacher is that the pupil's learning should extend beyond the limits of the school curriculum. The teacher hopes, and often comes to believe, that the study of chemistry or the reading of novels will lead to a continuing interest in science and literature; or that modes of thinking learned in a particular course of chemistry will be transferred to other topics, and that practice in writing English will enable the pupil to find ways of 'self-expression' in other aspects of his life. The psychologist asks if this is indeed the case. How much transfer is there from one learning activity to another, and under what conditions does the transfer take place? Does a pupil who has learned some chemistry find biology easier to learn, and how much easier, and in what ways? Once again this is a matter for psychological experiment, observation, and measurement. Similarly, if a pupil is expected both to learn chemistry and to think in a scientific manner, would it be more effective to teach the pupil two different sets of skills, chemistry and scientific thinking? What happens if we do? And do pupils who go on mountaineering expeditions learn to be 'self-reliant' and the like, or do they just learn how to climb mountains? To the psychologist it is a matter of definition and evidence.

Another point at which there is a gap between teaching and psychology is in the meaning of the word 'learning'. To the teacher, the pupil who cannot remember any of his list of irregular verbs has not learned them; to the psychologist, learning is a process which can be distinguished from remembering, as the two processes have different psychological characteristics. We discuss these characteristics later, but for the teacher retention is the essence of school learning, whereas to the psychologist the pupil who says he has learned his verbs but has forgotten them can be making a correct and reasonable statement.

Finally, there is a difference between the teacher's and the psychologist's assessment of learning. A pupil may be set the task of learning the life history of the eel. To find out how much he has learned, the teacher sets some kind of test, formal or informal. If the pupil knows enough about the eel to meet the teacher's requirements, the teacher is satisfied; the pupil has learned the life history of the eel adequately. But the psychologist would not accept this as an assessment of learning. If the pupil came to the topic already interested and informed on eels, he could satisfy the teacher, but to the psychologist no learning may have taken place. For the psychologist, the only proper assessment of learning is the difference between the pupil's behaviour before the learning process and after it. If the difference is large, then there has been a considerable amount of learning; if the difference is small, there has been relatively little learning.

THE PSYCHOLOGICAL STUDY OF LEARNING

The gap between the psychological study of learning and classroom practice is not absolute, but it cannot be completely bridged until the psychological theories of learning have been established by the methods of psychological investigation, and their relevance to classroom methods has been examined. To the psychologist investigating the processes and conditions of learning, the classroom situation is chaotic. Pupils are of different levels of ability, have different degrees of interest in what they are learning, have different motives for learning, and begin their learning from different levels of previous knowledge and skills. Some attend to the learning task for most of the time, others not. The same learning task may involve different psychological processes of learning, and different pupils may adopt different ways of learning the same task. Some may 'understand', others may be learning the same material 'by rote'. What different kinds of learning processes there are, and under what conditions learning is most effective, cannot be investigated until these various processes and conditions have been sorted out, analysed, observed, and measured. We begin, therefore, by following the psychologist's methods of inquiry into the process called learning, and see how far it takes us. The methods used in the study of learning are very similar to those used in the psychological study of other topics related to education, and, as we shall see later, the psychologist investigates such topics as remembering, thinking, intelligence, or personality by using the same kind of techniques.

The Psychologist's Methods of Investigation

The psychologist studies behaviour, and learning can only be examined in terms of changes in behaviour. Put in its simplest terms, psychological inquiry involves definition of the sector of behaviour being investigated, experiment or systematic observation of the conditions under which changes of behaviour take place, and methods of measuring differences of behaviour.

Learning may be defined as the process by which observed changes in behaviour attributable to active experience take place. Not all observed changes in behaviour are learned, so we must distinguish between changes due to maturation, or the natural process of growth, and changes due to experience. The word 'active' is used to distinguish changes due to learning from those due to accident, drugs, illness and deprivation. The definition implies that we are considering children as continuously acquiring new forms of behaviour, and modifying older ones; the learning is a necessary consequence of the child's activity. Though we aim at distinguishing different kinds of change of behaviour, in practice a child's behaviour is the outcome of the interaction between the processes of learning and maturation, as well as his physical and emotional condition at the time.

Maturation

We discuss maturation more fully in the next chapter, but to clarify the distinction between learning and maturation a few examples of maturational changes in behaviour are given. A baby of a few weeks old cannot walk upright, though it would appear that it could make all the necessary movements needed in walking, and its physical strength is adequate. Such a baby cannot learn to walk, because, in ordinary language, it has not grown yet to the stage of walking, or, in more technical terms, its nervous system has not yet developed to the point where co-ordination of the baby's movements becomes possible. When that point is reached the baby begins to make attempts at walking, which it can now manage, and if given opportunity will learn how to walk easily and efficiently. The change from crawling to walking behaviour had to await the natural process of growth, that is, maturation; when this is completed, learning may follow. Talking follows the same general pattern. Until the child's nervous system has grown sufficiently for his intellectual and physical abilities to cope with talking, the child cannot learn to begin talking. When he has developed these abilities he begins to talk, but whether he talks in English or French is a matter of learning. The most easily observed aspects of maturation are those involving physical growth, but, as we shall see, there is evidence that there are maturational changes in the child's intellectual, emotional, and social behaviour as well.

How do we know when Learning has taken place?

We have already emphasized that we cannot observe directly the process of learning; we can only observe changes in behaviour. Anything more is interpretation, which may be misleading. Thus, if we want to distinguish between a pupil who has learned 'parrot-wise' that a quarter and a quarter make a half, and a pupil who 'understands' that two quarters make a half, we can only make the distinction in terms of observed differences in the behaviour of the two pupils. If both pupils, when asked what is a quarter plus a quarter, give the same answer, "a half", then both pupils have learned to add a quarter and a quarter, as their behaviour has changed from the time when they could not give the answer; but no further difference is observable, so we cannot distinguish parrot learning from understanding. This distinction between rote and meaningful learning is one that has given the psychologists very great difficulty. There is evidence that the two pupils have learned, but there is no evidence that there is difference in the learning. For a time the psychologists tried to side-step this difficulty by trying to eliminate any possibility of understanding or meaning in their studies of learning by using nonsense material, such as lists of syllables like WUK, SOV, and so on, but even here it was found that the subjects tended to attribute meaning, sometimes indecent, to the syllables. This phase of the psychological investigation of learning is largely past now, and serious attempts are being made to clarify the relationship between learning and thinking. The problem, however, is far from being adequately solved; it represents one aspect of the gap between learning theory and teaching practice. Teachers tend to make the distinction between rote learning and understanding more readily than the psychologists can. If the teacher, quite reasonably, should ask the psychologist how to distinguish between the pupil who understands and the pupil who does not, the psychologist, equally reasonably, must reply that if there are no observable differences in behaviour, he cannot establish any difference.

The Need for Rats

The psychological approach to the study of learning requires the psychologist not only to define clearly and assess objectively those sectors of behaviour under investigation, but also to control the conditions under which learning is taking place, so that he may measure how changes in these conditions affect learning. How much repetition is needed to establish a simple learned response? How does strength of motivation affect speed of learning? How are motives, drives, and needs measured? Does learning take place in stages, or is it a continuous process? Do we learn more quickly at the beginning of a task, or at the end of it? How is the method of learning related to the difficulty of the task? Are there different patterns of learning, according to the nature of the task? What degree of similarity between different tasks is needed for the learning of one to have an effect on the learning of another? What are the effects of rewards for success in learning? Are immediate rewards more effective than delayed rewards? Does the same apply to punishments? How are responses most effectively extinguished, by delay, punishment, or withholding rewards?

To answer these and other such questions, the psychologist needs precisely controlled conditions, in which any changes in behaviour can be attributed to changes introduced by the experimenter, and to no other changes. The school learning situation, as we have seen, is very far from fulfilling these requirements. Pupils, as we have noted, do not all begin their learning from the same point, nor do pupils always know when their learning has been successfully completed. Very little school material is self-correcting.

To reduce the learning process to its most elementary form, where changes can be measured precisely and conditions can be controlled, the psychologist has to turn from the complex processes of human learning to the simpler forms of learning found in animals. Rats, pigeons, and dogs are frequently used in the study of the more elementary learning processes, and dolphins, monkeys, and apes for learning in situations requiring intelligence nearer to that of human beings. Rats can be set to run mazes with some confidence that each rat is learning from the same initial level of ability, and under the same conditions. Even then, for some of the more precise experiments, it proved necessary to breed special strains of rats, like the Wistar strain, to eliminate individual differences in ability. This attempt to breed out inherited variability in ability is an interesting story in itself. The result was to demonstrate that the inheritance of differences between individuals is as much a part of heredity as the inheritance of resemblances.

Though the study of learning in rats enables us to observe learning in its most basic forms, it does not follow that the findings can be applied directly to human beings. What happens is that a principle of learning derived from rats is then tried out in a human learning situation. If there are differences between the human learning process and that observed in rats, then we analyse this difference and return to the rats to observe the process in its elementary form. This reduction to the simplest and most easily controlled situation is essential to any scientific approach. To establish the basic essentials of learning in the laboratory is not too difficult; the main difficulty is getting the findings back into the complex and uncontrolled learning situation of a school class.

THE BEHAVIOURISTS' INTERPRETATION OF LEARNING

The psychologist, therefore, is virtually driven by the needs of his scientific approach to analyse behaviour into its most elementary units, and on the basis of these to develop his explanation of more complex forms of learning. One such elementary unit of behaviour is the Stimulus-Response unit, usually represented as S-R. Where such a unit of behaviour is inborn it is called a reflex; the new-born baby shows a number of such reflexes, a few others develop by maturation. Common reflexes are the response of coughing to a particle in the windpipe, blinking and eye watering to a particle in the eye, turning the head towards a sudden loud sound, or the contracting of the pupil of the eye in response to a bright light. The change in the environment is the stimulus, the change in behaviour which follows it is the response. The term 'stimulus' is particularly difficult to define precisely, as it involves the question of whether every response or change in behaviour must necessarily be associated with an identifiable stimulus. The question is of theoretical interest, but in practice most of our behaviour can be analysed into S-R units. These may be considered as the bricks of the structure of our total behaviour.

The human being is equipped with a small number of reflexes, not enough even to maintain life, so most of the S-R units of our behaviour are learned. Basically, the process of learning consists in acquiring new responses to a stimulus, or learning to make the same response to different stimuli. Learned behaviour is an extension of innate behaviour, but the adaptability of the human being is such that nearly all our behaviour is, in this sense, learned.

Behaviourism is the name given to a psychological theory of behaviour which begins from the principle that the basis for the scientific study of psychology is that the only observations which can be made are those of changes of behaviour. These can then be related to observed changes in the environment, which include observable changes in the bodily condition of the learner. Experiences like pain, hunger, satisfaction, thinking, and the like cannot be observed, and therefore cannot be investigated by the psychologist. Anger is not an experience to the behaviourist; it is an observable pattern of behaviour only. A behaviourist does not deny experience; if he puts his hand on a hot plate he reports pain like the rest of us. His argument is that no-one can observe his pain, they can only observe his behaviour. The approach aims at being wholly objective. The behaviourist approach is logically very strong; but though it has produced much valuable information about human behaviour, it has never been wholly accepted as the basis of psychological thinking. Before discussing the theory, let us examine in more detail how the behaviourist theory explains learning.

Classical Conditioning

The pioneer work on conditioning was performed by the Russian physiologist and psychologist, Ivan Pavlov, in the early years of this century. He was investigating the digestive processes of dogs. When food was presented to a dog, its mouth watered, the saliva was collected by a tube, and the amount measured. This response of salivating to the stimulus, food, is a reflex, called by Pavlov an Unconditioned Reflex (UCR). Then, as the food was presented, a bell was rung. This double presentation of the food and the bell was repeated several times; finally the bell alone was presented and the dog salivated as before, this time in the absence of food. A Conditioned Reflex (CR) had now been established, the response of salivating now being elicited by the conditioned stimulus, the bell. The original S-R of salivation to food remained. The dog had now acquired a pattern of behaviour which it did not have before; in other words it had learned to salivate to a bell.

This process of learning is commonly known as classical, Pavlovian, or respondent conditioning. There have been very thorough investigations into this kind of learning, and a number of its characteristics are now well known. First, there must be an innate or unconditioned reflex as the starting point for learning. Secondary conditioning is possible, such that when the CR, bell-saliva, is established, there is next a presentation of bell + light, leading after some repetition to the establishing of the secondary CR, light-saliva. This secondary CR is not easy to establish, and without the occasional reinforcement of a food presentation it fades out very quickly. Second, repetition is necessary to establish a CR; immediate learning does not take place. Also the rate of learning is not related to the intelligence of the animal. Third, if the CR is not periodically reinforced by the presentation of the unconditioned stimulus, food, the CR fades out. The flow of saliva to the bell diminishes and the CR is said to be extinguished. This is not the same as forgetting, which would be measured by the amount of saliva after an interval in which no stimulus of either kind had been presented. Forgetting appears to occur less rapidly than extinction. Fourth, there is the phenomenon called Stimulus Generalization. If a CR becomes established for one conditioned stimulus, the same response tends to be elicited by other similar or related stimuli. The dog salivates not only in response to the pitch of the original bell, but to bells of a different pitch, and indeed to any bell-like sound. This process of stimulus generalization gave Pavlov some trouble in his earlier inquiries, as it was found that his dogs began to salivate before the food was presented; they responded, by stimulus generalization, to the sound of the attendant's steps and the clink of the food cans. He found soundproof rooms necessary to observe conditioning in its basic form.

Finally, there is the allied phenomenon of Stimulus Discrimination. If, for example, a CR has been established for a red light and generalized to an orange light, it should be possible by withholding the unconditioned stimulus, food, to extinguish the CR to the red light, and to reinforce the response to the orange light. This is only possible if the dog can distinguish between red and orange lights of the same intensity. The way of finding out whether the dog is able to make such a distinction or not is to try the experiment. This is, in fact, the means by which the sensory discrimination of animals is investigated. By this means it has been established that cats, dogs, cattle, and horses are virtually colour-blind, and that most insects, fishes, birds, and apes are able to discriminate between colours. The attempt, therefore, to establish stimulus discrimination by using colour with dogs would not succeed; but if repeated with sounds of different pitch it is possible to demonstrate stimulus discrimination. What happens when, as in the colour experiment, the unconditioned stimulus, food, is sometimes presented and sometimes not presented with what to the dog is the same conditioned stimulus, a light? The answer is that learning takes place, if at all, much more slowly. And what happens if, when stimulus discrimination has been established for two sounds of different pitch, the pitches of the two sounds are brought close together, to the point that the dog fails to discriminate between them? The answer is that the dog begins to behave in a way very similar to that of a neurotic human being. To the behaviourist, neurosis is not a state of emotional distress, but a pattern of disorganized behaviour showing conflict between different responses to the same set of stimuli.

Classical Conditioning and Learning

As a theory of learning, classical conditioning is based on very sound experimental evidence and satisfies fully the behaviourists' demands for precise and objective observation of behaviour changes under controlled conditions. What conditioning theory fails to answer adequately is one of the critical questions in all learning, how does the new stimulus become attached to the existing response? The answer is almost certainly in terms of connections between neurones, or nerve cells; but our knowledge of the workings of the nervous system is still too limited for any adequate explanation.

Classical conditioning as a form of learning does not have much relevance in the school situation. The scheme of classical conditioning and the observed patterns of school learning do not fit each other very closely. Conditioned responses are easier to establish in animals than in human beings; the reverse is true for most learning. Repetition is necessary to establish a CR, but much human learning is achieved on one occasion. Repetition to prevent forgetting is not the same as repetition to establish a learned response in the first instance, though certain neuro-muscular skills like those involved in reading or handwriting may be an exception. But even here there is evidence that the learning of skills benefits from a period of rest, an observation expressed many years ago in William James's saying that we learn to skate in summer and to swim in winter.

It does not follow from what we have said about conditioning and school learning that classical conditioning does not play some part in the learning of children. D. O. Hebb has suggested that there are at least two kinds of learning, which he calls early learning and late learning. It could be, and there is some but not conclusive evidence to support it, that some of our early and basic patterns of behaviour are established by conditioning. The child who readily responds by temper, or by tears, may have established this pattern of responses early in life by a process of conditioning. Pavlov was led from a study of conditioning to a study of his dogs' temperaments, or habitual modes of response.

Aversion therapy, which is closely allied to conditioning, is being used with some success with both children and adults in eliminating undesired behaviour like over-eating, smoking, addiction to alcohol, and specific irrational fears. The drug apomorphine elicits the response of severe vomiting. The drug is given by injection so timed that the vomiting will follow almost immediately after alcohol is taken. Apomorphine plus alcohol are administered on a series of occasions, each eliciting the vomiting response. The apomorphine is stopped, and the CR, alcohol-vomiting, remains. To maintain the CR occasional reinforcement with the drug is needed. The patient seeks to avoid the vomiting response, and therefore avoids the stimulus, now alcohol. This follows the same pattern of conditioning as Pavlov's dogs with food, bell, and salivation. The additional element in the aversion therapy situation is the patient's motive to be cured of his addiction. This form of learning appears to succeed with some addicts, but not with the confirmed alcoholic.

Operant Conditioning

The main contribution of classical conditioning has been to the theory of learning and to the development of experimental techniques, rather than to the practice of learning. Psychologists studying the process of operant conditioning are more concerned with investigating the conditions under which learning takes place, and the ways and means of applying these conditions to ensure that the desired behaviour is acquired. B. F. Skinner, one of the leading exponents of this approach, talks about 'shaping' behaviour. In operant conditioning the learner plays a more important part. Pavlov's dogs did nothing but respond to the stimulus; they have been described as 'empty organisms'. In operant conditioning successful learning depends on the learner's behaviour, he is responding to a situation rather than to a specific stimulus. Skinner's learners, mainly pigeons and humans, are actively seeking a satisfying form of response behaviour; he describes behaviour, perhaps not too happily, as being 'emitted' by the learner.

A typical experiment in operant conditioning is one in which a rat is placed in a box fitted with a bar which the rat can press down, a device to produce a clicking sound, and a small tray into which a food pellet can roll. When a hungry rat is put into the box its food-seeking behaviour is characterized by a wide range of responses. The rat sniffs around the box, nibbles at the tray, scratches in the corners, or reaches up against the walls. The experimenter sounds the click, and a food pellet rolls into

the tray. This is soon discovered by the rat, and after a few trials
the rat learns to turn to the tray when there is a click. The next
stage is to connect the pressing of the bar to the clicking device.
As the rat moves about in the cage, it turns to the side which contains the bar. The click sounds and the rat obtains food. Soon the
rat learns to turn to that side to obtain food. Then the rat may
begin to scrape against that side. Again the click sounds, but,
after a few trials, only when the rat scrapes the side. The final
stage of shaping is when, during the scraping behaviour, the rat
presses the bar. Once again the rat obtains food; after one or two
trials the food is withheld from the scraping response, and given
only for the pressing response. The rat's behaviour has been
'shaped' so that the 'correct' response has been acquired by the
successive elimination of ineffective responses. The response of
pressing the bar has become established by reinforcement with
food; the other components of the rat's behaviour have become
extinguished by their failure to produce food.

As with classical conditioning, certain conditions have to be
fulfilled before learning takes place. If food fails to appear after
the bar is pressed, this response will fade out; it will be extinguished
like the others. Immediate and continued reinforcement of the
'correct' response is necessary for effective operant conditioning.
Repetition is also necessary, not only to establish the desired
response, but also to shape the total behaviour by extinguishing
unwanted responses. Stimulus discrimination is common to both
classical and operant conditioning; indeed, operant conditioning
may be considered as a process of successive stimulus discrimination in which the satisfying response becomes distinguished from
other responses. Finally, secondary conditioning can also occur.
The most frequently quoted example is Cowles's Chimpomat.
Chimpanzees learned to press a lever to obtain discs, which they
then learned to put in a slot machine which produced fruit. The
basic reinforcement was the obtaining of fruit, but the discs can
be considered as secondary reinforcement for the pressing of the
lever. Though some chimpanzees tended to save up discs, they
all ultimately cashed them for fruit.

Though Skinner and others have developed the concept of
operant, or instrumental, conditioning, the study of this kind of
learning began about 1900 with E. L. Thorndike's experiments
on cats. It was then known as Trial and Error learning. In a typical

experiment a cat was placed in a puzzle box, from which it could escape by pulling a loop of string. The time taken by the cat to escape was recorded for a series of trials; this time continued to be reduced till the cat could immediately release the catch and escape. Over the series of trials the correct response was established and errors eliminated. From his observations, Thorndike formulated a number of laws of learning, of which the principal one is the law of effect. This states that the response most effective in leading to satisfaction of the learner is most likely to become established.

Both Thorndike and Skinner were interested in the application of their learning theories to educational practice. Both investigated the effects of reward and punishment. Thorndike, who thought of learning as the establishment of neural bonds, or connections between stimulus and response, concluded that reward was more effective than punishment in establishing connections, and hence in determining behaviour. Skinner distinguishes between negative reinforcement and punishment. A pigeon placed in a cage where food can be obtained by the response of pecking a bar, receives food; this is a positive reinforcement of the pecking response. Other responses do not result in food; these responses are being negatively reinforced, and tend to become extinguished. Both positive and negative reinforcement have the effect of increasing the probability of the desired response. Punishment, on the other hand, is used to prevent a response occurring. If the pigeon pecks at the bars of the cage, and receives an electric shock, that response is punished, and the response ceases to be made. It appears that when punishment is given at intervals, it has the effect of holding an undesirable response in check, but it does not necessarily eliminate it. To return to the example of the drinker of alcohol, the effect of the apomorphine is to punish the response of taking alcohol. As long as alcohol is sought for satisfaction by the drinker, the response is only held in check and not eliminated; if by any means the satisfaction obtained by the drinking of alcohol could be removed, then by negative reinforcement the drinking response would be extinguished.

Thorndike also extended his findings on the trial and error learning of cats to the learning of arithmetic by school pupils. He investigated the conditions under which connections or bonds were formed between numbers presented to the pupils, and concluded that pupils learned multiplication tables according to much the same pattern of learning as the cats showed in escaping from the puzzle boxes. Skinner has developed a method of teaching, called Programmed Learning, directly derived from operant conditioning, in which the conditions found most effective in shaping behaviour are applied to school learning. Programmed Learning is discussed more fully in a later chapter.

MORE COMPLEX FORMS OF S-R LEARNING

As we have seen, the psychological investigation of learning tries to begin by isolating and observing the process of learning in its most elementary form, in this case the acquiring of an S-R unit of behaviour. Now that learning has been analysed into its elementary units, in which the processes of reinforcement, extinction, stimulus generalization and discrimination, and secondary conditioning are operating, the next step is to inquire how these elementary units and processes can be built up into more complex systems of learning which will not only adequately explain the observed features of school learning, but also enable us to predict the conditions under which such learning will be most effective. We are now beginning to close the gap between learning theory and school practice. We shall follow broadly the scheme proposed by R. M. Gagné in his book *The Conditions of Learning*. The development from simple to more complex patterns of learning can be thought of as a pyramid, in which each level is dependent on the establishment of the previous level.

Conditioning

The base of the pyramid is classical conditioning, where a general response is transferred from one precise stimulus to another. This can also be called 'signal' learning, as the stimulus is a signal for the response to occur. Salivation was the particular part of the total response Pavlov chose to measure; the dog's response was more general than salivation only. The second level is operant conditioning, where both the stimulus and the response are specific; behaviour is shaped by establishing a specific response (*e.g.*, pecking) to a specific stimulus (*e.g.*, a bar). A Pavlov dog responds to the signal bell by setting the whole digestive process in motion; a Skinner dog will learn to 'shake hands' for a titbit.

Chaining

This scheme of learning consists of a number of learned S-R units being connected in a series in definite order, the response of one unit frequently being the stimulus of the next. Many routine activities are examples of chaining. Putting on clothes in the morning is one example, where each step tends to follow the other in a definite sequence. The sequence of starting a car is a chain of S-R units—insert key, switch on, check gear lever, start engine, look in mirror, depress clutch, release hand brake, and so on. If the series is broken—for example, by not having gear in neutral, or not releasing the hand brake—then the chain is ineffective, and successful accomplishment of the task involves other kinds of learning. Much rote learning in school follows this scheme of chaining. A pupil learning a poem by heart is learning a chain of verbal responses, in which one word, or group of words, acts as the stimulus for the next. If the sequence is broken, prompting by supplying the next word as stimulus will set the pupil off on the chain once more. If he learns the poem stanza by stanza, the last words of each stanza become the stimulus for the first words of the same stanza, and a circular chain is formed in which a prompt of the first words will set the pupil repeating the stanza. Also, the pupil who, when asked what is six times eight, has to proceed through the whole chain of the six times table, is not unknown to teachers. The pupil learned the table as a chain. There are many other instances where chaining is the system of learning: playing a musical instrument, serving a tennis ball, sawing wood on a mitre block, setting up a retort stand, or typing a group of words are all examples. It is not enough for a typist to tap the correct key for each of the letters e, n, o, p, r, s to learn to type the word "response"; the sequence must be learned as well. Much of the learning of what are called skills involves this process of chaining, and such chains appear to be relatively permanent elements in our learned behaviour. Extinction does take place, by failure to reinforce. As the main reinforcement is the successful performance of the activity, occasional exercise of the behaviour pattern tends to keep the chain established.

Verbal Association and Multiple Discrimination

One of the difficulties of the S-R explanation of behaviour is found in the use of such terms as 'verbal behaviour', 'verbal stimulus', and 'verbal response'. The behaviourists rightly point out that speaking is just another observable form of behaviour like blinking or grasping, except that it is performed by a different set of muscles. Thinking cannot be observed, so, to the behaviourist, learning to use language can only be defined in terms of learning responses to verbal stimuli, or learning verbal responses to stimuli of different kinds. Pavlov's dogs learned to salivate to the sound of a bell, but could equally have learned to respond to the spoken word "bell". The same applies to operant conditioning. A child is offered a sweet, and learns to say "Thank you" before getting the sweet. The sweet reinforces the verbal response, and the child has learned a desirable form of behaviour. The teacher points to the word "dog" in a reader, and asks, "What does this word say?" The pupil's verbal response is, "Dog". A pupil is asked, "What is six times eight?" and responds, "Forty-eight".

The S-R theory has no difficulty in explaining certain types of language learning. A co-operative parrot can learn to respond to "Five and five" by "Ten". A cageful of parrots could learn the multiplication tables; they may sometimes forget, but so do children. The difficulty with language arises when we consider how the pupil learns the response, "triangle". He cannot be presented with all possible triangles as stimuli; but when presented with a particular triangle which has not been presented before he responds with "triangle". Later he will learn about the properties of a triangle which is not equilateral, scalene, or isosceles, but all of these. The immediate difficulty of reconciling S-R verbal responses with the more extensive use of language can be met by regarding language as having two functions. One we call 'signal' language, the other 'sign' language. The example of the word "triangle" represents sign language, and this function is discussed later in connection with concept learning. If we confine our discussion to the use of signal language we can proceed to examine the next two levels of the learning pyramid, verbal association and multiple discrimination.

Signal language is the type of verbal behaviour we have been discussing in S-R terms. The word "bath" to a child is a signal which is the stimulus for a chain of responses, not necessarily the same for each child. The pupil who learns to recite a stanza of verse is chaining a series of verbal responses. Verbal association goes one stage beyond pure chaining. The basic form of verbal association is naming objects or actions. The structure, in S-R terms, is the object as stimulus (*e.g.*, a pencil) with the response of noting its characteristics, followed by the verbal response, "pencil". In verbal association there is a mediating link, in this case the observation of the properties of a pencil and the identification of them as the appropriate stimulus for the word "pencil". A similar link may be found in the verbal associations formed in learning a foreign language—for example, French "cheval", link caval(ry), response "horse". Or the link may be a picture of a horse. It is evident that the S-R theory is beginning to get into difficulties, but if the signal use of language is adhered to, the process is still adequately explained.

The level of learning called Multiple Discrimination depends on verbal association. The teacher who learns the names of the pupils in his class is learning by this process. He learns to discriminate between a number of initially similar stimuli, in the shape of pupils in a new class, and attaches to each pupil the appropriate response, the pupil's name. He does not need to ask what is the meaning of the words "Mary Jones"; they remain a signal. The pupil who learns to distinguish between 3 + 4, 3 − 4, and 3 × 4, and to respond with the appropriate chain of S-R units is learning by multiple discrimination. Multiple discrimination is a higher level of learning than stimulus discrimination as observed in dogs. The dog can only discriminate between stimuli presented to it, and then only within very limited numbers. The dog cannot name the different stimuli; it is the use of language which makes multiple discrimination possible. Much of a pupil's progress in a school subject depends on learning to discriminate differences in stimulus situations and make the correct chain of responses. Most of it is in terms of verbal behaviour. Taking geography as an example, the pupil learns to discriminate between the different symbols used in maps, between the features of different regions, climatic, topographical, economic, and so on. Many of the responses consist of naming responses, including definitions. The level of learning is still what teachers might call rote learning, but this level is a necessary step in the pyramid, and more complex forms of learning cannot develop without a foundation of more elementary learning. The geographer cannot develop theories or concepts without first having acquired the basic information on which generalizations and classifications can be built.

Concept Learning

So far, the S-R theory of behaviour has been able to account satisfactorily for the processes of learning. Most animal learning ceases at the chaining level, and by limiting the use of language to signals, human learning can continue in S-R terms to the multiple discrimination level. But at this point the S-R explanation breaks down. The difficulty is in accounting for the findings of an experiment like that of Harlow on learning by monkeys. The monkeys learned, by operant conditioning, to obtain food when the middle one of three lights was on. They were then transferred to a situation in which the food was placed in the middle box of three. The monkeys who had learned to respond to the middle light learned to respond to the middle box more quickly than a control group of monkeys who had not previously learned to respond to the middle stimulus. The stimuli, boxes and lights, were very different; and stimulus discrimination is not an adequate explanation. What is new in this learning situation is the concept 'middle', which is a classification made by the learner, and not a character of the stimulus. Though we can identify a light as red, or bright, or large, we cannot describe that light as middle. The stimulus itself remains the same whether the learner classifies or not.

There is no doubt but that much human learning, and some learning by the more intelligent animals, is concept learning. The human learner has the advantage of language, and at this stage the use of language as a sign enables human learning to proceed beyond animal learning. Sign language is used to represent the properties of a class of stimuli. 'Dog' as a signal may mean, "Look at the dog" or "Beware of that dog", but as a sign it represents the class of animals which have the characteristics common to all dogs. Concept learning depends therefore on a system of signs, of which language is the most extensive. The difficulty of the S-R learning theory in explaining this process of learning lies in the identification of the stimulus in the S-R unit. The learner is responding to his classification, and though the response may be observed, the stimulus cannot. Explanations in terms of S-R theory have been advanced in terms of stimulus generalization, internalization of the stimulus, and chaining from 'light' to 'middle light' by verbal association, but none of these is wholly convincing. The essential difficulty remains; pupils who have learned to discriminate between three spoons and four spoons can discriminate between three books and four books without having to go through the same learning process again in a different stimulus situation.

Principle Learning

Though the S-R learning theory appears to fail to explain the features of the higher levels of the learning pyramid in terms of observable S-R units of behaviour, the discontinuity is in terms of theoretical explanation rather than of the development of learning behaviour. Concept learning can only be attained on the basis of previous and more elementary forms of learning. In the same way the level of principle learning is developed from concept learning. Essentially, principle learning is the learning of a chain of concepts. Thus the grammatical principle that a subject in the singular is followed by a predicate in the singular form implies the concepts of 'singular' and 'subject' and 'predicate'. The principle that the area of a rectangle is obtained by multiplying the length by the height depends on linking the concept of area with the concepts of length, height, and multiplication. If the verbal stimulus, "area of a rectangle", were a signal for the verbal response, "length times height", the level of learning would be chaining of verbal S-R units; the test of principle learning would be to find whether the pupil could find the area of a number of rectangles of different dimensions.

Problem Solving

This form of learning represents the peak of the pyramid. Problem solving can be regarded as the chaining of a series of principles. To solve a problem the learner must have an understanding of the nature of the solution. Even if the procedure is by trial and error, he must be able to recognize the solution when he finds it; otherwise the problem remains unsolvable. For example, a pupil has learned the principle that the area of a rectangle is length times height. He is presented with a parallelogram and asked to find the area. He can link at least two sets of principles; the first is the principle that he has learned for the area of rectangles; the second is the principle that cutting a plane figure into different pieces does not alter the total area. He cuts off the sloping ends of the parallelograms, and fits them together again to form a rectangle, whose area he can find. Alternatively he can use the principles that 'rolling up' a parallelogram does not affect its area, and that the curved surface of a cylinder can be peeled off to form a rectangle; again he has solved the problem by learning to chain a series of principles. He has learned how to find the area of a parallelogram.

We should emphasize that problem solving is not a different kind of learning from the previous types; it is the extension from concept learning to principle learning to problem-solving learning, and each depends on the mastery of the previous level. Any kind of 'discovery' learning in which the pupils have not established the concepts and principles involved is ineffective. A class of young pupils are shown the experiment in which a metal ball is shown to be just too big to pass through a metal ring. The problem is to get the ball through the ring. The ring is heated, expands, and the ball passes through. What have the pupils discovered? The answer depends on what principles the pupils have already learned, and whether they have learned to link them together in this kind of problem. With young children it is probable that one principle they have learned is that people do not go to the trouble of heating the metal ring so that the same thing will happen again. They have learned to expect something different, so the passing of the ball through the ring comes as no surprise. The other probable principle is magic. When a conjurer waves his wand over an empty hat, he is expected to produce a rabbit from it, which is magic, and not to show a still empty hat, which is science. What the pupils have almost certainly not learned from the ball and ring experiment is how to solve a problem by using the principle of the expansion of metals when heated, because it is unlikely that young pupils have learned such a principle. The test would be to get them to remove the metal cap from a container on to which it had been too tightly screwed. They may have learned to do so independently at a lower level of learning, but problem-solving learning implies learning how to reach a solution from 'first principles'.

HOW WELL DOES S-R THEORY
EXPLAIN LEARNING?

By now we have departed rather far from the earlier S-R pattern of learning; we have ceased to mention S-R units, repetition of presentation, establishment of responses, reinforcement or extinction. We have also ceased to quote evidence from experiments on animal learning. The departure from basic S-R theory took place at the level of concept learning; but before going on to examine other theories of learning which are more concerned with Gagné's higher levels of learning, let us see to what extent the S-R theory of the behaviourist psychologists can contribute to our understanding of the process of learning. It must be kept in mind throughout that any single learning task usually involves learning at different levels at the same time. A pupil learning the principles relating physical geography and economic geography cannot learn effectively if he does not know the symbols used in maps, or the meaning of words like 'alluvial' or 'entrepot'. The virtues, whatever they may be, of Livy's history of Rome are lost to the pupil whose Latin vocabulary is inadequate.

As we have said, the behaviourist approach is logically a very strong one. It requires that our evidence should be objective and precise, and therefore concentrates on observable behaviour and defined units of behaviour like the stimulus-response unit. The behaviourists lay great stress on learning, by which new S-R units are acquired to build up the extensive and complex range of our behaviour, and claim that a knowledge of how such S-R units are learned would enable us to direct and predict behaviour, which is what the teacher is aiming to do. But the behaviourist theory has never attracted favourable attention from teachers. Possibly it is considered too mechanical, possibly teachers are devoting most of their attention to those levels of learning where the behaviourist explanation is least satisfactory, possibly the insistence on objective and precise evidence prevents teachers from making those very generalized interpretations of pupils' behaviour which they are prone to do, and reveals how inadequate our knowledge of learning often is.

Psychological Assessment of Behaviourist Learning Theory

There are also some objections to the behaviourists' S-R theories of learning on psychological grounds. A satisfactory theory should take into account all available observations, should classify the relationships between the observations in a logically consistent system, and should thence predict what behaviour will be the outcome in known conditions. Behaviourism is open to criticism on the first requirement, is sound on the second, and, within its limits, sound on the third.

The first psychological difficulty with S-R learning theory is that it tends to assume the learner is passive, a responder to stimuli rather than a seeker of stimulation. Model rats can be constructed which, by means of signals from a sensitive set of metal whiskers, can run a maze in the same way as live rats, and like them can learn to improve their performance. Other mechanical and electronic models can be made which show all the features of the learning required by the S-R theory. Computers working on S-R type units can be made to acquire conditioned responses, and learn not only to play draughts, but to learn to play better and better till they are virtually unbeatable. Such models are very efficient learners up to the level of chaining. They cannot learn concepts; these have to be fed into the model by the programmer.

The psychological observations, however, do not indicate that the model adequately accounts for all behaviour observed in a learning situation. The live rat who has succeeded in running his maze does not switch off; he sniffs around, tries to get out of his box, and may run the maze backwards to escape. He is, as we said, a seeker of stimulation. This is even more marked in chimpanzees and humans. They make their own activities and when deprived of stimuli become neurotic. A bored pupil is by no means an inactive pupil.

Another psychological objection to S-R theory is that the experimental evidence is mostly obtained from learning situations in which the experimental conditions are such as to prevent any forms of learning other than the most elementary. The behaviourist's method of studying learning in its most elementary form, and under conditions of precise experimental control, leads to the learner becoming 'stimulus bound'. The animals are in boxes where only the experimental stimulus is presented, all other sources of stimulation being excluded. If Leonardo da Vinci or Isaac Newton were placed in a box where their food depended on their tapping a lever every time a click sounded, they would behave in the same way as a pigeon. The nature of the experimental evidence used by S-R theorists tends to limit the evidence to that which supports the theory. It should be added that behaviourists are not alone in this practice.

The final psychological objection follows from the previous ones. The prediction of behaviour by inference from theory is a necessary part of any adequate explanation. The learning progress of a pupil who is improving his fluency in French by conversation, or of the adolescent who is learning to cope with the apparently unpredictable behaviour of his girl-friends, is not easily explained in terms of S-R units. It is possible, but the structure of S-R units is so complex as to be virtually useless for prediction.

Despite these shortcomings, the contribution of S-R psychology to learning theory and to interpreting behaviour in general is by no means negligible. The fact that they exclude experience as evidence is not an adverse criticism; the fact that the S-R theory does not account for more complex observed behaviour is. The main contribution of S-R theory has been to force psychologists to adopt more exacting standards of evidence and more precise thinking about learning than they would otherwise have done. For the teacher the lesson of the behaviourists is that a much more careful distinction needs to be made between what is known about learning and what is not known.

The other contribution by the S-R theorists is that they have provided a thorough and precise explanation of certain kinds of learning which do occur in the school situation. Operant conditioning does work in practice if the conditions are suitable; Programmed Learning is a case in point. Rote learning and the learning of skills have a place in the education of school pupils, and the S-R theory has clarified the processes by which this kind of learning operates. Aversion therapy is not the whole solution to emotional conflicts, but it is one effective technique in the hands of the psychologist.

COGNITIVE STRUCTURE

It was the lack of correspondence between the S-R theory of learning and the observed behaviour of learners in the more advanced forms of learning which led other psychologists to attempt to analyse and interpret learning behaviour from the other end. The behaviourists attempt to build up an explanation of behaviour as an increasing, complex system of S-R units. The cognitive structure theorists or, as it is easier though rather old-fashioned to call them, the Gestalt psychologists, begin by identifying the pattern of this system, and proceed to examine the properties of this pattern or organization. The word *Gestalt*, which is German for "form" or "configuration", gives a clue to their basic concept. To the Gestalt psychologist, learning is an organizing activity of the learner and is best observed when the situation permits this organizing activity to operate most freely. The evidence therefore tends to be drawn from observation of the more intelligent species of animals and from human beings.

Both behaviourists and Gestalt psychologists agree that learning is a modification of previous behaviour to a change of needs or circumstances. The difference lies in the part played by the learner in the process, and in the interpretation of the stimulus. For S-R theory, the learner is a responder to an identifiable stimulus, a bodily change, a light, a lever, a spoken word. In cognitive structure theory, the learner is an organizer, responding to his perception of the pattern of the whole situation; in one context a light may mean "food", in another "stop", and in another may be irrelevant. The kind of stimulus presented, therefore, depends not only on the nature of the stimulus, but on the cognitive structure of the learner, which in turn determines how the situation is interpreted. The same rattlesnake is interpreted as an interesting object by a young child, who reaches out for it, but as a dangerous object by an adult, who retreats from it.

Herbart and the Apperception Mass

Though we may be tempted to attribute the first theory of cognitive structure to the Greek philosopher Plato, with his system of ideal forms, the first real attempt to express it in psychological terms was made by the German, J. F. Herbart. In 1824 he published a method of teaching based on the theory that the mind consisted of systems of ideas. Each idea had its own energy, striving to reach a state of consciousness. Like ideas associate with each other, and disparate ideas repel each other. Groups of associated ideas were called apperception masses, and the largest and best organized apperception masses were those which occupied consciousness at any given time. A new idea was presented, and the related apperception mass would emerge into consciousness. For example, the word "Hiro" is presented. For most people, this calls up the apperception mass of Japan, cherry-blossom, Fujiyama, the Mikado, geishas, oil-tankers, the atom bomb. But "Hiro" is an American Indian word, which now calls up the apperception mass of tepees, eagle feathers, canoes, and Indian braves. The word means, "I have spoken", which calls up the further apperception mass of camp-fires, circles of wigwams, and pipes of peace. It is in fact the origin of the name of the Indian tribe, the Iroquois, the people who say, "I have spoken". The unknown word is now firmly embedded in its apperception mass, its meaning has been learned and is not likely to be forgotten easily.

Methods of instruction based on Herbart's scheme of apperception masses consist of five steps:

Preparation: the calling into consciousness of the appropriate apperception mass.

Presentation: the presenting of new material to be associated with the apperception mass.

Association: the organization of the new material into the apperception mass, by showing its relation to existing ideas.

Generalization: the reorganization of the apperception mass to include the new material.

Application: the relating of the newly acquired apperception mass to various situations.

As a method of instruction this is effective enough, and there is a resemblance between apperception masses and cognitive structures. But the weakness of Herbart's psychological theory becomes apparent when we begin to ask such questions as, "How do we identify an idea?" "How does it appear as behaviour?" "How do we measure its energy?" "What are the conditions that determine the formation of apperception masses?" "How do they change?" "How can we predict if an apperception mass will become conscious?"

Gestalt Psychology

The more scientific investigation of cognitive structures was begun by a group of German psychologists. The principal members of this group, Köhler, Koffka, and Wertheimer, directed their attention to the investigation of perceptual experience, on the basis that what we respond to is not the physical character of the stimulus, but the meaningful patterns into which we have organized the stimuli. We cannot perceive the external world except as organized, as a system of Gestalts (or, in German, *Gestalten*), and it is the pattern rather than its component parts that determine the nature of our cognition or awareness, and therefore our behaviour. A melody can be transposed so that no single note remains the same, yet the melody is recognized as the same. Conversely, the same notes can be rearranged to form distinctly different tunes. If we look at Fig. 1 it is perceived as a rectangular table with a circular dish on it.

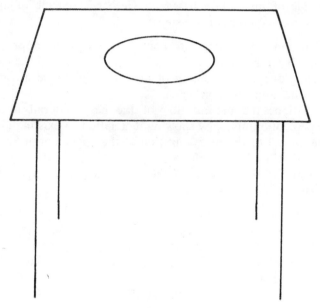

Fig. 1

The table is, however, not drawn as a rectangle, nor is the dish circular. In our daily experience we seldom see dishes as circular or tables as rectangular, as it is only when they are at right angles to our line of sight that they would be seen as such. The Gestalt interpretation is that we perceive in terms of what we know rather than what is physically presented to our senses. In our cognitive structure dishes are circular and tables rectangular.

The next step is to examine the properties of these *Gestalten*. There are three main properties of these cognitive structures, figure on ground, closure, and meaningfulness. Consider Fig. 2:

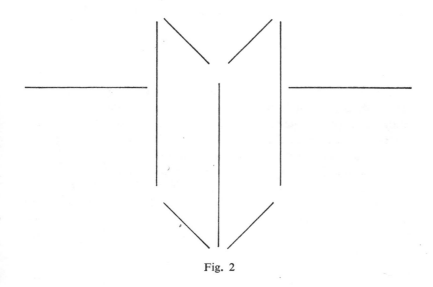

Fig. 2

This consists physically of a set of black lines on white paper. But it tends to be perceived as a folded sheet of paper resting on a table or similar surface. The folded sheet is perceived as the figure, and the white of the page as the ground, such that the figure, the folded sheet, appears to be in front of the ground, which tends to be perceived as continuing behind the sheet. The organization can change, so that the sheet appears as upright with the centre fold pointing outwards; at other times the sheet is perceived as lying with the folded edge on the table, open like a book. With a little effort the Gestalt can be changed again, this time to be perceived as a window in a triangular recess in the wall of a room. Here the previous ground becomes the figure and the surface of the sheet becomes the ground, the space outside the window. What is most difficult of all is to perceive the drawing as neutral, as nine lines on a white page.

Fig. 2, therefore, is readily perceived in terms of figure on ground. Closure is demonstrated by the fact that each of the lines is separate, but that our perception of the figure as a folded sheet leads us to perceive it as a complete pattern, and we close the gaps between the lines. Meaningfulness we have already mentioned; it is the tendency to perceive the pattern as that of something known, not just as a meaningless figure. Most of the work of the Gestalt psychologists was done with visual perception, but the processes of organizing as figure on ground, closure, and attributing meaning are present in other modes of perception. When a pupil is listening to a teacher, the teacher's voice is the figure and the other noises become the ground. We are not always aware of the extent to which closure occurs in speech; it is rather more than we suspect, and meaning can be attributed to very indistinct and garbled speech. The organization of heard sound into figure and ground can be demonstrated by recording a conversation between two or three people on a tape recorder. The recorder does not organize, so the background noises are much more conspicuous, and the speech of two people speaking at the same time is difficult to distinguish. The relationship between organization in *Gestalten* and attending is obvious. Attention implies organization and selection.

Cognitive Structure and Learning

According to the view we are examining, learning is a process of acquiring new cognitive structures by adapting, differentiating, and extending existing cognitive structures. This can take place by an increasing differentiation of figure and ground or by a reorganization of patterns of interpretation to meet different needs and different situations. In Gagné's scheme, a concept is roughly equivalent to cognitive structure—that is, a system of knowledge and mode of thinking in terms of which we interpret our experience and behave accordingly. The word "dog" is a sign for a cognitive structure, which may be very simple; a school subject like geometry is also a cognitive structure of great complexity. Gagné's multiple discrimination is parallel to the increasing differentiation of figures on ground, and his problem solving represents the process of reorganizing cognitive structures to meet different needs and situations. The more elementary forms of S-R learning have no parallel in cognitive structures; the experimental conditions tend to exclude cognitive structure, and whether a pigeon is capable of developing a cognitive structure or not is largely a matter of definition.

The learning may take place in the two main ways we have mentioned. The increasing differentiation of cognitive structures may be illustrated by a pupil learning elementary arithmetic. He organizes his responses to numbers in a series of cognitive structures, the earliest of which is probably counting. He then learns to differentiate adding from subtracting, and proceeds further to the cognitive structures called multiplication and division. He later differentiates his system of numbers into fractions and negative numbers and so on. During this process of differentiating his rather simple system of thought about numbers, he is learning various number combinations by a process best explained in S-R terms. Another way in which differentiation may occur is demonstrated in the sentence, "They are eating apples". This statement at first sight represents a relatively simple cognitive structure. But we can differentiate, by emphasizing each word separately. It is they, not we, who are eating apples. They *are* eating apples (and don't argue). They are eating apples, not cookers. They are eating apples, not pears. The cognitive structure has become more complex.

Reorganization of cognitive structures to adapt to new situations is the other main way of learning. The reorganization may lead to the recognition of similarities in situations previously interpreted as different. For example, English *chief* is recognized in French *chef* and in turn in Latin *caput*, and this again in English *captain*. Further reorganization may lead to the recognition that the 'p' in Latin has become 'f' and therefore that the Latin *piscis* has become Old English *fisc*, with the modern English pronunciation of fish. Reorganization to adapt to differences arises in much the same way. Four men take four days to build a wall, how long for one man? Four ships take four days to cross the Atlantic, how long for one ship? The pattern appears the same, but the cognitive structure has to be reorganized for the second; otherwise the answer conflicts with the cognitive structure relating to sea voyages. When this reorganization occurs, the process is known as Insight, the English translation of the German word *Einsicht*. There is a tendency to use the word Insight only when the reorganization is spontaneously performed by the learner.

This need not be so, as Insight can be created by teaching and demonstration; this is what Herbart's method aimed to do.

Köhler's Apes

In the same way as Pavlov conducted the classical experiments on conditioning on dogs, and Thorndike the classical experiments in trial and error learning on cats, Köhler conducted the classical experiments on Insight on apes during the First World War. In one of his experiments a bunch of bananas was hung from a hook in the roof of the cage, beyond the reach of the apes. A stick was also placed in the cage. The ape might make a few unsuccessful attempts to reach the bananas, and then turn its attention to the stick. Some apes, after playing with the stick, related the stick to the bananas and quickly used the stick to knock down the bunch, or climbed rapidly up the stick and took a flying leap at the bananas. Other apes continued to use the stick as a plaything, or as something to hit other apes with. In another experiment, the apes were given two boxes which, when placed on top of one another, provided a platform high enough to reach the bananas. Most apes learned to build such a platform, and little repetition was needed for them to learn how to reach the bananas in later trials. One ape, after a first success, could apparently not remember how to arrange the boxes. Its behaviour suggested it knew the second box fitted somehow into the pattern; it kicked the box around the cage and finished by thumping it violently. In another experiment, requiring three boxes, one of the apes removed one box, leaving one of the more intelligent apes with two boxes. This ape built a platform of two boxes, then took the lower box and attempted to place it on the upper box. The idea was sound, but the ape got no bananas.

How is this translated into Gestalt and cognitive structure theory? The apes are responding to the situation as they have organized or structured it. In its simplest form, the first pattern may be described as: Hungry ape → unclosed gap → bananas. The ape's previous cognitive structure may lead it to behave in its customary manner of jumping up for the bananas. This is unsatisfying, the gap persists, and the ape restructures the situation. The new structure may be: Ape → another ape → stick to hit it with. The gap between the ape and the bananas remains, and Insight takes place when the ape again reorganizes the structure into: Hungry ape → stick to climb up → bananas → satisfied ape. The ape has learned to obtain the bananas, there is no tension arising from an unclosed gap, and whether the ape can repeat the behaviour later appears to be mainly a matter of remembering.

The ape who could not remember how to use the box had retained an incomplete cognitive structure, and failed to attain Insight on this occasion. The ape who tried to place the lower box on the upper one did achieve insight; but this instance is given to stress the fact that Insight or 'understanding' does not necessarily mean the same as reaching a correct solution. The learning of these apes is not unlike that of school-children. There is the pupil who learns how to tell the time from a clock, and then forgets exactly how to do it. The ape with the two boxes had the same difficulty as the pupil who learns "walk—walked" and then says "drink—drinked", or who learns the proportion sum about the four men building the wall, and applies the same structure to four ships sailing the Atlantic.

ASSESSMENT OF COGNITIVE STRUCTURE AND S-R LEARNING THEORY

The psychological account of learning in terms of cognitive structure has certain attractions for the teacher. It deals more directly with the kinds of learning that the teacher is concerned with, the higher levels of learning in Gagné's scheme, which the S-R theory did not adequately explain. Also, the cognitive structure theory lays much greater stress on the individual differences between learners. The S-R theory does not require examination of differences; the theory is developed on the basis of the elementary units of S-R learning, common to all learners, which can be acquired equally by men, monkeys, dogs, and pigeons. For S-R theory, differences between learners do not lie in the process of learning, but rather in the number of S-R units which can be established and linked together; the intelligent pupil is the one who has acquired the largest store or repertoire of responses. The explanation is logically consistent, but is not very fruitful for understanding differences in ability among children.

S-R theory also tends to limit differences in motivation for learning. In the experimental work on which the theory is based, the learners are usually provided with a defined and often ready-made motive. The rats learn faster when they are hungry or when given electric shocks for errors. But, though effective, this kind of motivation is not used on pupils, who learn nevertheless. Both theories are agreed that the motive of need, or drive reduction, leads the learner to modify his behaviour to obtain satisfaction. But the normal activity of the wakeful individual also appears to be a motive for learning. As we discuss motivation in a later chapter, we shall not pursue the discussion here.

Another aspect of individual differences among learners is that the cognitive structures which they acquire do not wholly depend on the conditions under which the behaviour is elicited. As we have noted, in S-R learning the learner is constrained to learn the prescribed response; he is conditioned, or his behaviour is 'shaped' to a given response. The nature of the cognitive structure developed by the learner depends on a number of factors peculiar to each learner. Again, as we shall be discussing these more fully later, we only mention them. It is a common observation that children differ in intelligence, which can be interpreted as saying they have different capacities for acquiring cognitive structures. It is also a common observation that the capacity of younger children for acquiring cognitive structures differs from that of older children; in other words, learning depends on maturation. And finally, cognitive structures depend on previous learning, which may vary from one person to another.

The other major difference between S-R and cognitive structure theory is that cognitive structure is a field theory; that is, the learner is responding to a situation, or a pattern of relationships, rather than to a unit stimulus. The single stimulus does not seem to the cognitive structure theorists to have any meaning in itself, it only has meaning in its context or situation; this attributing of meaning, they claim, is more closely allied to human learning than is the responding to an isolated element, the stimulus. Response to relations and context is the elementary form of most behaviour and learning.

The attractions of the cognitive structure interpretation should not blind us to its very real weaknesses. For one thing the explanation cannot account satisfactorily for a number of kinds of learning which undoubtedly occur both in school and out of it.

Learning by conditioning, either classical or operant, does not fit into the theory of cognitive structures; the concept of cognitive structure is as irrelevant to Pavlov's dogs or Skinner's pigeons as the concept of conditioning is to Köhler's apes. Nor does the large area of school learning which includes rote learning and the learning of skills owe anything to cognitive structure theory.

Another weakness of the cognitive structure theory of learning lies in the difficulty of predicting whether Insight will be successful or not in any given situation. Achieving Insight is not the same as achieving a solution, as witness the ape with the two boxes. What the cognitive structure theory fails to provide is a technique for directing or controlling the learner's final behaviour. This is what the S-R techniques, such as operant conditioning, do provide; behaviour can be 'shaped' and S-R theory indicates how it can be done. In cognitive structure theory, Insight may lead to an incorrect solution, or to an undesirable form of behaviour, and there is no evidence that a pupil learns from his mistakes, especially if he does not know that they are mistakes, and why they are mistakes. In school learning the pupil does not acquire cognitive structure by spontaneous Insight. Either the material must be self-correcting, which is uncommon, or the teacher presents to the pupil a cognitive structure such as a system of number relationships, language structure and usage, or scientific definitions and techniques, which provides the pupil with a model on which he can organize his own system of cognitive structures, and against which he can verify them. If the model structure is beyond the learner's capacity, then the learner falls back on piecemeal trial and error learning, where the S-R theory and methods are more helpful.

This difficulty represents one aspect of the most serious objection to the cognitive structure theory. The theory is neither objective enough nor precise enough to be applied with confidence in any given situation. Changes in behaviour can be observed, but cognitive structures cannot; they can only be inferred from behaviour, and the inference may be wrong, which introduces an additional source of error in interpretation. Further, the conditions under which cognitive structures are acquired, and under which they are modified, are not known at all precisely; in contrast, the S-R theories can specify the process of learning, such as reinforcement, extinction, generalization, and discrimination with a considerable degree of precision, though at the cost of restricting the areas of behaviour studied. By limiting the forms of learning studied to those common to all learners, the S-R investigations have established the conditions of effective learning; by accepting as part of the learning process the very wide range of individual differences in the learner, the cognitive structure theorists have made similarly precise findings almost impossible to establish.

Learning Theories and Practices

Which approach to the interpretation of learning is most likely to develop a more complete understanding of the processes by which pupils learn? Probably the behaviourist theory holds most promise. The basic elementary learning processes have been scientifically investigated, and techniques which are known to be effective have been developed. There is still a long way to go, but the analogy of other sciences, medical science for example, suggests that this method of investigation in the long run may be the most rewarding. Conditions such as mental illness are beginning to be treated successfully by specific drugs, whose properties have been precisely and objectively investigated.

The psychologist wanting to undertake further research into the processes of learning is faced with a choice between extending the growing edges of the S-R theory of learning, or attempting to reduce the cognitive structure theory to a more objective and precise formulation, leading to hypotheses which can be experimentally verified. The teacher is not faced with such a choice. He has in his school pupils whose activity covers the whole range of learning processes. His problem is to ascertain what kind of learning is most fitted to the pupil and to the learning task, and select, from what evidence and techniques the psychologist can provide, the conditions and methods which will make the pupil's learning most effective. Bugelski's gap still remains, but perhaps it is not quite so wide if it is recognized on the one hand that there is no psychological theory applicable to all kinds of learning, and on the other that school learning is not one single process, but usually a complex of learning processes involving different techniques and different levels of behaviour. At certain points the theory and the practice meet, at others the gap has yet to be bridged.

2

Maturation

Though we have defined learning in terms of observed changes in behaviour, not all changes of a child's behaviour can be attributed to learning. There are changes which are the result of the child growing older and developing new patterns of behaviour with age. The natural process of growth in a living organism we call maturation. Changes of children's behaviour due to maturation are particularly difficult to identify, as the pattern of development is by no means as clearly reflected in behaviour as it is with the lower orders of animals. The progress of a frog from an egg to a tadpole to the adult frog can be plotted exactly almost on a day-to-day basis. But children follow a much less rigid schedule of development; the time span is in years rather than days, the child's capacity for adapting behaviour by learning is much more extensive than that of any other organism, and most of the changes in the child's observed behaviour are the outcome of interaction between learning and maturation. Where the behaviour is least affected by learning, as in physical growth, maturation can be most clearly observed. Where learning plays a large part in determining behaviour, as in intellectual or social development, the scheme of maturation can only be observed in the broadest of outlines.

One result of the increasing volume of information becoming available about children's development and behaviour is that the study known as child psychology or child development has tended to break up into the study of different sectors of the child's behaviour. The psychologists have had to follow their usual practice of analysis, definition, observation, and assessment, and various sectors of behaviour have been investigated independently. Though each child behaves as a single person, growing according to a pattern common to all children, but with marginal individual variations, the whole process is so complex that interpretation without analysis would only result in confusion. In the same way as separate chapters on such topics as learning, maturation, intelligence, or personality are necessary, so within the study of maturation the process has to be dealt with in sectors and not as a rather shapeless single topic. In this discussion we shall be dealing mainly with the physical and cognitive development of children as far as these can be attributed to maturation. The cognitive aspect of development is that which is concerned with processes such as perceiving and thinking. Discussion of the sectors of social and personality development is reserved for later chapters. Our main task here is to try to separate from those components of behaviour which are acquired, those that reflect the common patterns of growth in children, and to examine what their characteristics are.

The Physical Basis of Maturation

In the last analysis changes of observed behaviour must be attributed to changes in the physical constitution of the body, however obscure to us these at present may be. As we did with learning, let us first look at the process of maturation in its most elementary and therefore most easily observed form. There is a well known investigation by Coghill into the maturation of the behaviour of salamander embryos, organisms which are relatively uncomplicated, but nevertheless by no means simple.

He found that in the early stages of their development the embryos did not respond to the stimulation of a touch, though electrical stimulation showed that each muscle of the embryo was in working order. A day or so later the embryo responded to a touch by moving the head part. Shortly after, the embryo responded to the same stimulus by forming a coil or C shape, and later still, when more fully developed, by forming an S shape. There are two interesting features about this experiment. The first was that when sections of the salamander embryos at each stage of maturation were examined under the microscope, the development of behaviour was found to correspond to the physical growth of the organism's nervous system. In the first stage, the embryo had not yet grown nerve fibres connecting the muscles on one side of its body with these on the other side. When the physical growth of these nerve fibres was complete, and not before, the organism was able to make a response in which the muscles on the two sides of the body were co-ordinated. The other interesting feature is that the responses to the touch stimulus followed the same sequence of movements as the organism follows in developing the ability to swim. The series of S-shaped movements were those which propelled it through the water. It would be wrong to say it "learned to swim", as learning was in no sense the cause of the organism's change of behaviour.

There is little doubt but that the same process of physical growth of the nervous system underlies much of human maturation. But we cannot study the development of children in the same way as Coghill used for salamander embryos. Apart from obvious humanitarian reasons, the child's nervous system even at birth consists of nerve cells counted in the hundreds of millions, and the behaviour of children is much more adaptable than that of salamanders.

The maturation of the sex organs and the accompanying drive for sexual satisfaction is directly due to the maturation of certain physiological processes in the growing child. Yet the appearance of sex behaviour in adolescents does not directly reflect this development. There is, for example, some doubt as to whether earlier sexual components in the younger child's behaviour are not repressed by social disapproval; sex is recognized socially as an adolescent 'problem' and the expression in behaviour of the maturational stage reached is shaped very powerfully by the prohibitions of adult society. This is a case where the social environment conspires to prevent learning, and in the five- or six-year-olds, a possible maturational stage may never be observed because society is not willing to recognize its existence.

HOW DO WE STUDY MATURATION IN CHILDREN?

The result of this interaction between learning opportunities and maturational changes in children is that we can only use certain very broadly based tests to establish if changes in behaviour arise directly from maturation. If children brought up in different environments, that is with different expectations of the behaviour appropriate to their age, all tend to go through the same sequences of behaviour, we can assume that these sequences are basically maturational. Thus, in the first few months of life all babies make speech sounds in much the same sequence, from crying to babbling. Up to this point development is maturational, and babbling words like mama, papa, dada, and baba are common to the nursery language of nearly all societies. This stage coincides with the beginning of language, as distinct from vocalization, or the production of speech sounds. When the speech sounds are being co-ordinated in the learning of a language, the Bushman baby retains a set of clicking sounds, which the European child loses in the process of learning his particular language pattern, and which he cannot later learn adequately. When different languages, often reflecting different patterns of social behaviour and possibly different structures of thought, are being acquired, any common maturational element becomes increasingly difficult to identify.

Another test is the extent to which children are able to learn certain new forms of behaviour. In so far as the performance of certain activities depends on the development of the abilities necessary to learn the task at all, the failure of children to learn is an indication that the necessary maturational level has not yet been reached. It is not possible for a child under six months to learn to walk however hard we try to teach him, because he has not yet grown the nervous machinery necessary to co-ordinate his movements. Reading and handwriting are in the same class of activity; reading depends on co-ordination of the eye muscles and on perceptual organization, handwriting also depends on the co-ordination of muscular movement and perception. Where the behaviour is overt—that is to say, it can be directly observed—the establishment of maturational stages of development is not too difficult.

But not all maturational changes are directly reflected in overt behaviour. In children's drawings, for instance, we can observe two sequences of maturational development. One is in the overt behaviour of manipulation of the crayon or pencil, which we shall call draughtsmanship. Young children have not yet developed the muscular co-ordination for precise control. The other aspect is the child's organization, the cognitive structure of the scene he is representing. Seven-year-olds, drawing a familiar scene like a street, tend to organize their drawing on a common basic pattern. The typical drawing is in layers, blue sky at the top (where the sun is), then empty space (where the air is), then a row of houses of equal size seen front on, and then two parallel lines for the road (where the cars are drawn side on). Each object occupies its own space and is drawn in its complete form. There is no definable point of view from which the scene is observed, and no attempt at the representation of distance. Draughtsmanship may vary in precision, but the cognitive structure represented seems to be remarkably rigid. Attempts to teach perspective to children of this age end in failure. The child may, under pressure, adopt some of the tricks of the trade; houses may become smaller, but the fronts remain rectangular. Eleven- and twelve-year-olds become increasingly critical of their system of representation, and attempts at introducing a new system involving perspective begin to appear. The earlier cognitive structure no longer satisfies the child, and a new set of techniques are being acquired to express a more mature system of interpretation. This system is no more an objective representation of the actual scene than the earlier one. College students very frequently draw a street as it would be observed from a point about twenty feet above the centre of the street—not a usual point of observation. What we are observing is a change in the cognitive structure reflected in the drawing; the visible scene is the same for all. The inability of the younger children to adopt the system of perspective indicates that the development is maturational.

Differences in Rate of Maturation

There is very little difference between one salamander embryo and another, and indeed between one baby and another, so that it is possible to identify not only the sequence of maturational changes, but also the age at which they will become evident. As children grow older differences in rates of development become more marked, not only between children, but also between sectors of behaviour in the same child. These differences are already evident during the child's school years; some children entering school are able to begin to learn to read, but some are not. Sexual maturation may develop anywhere over a span of about three years, boys being later than girls. In school pupils, we have to think of maturation in terms of sequences rather than in terms of age. The order of maturational development is relatively uniform, the age at which the various stages are reached may vary considerably.

This situation contains a warning for the teacher. There is a danger that the teacher may claim a maturational change as a success for a particular method of teaching or learning. With children learning to read, there is a maturational element in their progress during the first twelve or eighteen months of school life. This involves muscular co-ordination of the muscles of the lens and eyeball, the possibility of asymmetrical growth of the eyeball leading to long-sightedness, and fusion of the images from the retinas of the two eyes. There is probably also a maturation of perceptual organization of the visual field, and a maturation of cognitive structure involved in the interpretation of what the process of reading is about. A teacher may concentrate on reading instruction and practice, and the pupil will begin to learn to read. But unless there is a carefully controlled comparison with a parallel group of children who have not received the same teaching, it is very difficult to distinguish whether the pupils' progress is due to teaching, or to maturation which would have occurred in any case, or to both.

Methods of Study and Sources of Information

In the investigation of learning much of the evidence was obtained from experimental work on animals. This method will not help in the study of maturation, as the sequence of maturation is not the same for each species of animal, nor can findings from animals be transferred to human beings, except in the most fundamental of processes. We therefore draw our evidence from direct observation of human behaviour and, as we have seen, this is not altogether easy. Different physical and social environments present the growing child with different learning tasks, but if we draw our evidence from children in much the same type of environment, it is possible to trace the broad sequences of maturational development. The inquiries of Piaget, for example, into the maturation of cognitive structures in children were conducted on French-speaking children, but it is becoming evident that most of his findings are equally applicable to English-speaking children in the context of the same general type of society. Whether they would equally apply to Eskimo or Australian aboriginal children remains to be seen.

There are four main sources of information about the sequence of maturational development in children. There are studies based on systematic observation; these studies can be classified into two types, longitudinal and cross-sectional. The second kind of study is the controlled experiment, the third may be called assessment studies, and the fourth may be called the intensive inquiry. We consider each of these in turn.

Systematic Observation

Longitudinal studies are those in which a sample of children are observed at regular intervals over a period of time, mostly measured in years. The purpose of most of these studies is not primarily to study maturation as such, but incidental evidence about maturational development can be gleaned from them. Such studies as the Berkeley Growth Study in California, or the current National Child Development Study in Britain, give a picture of the developmental sequences of behaviour in a representative group of children. Much of the evidence is about physical growth, and it is on the basis of such surveys that we can trace the order of events in physical growth and, more important, the range of variation between different children. As the children grow older, such studies extend their inquiries to educational and social aspects of the children's development, but by that stage the maturational element often tends to be obscured by environmental differences.

The other type of systematic observation, which we have called cross-sectional, differs only in method from the longitudinal study, in that in the longitudinal type of study the same children are observed over a period of years, whereas in the cross-sectional studies a representative sample of children of each age is taken, this sample being regarded as typical of children at that stage of their development. An example of this type of study is that of Gesell and his colleagues. On the basis of extensive observation of children in North America, he has published detailed descriptions of the typical behaviour of children of different ages, covering a very wide area of children's activities and characteristics. The accounts given in *The Child from Five to Ten* illustrate his method. Some forty pages are occupied by description of the typical eight-year-old. The eight-year-olds are described as being physically active and well co-ordinated, sociable and fond of company; girls are beginning to be careful about clothes, but not so the boys. They are adventurous but not prudent, as they have lost the caution characteristic of the seven-year-olds without having yet gained the experience of the older child. They tend to be impatient and demanding of immediate attention, though they can behave well outside the home, and on occasions within it. They organize groups and clubs, but these are generally short-lived; they enjoy games and activities which are organized and supervised for them, but left on their own they tend to run wild. For most of them school is enjoyable, they are beginning to read for pleasure, they can write in a reasonably clear hand, and they enjoy arithmetic as long as there is some novelty or variety. They are keenly aware of their own property; they are great collectors but their desire for system and order in their collection exceeds their ability to keep such order. They have a good sense of direction, can find their way around their neighbourhood, and can distinguish left from right not only in themselves but also in other persons.

This is but a summary of the kind of systematic observations made by Gesell for children of each age. There can be no doubt about its value; its virtues are that it is comprehensive and based on extensive and careful observation. But such surveys, both longitudinal and cross-sectional, are but the first steps. They map out the field of development, and indicate the paths that further inquiries can follow. Gesell describes the typical child; we next ask what is the range of differences among children in their development, how much is common to children in different environments, and, above all, what is the theoretical explanation of these observations, so that we can explain relationships between our observations and predict the course of the children's future behaviour.

Controlled Experiment

The experimental method is one of the most powerful weapons of the scientist, and has been the basis of much of the development in the physical sciences. Coghill's work with salamander embryos, relating the behavioural maturation to the physical maturation of the nervous system, is one instance of its application to biological growth. The possibilities of applying the experimental method to children's growth are limited, and most are designed to distinguish between learning and maturation as determining factors in behaviour changes. The most frequently used experimental method is that called co-twin control. This method depends on the fact that identical, or monozygotic, twins have the same genetic constitution, and that the maturational development of both will therefore follow the same lines at the same rate. About one in eighty-five births is a twin birth. Approximately three-quarters of these twins are fraternal or dizygotic twins, who may be regarded as brothers or sisters who are born at the same time instead of at different times. They show the same degree of genetic similarity and difference as do other children in the same family. The monozygotic twins, on the other hand, may be regarded as the same individual in duplicate. They are assumed to begin life as one fertilized egg cell, which at a very early stage of its development splits into two embryos, each with the same genetic constitution. A pair of normally developed identical twins are at birth as alike as any two human beings can ever be, and therefore if the environment of one twin is different from that of the other, any resulting changes in behaviour can confidently be attributed to learning, as maturational development is the same for both. The method is, of course, not infallible. Only a few such experiments can be conducted on any one pair; the effects of environmental differences can be cumulative. Most experiments tend to be conducted when the twins are still at an early age, when their upbringing has been the same for both. The other difficulty is that it is not possible to be absolutely certain that any given pair of twins is monozygotic. There are a number of tests of identity, blood groups, hair and eye colour, pattern of hair growth, and so on, which can be used to establish with a high degree of certainty, say about a million to one, that the twins are not fraternal; but absolute certainty cannot be established, and more than one co-twin experiment has been performed on twins who were later suspected to be fraternal.

One of the best known experiments on monozygotic twins was that which used a pair of one-year-old twin girls, known as T and C. The experiment began when the twins were 46 weeks old. From the age of 46 weeks to 50 weeks T (the trainee) was given encouragement and teaching in the climbing of a short set of steps. She succeeded by the 50th week, and two weeks later, by the 52nd week, was able to climb the steps in 26 seconds. Meantime, twin C (the control) was given no opportunity of learning to climb up steps. When she was 52 weeks old, she was introduced to the steps and, without previous teaching or encouragement, climbed them at the first attempt, taking 45 seconds, as compared with the 26 seconds taken by T at the same age. Twin C was then given practice in climbing, and two weeks later, at 54 weeks old, could climb the steps in 10 seconds, a better performance than T's. Though a single experiment proves very little, this is typical of the kind of experiment which can be conducted in inquiries into maturational development, and demonstrates certain general principles very relevant to education, which we discuss more fully later. It should be kept in mind, however, that the body of experimental evidence on which learning theory is based is very much more extensive than the corresponding experimental evidence available for any theory of maturational development.

Assessment Studies

These are indirect sources of evidence in that such studies or tests were not devised primarily to provide information about maturation. One main source is the standardized individual intelligence test, such as the Terman–Merrill Binet test or the WISC (Wechsler Intelligence Scale for Children). These tests consist of a number of small problems, or requests for common information, which are given to children of different ages, and the acceptable answers are those which can be given by approximately half the children at the appropriate age. Thus, by examining the nature of the acceptable answers, and the commoner types of failure, we can gain some idea of the development of children's thinking. For example, in the Binet Test, children aged three-and-a-half years are shown a picture of some children arriving at the door of a house for a birthday party. The three-and-a-half-year-olds are expected to be able to name three objects or persons in the picture, or to give a simple description of part of the picture. The same test is also given to six-year-olds, who are expected to bring together the component elements of the picture and to describe or interpret the situation as a whole. The age sequence is from enumeration of items to description to interpretation. Another test, for seven-year-olds, is copying a simple diamond-shaped figure. The less mature child tends to draw one side, then to draw the corner (almost like ears on the figure) and then the next side, and so on. The more mature child does not draw corners separately from the joining sides.

A similar sequence of development appears in the child's definitions of words. One item in both WISC and Binet tests is called Vocabulary, in which a series of words are said to the child, and he is asked "What does . . . mean?" The form of the question is very noncommittal, and the child interprets the kind of answer expected in terms of his level of maturation. The six-year-olds tend to answer in terms of use or appearance; an orange "is yellow" or an envelope is "for a letter" are acceptable as answers and are characteristic of that age. The ten-year-olds tend to define more readily in terms of description, or of other words of the same meaning: for example, scorch is "to burn" or "to make something brown". The older child and the adult define more formally: for example, ambergris is defined as "some kind of jelly thing they take from whales", or incrustation as "crust formed by the evaporation of water". Even when the definition is wrong in fact, the form varies with age. Philanthropy is defined as "a place where they take in old clothes for the needy". The content is wrong, but the form is mature. These are but some examples of the indirect evidence about maturation which can be derived from what we have called assessment studies. In general, psychological tests, particularly intelligence tests, can be a mine of information on aspects of psychology beyond those they were devised for.

Intensive Inquiry—Piaget

This source of information refers particularly to certain detailed studies concerned directly with the process of development in children, but can also include less formal investigations of children's behaviour with the maturational component in mind. The outstanding contributions directly concerned with the maturation of children's thinking are the studies of Jean Piaget and his colleagues. Originally trained as a biologist, Piaget applied the methods and thinking of biology to a series of intensive studies of the development of cognitive structure in children. His method was to present children with a small problem, to observe how children solved it, or failed to solve it, and, by questioning the children, to interpret the logical processes in terms of which the children did their thinking. He has devised a large number of such problems, often very ingenious, and we can only give a few samples of his procedure.

A child about five years old is shown two glasses of liquid, say lemonade. The two glasses are of the same size and are filled with equal amounts of lemonade. The lemonade from one glass is then poured into two smaller glasses, and the child is asked who would now have the most lemonade, a child who has the two small glasses or a child who had kept the original glass. If the child answers, as a number of them do, that the one with the two glasses has more, or less, lemonade, he is asked to mark with a rubber band the expected level of lemonade in the larger empty glass. The lemonade is then poured back into the original glass and some children express surprise that the level is the same as in the other undisturbed glass. Such children appear to accept without difficulty the idea that the quantity of lemonade can be changed by transferring it from one glass to two, or more, smaller glasses. Around the age of seven, however, most children, instead of judging that the amount of lemonade has changed, give answers such as, "It's still the same, because I saw in the other glass that it was the same." Such children are confident that the amount of lemonade has not been changed by transfer from one glass to others. An extension of the same inquiry is to pour the lemonade into another glass that is either tall and narrow, or that is short and broad. Again the less mature child is prepared to state the quantity of lemonade changes if it looks to be more, or less, to him. The more mature child is sure that the quantity must be the same, as none has been added or taken away. There is an interesting intermediate stage, at which some children intuitively think that the amount cannot have changed, but support their judgement by the (unnecessary) argument that the height of the tall glass is balanced out by its narrowness, and therefore the amount should be the same.

Piaget and his colleague Bärbel Inhelder have explored other aspects of the development of children's thinking in the same way. A set of six egg-cups is placed before the child, and he places an egg in each cup, making a one-to-one correspondence between eggs and cups. The eggs are removed from the cups and placed in a cluster in front of the row of cups. "Are there now more or fewer eggs?" The eggs are spread apart, and the same question asked. Once again the less mature children are prepared to say that the six eggs are more or fewer than originally. Another type of problem presented to the child consisted of a table-top model of three mountains, each of a different colour. The child saw the model from one point of view only, but was asked to identify himself with a doll, and asked to say what the doll would see when placed in different positions. Children of about seven or eight years old tend to attribute their own point of view to the doll, and appear to have difficulty in describing relationships between the mountains which are very much different from what they see themselves. Ten-year-olds are much more able to correlate relationships of left and right, and in front of and behind, from a viewpoint other than their own.

For older children, a typical problem was to present the children with five beakers of colourless liquid. These five liquids, which can be called A, B, C, D, and E, were respectively dilute sulphuric acid, water, oxygenated water, thiosulphate, and potassium iodide. The mixture A + C + E produces a yellow liquid, to which B can be added without producing any change, but to which the addition of D bleaches out the yellow. The production of the yellow liquid and its bleaching were demonstrated to the children, but the liquids used were not identified. Three methods of attack were noted, according to the maturity of the child's thinking. The least mature pupils attempted to reach a solution by random trial and error, mixing one liquid with another and tending to try only two liquids at a time. Older pupils tried a mixture of more than two, but where they succeeded in obtaining yellow, they attributed the change in colour to the addition of one liquid only; it did not occur to them that when E was added to A and C both A and C were necessary before E could act. These pupils also stopped whenever they obtained a solution; they did not consider whether there were other possible combinations that would give the same effect. The most mature pupils set about the test systematically, trying first each possible pair and then proceeding to groups of three liquids. Nor do they stop when a solution is reached; they tend to continue and check that only one combination will produce the required results.

Intensive Inquiries — Other

We have spent some time describing Piaget's methods of inquiry because both his own work and investigations which have been inspired by himself and his colleagues have so far provided the most extensive body of evidence on which a system of maturation can be established. What that system is, we discuss shortly.

There have been parallel inquiries, such as those by J. S. Bruner, an American psychologist interested particularly in the processes of thinking. He approaches the question of maturation in much the same way as Piaget, and develops from his observations a theoretical scheme which is in many ways also similar to Piaget's. This also we discuss later. But material for less formal inquiries is available to any teacher, as the sequence of maturation investigated by Piaget and Bruner shows itself in many sectors of a child's behaviour. From the classroom we can take two such sectors. Children's drawings are best studied on the principle that the child draws what he knows rather than what he sees. We have already outlined the main sequence of the development of children's drawings; further study enables us to identify with some certainty the maturational stage the child has reached, and more significantly to distinguish between what is the child's own production and what has been contributed by a teacher who tries to establish techniques too mature for the child. Language is another fruitful source of information about the development of the patterns of children's thought. Sentence structure is probably the best index of the developing cognitive structure of children. Vocabulary is also related to maturation, but is more sensitive to differences in learning than the structure of the child's statements. A distinction between the elementary structure of a set of statements strung together with "and then", "and so", "and when", and the like, and more complexly co-ordinated single statements is not difficult to make. Indeed, a straight count of the number and variety of connectives and prepositions used by a pupil is as good an index of a child's level of thought as any. It does not necessarily follow that the child who is most mature is the most efficient; a pupil acquiring a new pattern of thought may not have acquired the technical skills in language to express himself clearly.

Before examining the theoretical interpretations of maturational changes, it is worth repeating that any observed sector of a child's behaviour is a compound of maturation and learning. Very little human behaviour, especially after the first few months of life, is acquired by maturation alone. Most of it is learned, and it is only where the maturational stage of development is incompatible with the nature of the learning task that it is possible to distinguish the two processes; the learning of perspective drawing is an instance. Normally, the progress of maturational change is dependent on opportunity for experience and activity being available to the child. Piaget, for example, lays considerable stress on the need for appropriate manipulative and social experience for children to progress through the various sequences of development we are about to discuss.

THEORIES OF MATURATION

From the brief review of sources of information and methods of study of the process of maturation, there have already emerged certain broad sequences of development. As we are confining ourselves to physical and cognitive development, we only mention here that there are parallel developments occurring in the social and personal aspects of the child's behaviour. Developmental theories of personality, like those of Freud or Erikson, we reserve for later discussion, but it must be remembered that the different aspects of development are distinguished for the sake of coherent discussion, and for any given child, his emotional and social needs are directly related to his intellectual interpretation of the personal and social situations he finds himself in.

Physical Maturation

It is not the function of a discussion of psychology as related to education to present any detailed or comprehensive scheme of the physical development of children. The relationship between physical development and cognitive development is not very close; that between physical maturation and personal and social development is probably more significant. By the time a pupil has passed the age of seven years, his level of physical maturation is adequate to meet nearly all educational requirements with the possible exception of certain special physical activities like handstands or playing some musical instruments. Before that age, physical maturation can be an element in the pupil's progress; the earlier stages of reading, for example, depend on maturation in eye movement and other aspects of vision.

There have been various attempts to identify recognizable stages or phases in the physical development of children, but the evidence tends to suggest that during school years the process of physical maturation is a continuous one, without any marked transitions from one stage to another. The one exception to this is the 'adolescent spurt'. Sexual maturity begins to develop in girls at some point between the ages of eleven and fourteen years, and in boys between twelve and sixteen years. This is accompanied by a distinct increase in the rate of growth, particularly in height. This adolescent spurt lasts over a period of between two and three years normally and tends to be characterized by a temporary loss of muscular co-ordination, showing itself as clumsiness and awkwardness, and the period ends with the boy or girl having developed a relatively much greater muscular strength than he or she had previously. The spurt occurs in boys about two years later than in girls, but in both sexes it is possible for one individual to have virtually completed the process while another of the same age is still in the early stages of this development. These differences can give rise to social and personal problems, but there is no evidence to suggest any corresponding spurt in intellectual or cognitive growth. Where different stages in cognitive development are recognized these do not appear to be directly related to physical growth.

Cognitive Maturation—Bruner

As with physical maturation, the rate of cognitive development varies from one child to another, and the interest of psychologists has been in establishing stages showing different patterns of cognitive structure in children, the chronological age assigned to any stage being only approximate. Bruner begins by considering the ways children use to represent their environment. Throughout our conscious life information is flooding in through our senses. To interpret this information we must select, which is a function of attention, and we must select according to some coherent system. It is the structure of this system that Bruner finds to change and develop as children grow older. The young child has the same sensory equipment as the older child; his eyes, his ears, and other sense organs function just as efficiently. He probably has greater need of protection from the flood of experience; it is the function of cognitive structure to select from this unending stream of information and to order it in a pattern comprehensible to the individual. We have already suggested how this process might be operating in children's drawings and language.

The first stage in the development of cognitive structure is called by Bruner the stage of enactive representation. Here the child interprets his experience in terms of appropriate motor response. His model of the world is essentially a structure of active responses. This mode of representation of our environment remains with us throughout our lives, as in such activities as tying knots or climbing stairs. The difficulty of representing a spiral staircase without action is a relic of the enactive stage, which is much more widespread in children than in adults. The process of development is illustrated by one of Bruner's experiments in which children from three to twelve years old were given a board with a number of pegs inserted in it. A ring was placed on a peg in a particular position on the board, removed, and the children asked to replace it on the same peg. None of the children had any difficulty as long as the board was presented to them in the same position as in the demonstration. But when the board was rotated through a right angle, the younger children had difficulty. The motor pattern of response was not the same. The older children, from five years or so, had little difficulty. These children had reached the second stage in the maturational sequence, the stage of iconic representation.

Iconic representation involves the use of visual, motor, and other forms of imagery, as distinct from direct behavioural response. The ability to represent experience of a previous or imagined situation in terms of imagery (Greek: *eikon*, an image) is characteristic of the iconic stage. The child can now apparently construct a visual image of the board rotated through ninety degrees, and a motor image of the response of placing the ring on the peg.

About the age of seven, children were beginning to reach the third stage, that of symbolic representation. Here the ring can be correctly placed whatever the position of the board, by formulating the row and column of the peg on which the ring is to be placed. The child no longer needs to construct an image representing the board as it would be perceived in different positions; his formula is adequate and satisfying. The well-known riddle about which is heavier, a pound of lead or a pound of feathers, can illustrate the transition. To the iconic mode of thought, the riddle involves the image of lead and of feathers; lead has the perceptual quality of heaviness, and feathers of lightness. The symbolic representation is in terms of pound weight, the perceptual qualities being largely irrelevant.

The transition from iconic to symbolic representation involves the extended use of language as a system of signs. Symbolic representation is impossible without some system of language, and there is also evidence that practice in language leads to greater proficiency in symbolic thinking. An inquiry by the Russian psychologist, Luria, demonstrates this relationship. The subjects of the inquiry were a pair of identical twins, both of whom suffered from a condition of retarded speech development which they inherited from their mother. Both the retarded development in the use and understanding of speech, and the fact that as identical twins they were always at the same stage of development, resulted in the twins being able to communicate with each other without much need for language. In fact, when the inquiry began, the twins were using a very primitive language in which the word was not separated from the action; that is, they only used words when the word was accompanied by the appropriate action. Pointing and exclamations were the main method of communication. In Bruner's terms, they were still in the enactive stage.

The first step in the experiment was to separate the twins and place each with a different group of children in a kindergarten. Both twins rapidly progressed to a more symbolic representation of their experience. Language structure became more complex, and was used for narrative and planning; their play activities expanded and their intellectual competence increased. Then one twin was given further training in the use of language. The result was that he later showed a superiority in his command of thought processes and a greater awareness of the logical structure of language. Though these twins were a rather special case, Luria's findings are of general application. 'Saying' a procedure, as in arithmetic, often helps children to learn.

Most of the maturational changes found by Bruner occur in the early years of the pupil's school life. Though he continued his studies of the thinking processes to the level of college students, Bruner did not identify any further development in the sequence beyond symbolic representation. His studies of the thought processes, to which we shall return in a later chapter, are therefore concerned with the elaboration of the symbolic stage.

Cognitive Maturation—Piaget

Piaget's scheme of cognitive development is based on the emergence of different kinds of structure of interpretation and modes of thinking as the child grows older. These follow each other in a regular sequence which is defined in terms of the process by which each stage is reached and the features of the mode of thought characteristic of that stage. Each completed stage represents the beginning of the transition to the next, so that the development is in process all the time. There are no resting places.

Piaget recognizes three main kinds of cognitive structure:

(1) Sensori-Motor.
(2) Concrete Operations.
(3) Formal Operations.

The first stage of maturation is the establishing of sensori-motor structure. This is not unlike Bruner's enactive phase, and the child is still tied to his perceptual experience, responding to the appearance of things around him. He may reach for the moon, but he is also learning the properties and relationships of things in terms of what he can and cannot do with them. There is little yet that can be called thinking; the child has not yet 'internalized' his behaviour.

The first stage takes place mainly in the first two years of life. The next stage is the development of a structure of concrete operations, which is founded on and emerges from the behaviour and experience acquired in the earlier stage. The completed structures of concrete operations are reached at various points between the ages of seven and eleven years. During the development phase of concrete operational thinking, the child becomes able to internalize his operations—that is to say, he can form images of his experience and form relationships between objects which he does not actually manipulate. He uses language, drawings, and symbolic play activities to establish and to represent his thinking. These operations become reversible. Piaget defines reversibility as "the permanent possibility of returning to the starting point of the operation in question". In the demonstration with the glasses of lemonade (p. 48) the older children accepted the concept of the conservation of the quantity of lemonade, because they could envisage the operation of pouring out the liquid in reverse, so that if the liquid were poured back it would be the same as at the beginning of the whole procedure. The less mature children could only judge on what they saw before them. So with the egg and egg-cup demonstration. The less mature children could make a one-to-one correspondence between eggs and egg-cups when they were visible to them; when the perceptual pattern was broken by clustering the eggs, they could not establish again the original pattern by mentally putting the eggs into the egg-cups whence they came.

The structure of concrete operational thinking is not acquired in one step. The child about seven years old takes the first step to thinking in concrete operations. By informal experiment with his environment and by extending the range of his behaviour, the child builds up step by step a system of thought in terms of which he increasingly comes to interpret his experience. Thus a pupil who has established the concept of the conservation of quantity by the age of seven would then be expected to proceed to acquire the concept of the conservation of weight, and later of volume, by interpreting his experiences and observations in terms of the same kind of thought structure. He may accept, for example, that a ball of Plasticine remains the same in quantity and weight, however the shape may be changed, but he may not yet be certain about the constancy of its volume. Or he may accept that the amount of substance remains the same for a ball of clay, however shaped, but not accept the same concept for a rubber band when it is stretched. During this stage the child's thinking is largely restricted to dealing with concrete situations; he does not generalize easily, but builds up systems of thought composed of elements derived from his extending range of experiences.

It is from the foundation of these systems of concrete operations that the final phase emerges, the development of formal operations. This development takes place roughly between the ages of eleven and fifteen years; after fifteen, formal operations have normally become established as the structure of adult thinking. Formal operations are so called because the child begins to think in terms of the form of a logical relationship or structure, independently of the content. The child begins to think in terms of propositions rather than particular instances, he can play with propositions and discuss what is not and what might be; hypotheses begin to have meaning, and his thinking can be ordered in systematic schemes and procedures. The difference between concrete operational thought and formal operations can be illustrated in many ways. It is the difference between applied arithmetic and algebra. Pupils in the concrete operations stage will ask, "What is x?" and want an answer in concrete terms which they can understand. Such pupils can understand a parabola as representing the flight of a ball, but they cannot identify the co-ordinates. The ability of the more mature pupils to order their thinking in terms of hypothesis and system is illustrated by the experiment on the five liquids we described earlier. A similar demonstration requires a rod balanced on a spindle, and weights which can be attached to the rod. The children are given two unequal weights and asked to balance the rod. Those in the concrete operations phase set about solving the problem by fairly systematic trial and error. The first correct solution satisfied them; they did not relate weight to the distance from the fulcrum, and when given another two unequal weights solved the problem afresh by trial and error as before. They observed that the heavier weight needed to be nearer the spindle, and that the distance of the weight from the spindle affected the balance, but they could not combine these two independent observations into a formal relationship of weight and distance. Those children who had attained a structure of formal operational thought could combine the two observations and though most were unable to express the relation formally, could easily solve the problem with different weights by applying the principle of weight times distance.

The development of a structure of formal operations implies detachment of interpretation from immediate personal experience. The relations are handled as a pattern existing in itself. We noted that the immature children could not separate the spatial relationships of the three mountains from the particular view that the child had. From the age of twelve years or so, this problem ceases to give difficulty; the relationship between the mountains is perceived as a formal system, which can be applied in various different instances, and apart from a certain inefficiency in applying the formal relationships, the pupils know what has to be done. But again, formal operations are not attained in one step. The pupils who could manage the three mountains problem would tend to have difficulty with other components of their experience. A number of boys were shown how to operate a simple air pump. All the boys understood thoroughly the operation of the pump and the principles on which it worked. This set of boys, the teacher boys, were then asked to teach the workings of the pump to another set of boys, the pupil boys. The teacher boys had not established completely the structure of formal operations, with the result that they taught the pupil boys those aspects of the topic which they, the teacher boys, had found difficult or interesting. If the pupil boys had difficulty in understanding the operation of the pump, the teacher boys could only repeat the rules, and if the teacher boy did not have the same difficulty as the pupil boy, the teacher boy seemed to have great difficulty in understanding how anyone could not understand an operation which, to the teacher boy, was perfectly clear. The more mature teaching boys, functioning nearer the level of formal operations, could expound the working of the pump independently of their own difficulties, but the exposition was not selective in relation to the needs of the pupil boys, but was a complete and systematic discussion of the pump as a topic in itself. We have here two levels of development towards formal operations; one is completed, the understanding of the pump, whereas the other, the teaching of the pump, has not yet been reached. The experiment has also obvious relevance for any educational method which involves one pupil teaching another.

We have discussed Piaget's theoretical scheme of cognitive development because it is to date the most comprehensive and enlightening. Both Piaget's own work and that which he has inspired have added greatly to our understanding of the way children think, and how they interpret their experience. Essentially what Piaget is trying to do is to find the logical systems according to which children order their thinking at different ages. From this arises one of his major contributions to our understanding of children's behaviour. He has shown that the logical systems underlying children's ordering of their thinking are different in quality from those of adults, and the younger the child the greater the difference. Our accepted principles of logic apply only to the phase of developed formal operations; the children at the stage of concrete operations have a fairly consistent system of logic, but it is of a different quality. It is his convincing demonstrations that children's modes of thought are different from ours and are in themselves fairly consistent that is Piaget's distinctive contribution to child psychology.

He has also performed a useful service by his insistence on the intimate connection between maturation and learning. There has been a tendency among psychologists to contrast the changes in behaviour which have been learned with those arising from the process of maturation. It may appear rather surprising to state that Piaget's theories of learning lean towards an S-R interpretation rather than one in terms of cognitive structure. But to Piaget, cognitive structures are not learned; they are part of the same sequence of growth as leads an egg to become a tadpole, and a tadpole a frog. These cognitive structures provide the logical scheme by which the child organizes his learned behaviour. By learning more and more responses to a wider and wider range of stimuli, the child is able to integrate his behaviour into the logical system appropriate to his stage of cognitive development. His system of interpretation, or his cognitive structure, develops and becomes established, giving his behaviour a foundation of confidence and consistency; then by the natural process of development his body of learned responses becomes reorganized into a new system, in the same way as the bodily structure and physiological processes of the tadpole are reorganized to those of a frog. Educationally, according to Piaget, the need of the child is not to be taught how to organize and understand his experience, but the provision of as wide a range of stimulus situations as will enable the child to establish his appropriate systems of thought on as wide and as firm a basis of learned experience as possible.

The other feature of Piaget's thinking on maturation is his insistence on the sequence of development. His stages of development are not clear cut, and the rate at which children progress through them may vary, but Piaget insists that the sequence of stages is virtually the same for all children. Age norms he regards as largely irrelevant; what matters is the stage the child has reached in the sequence of development. Inhelder, for example, considers that mentally handicapped children pass through the same sequence as other children, but more slowly; the more severely handicapped may never attain the stage of formal operations before intellectual maturity, when maturational development ceases. Besides the stress on the uniformity of sequence among children, Piaget also stresses the rigidity of each stage. The child is the prisoner of his cognitive structure, and cannot think in terms of any scheme other than that which he has built for himself. In one experiment, Smedslund used a ball of Plasticine, weighed it, and then flattened it out, asking if it was the same weight as before. He then reversed the process, but before weighing the re-formed ball he removed, unknown to the child, a small piece of Plasticine, so that on the second weighing it became lighter. Children who had not yet attained the concept of the conservation of weight accepted this without difficulty, but those who had, refused to accept that it had become lighter, and rejected the evidence of the scales.

In education, it is possible that Piaget would approve of a policy of withholding from the teacher any information about the child's chronological age. The teacher would then require to teach the children as he found them, and would have to ascertain the pupil's maturational level before beginning to teach in the manner most appropriate for the pupil. This, however, is by no means as easy as it sounds.

THE ASSESSMENT OF MATURATION

The value of the contributions of Piaget, Bruner, and others to our interpretation of children's behaviour should not blind us to the large gaps that are still present in our knowledge of the matura-tion of cognitive systems, and to the inadequacies of the evidence and interpretation of even such well investigated schemes as Piaget's. The most firmly established evidence is that derived from twin studies, but this is obviously of limited scope.

In order to obtain reliable information about the maturational processes in children, we require to identify and to assess both the sequences of maturational changes in behaviour in children, and the extent to which children differ in their progress through these sequences. To identify maturational changes is, as we have seen, not easy; learning is necessarily present at each stage of a child's development, and only a rough approximation to assess-ment of maturation can be made, on the assumption that learning opportunities are approximately the same for all the children in the sample under observation. Also, we lack adequately standar-dized tests of maturation. In the sector of social and personal maturation they virtually do not exist. In the more intensively studied field of cognitive maturation, they are being developed. The new British intelligence test contains items derived from Piaget's experiments, but its effectiveness can only be established after some years of use. The main difficulty is that most tests of cognitive ability or intelligence are tests of what can be called competence; that is, the child is presented with a series of small problems involving various aspects of the thinking process, and the assessment is based on how many he can solve correctly. The method used to solve them is not recorded, or only recorded incidentally. What is now becoming necessary is to distinguish in practice what has already been distinguished in theory, the difference between maturity and efficiency. Let us illustrate by comparing two babies, who are crossing the floor of a room. The more mature baby will attempt to walk, the less mature will crawl. The crawler is the more efficient of the two, and would win a race. Or consider two pupils of about the same age who draw a street scene. One displays rather immature composition, with the structure of layers we have already mentioned, and each object occupying its own space. The draughtsmanship is good, and the contents of the drawing are lively and well arranged within his system of space. Another pupil, somewhat more mature, attempts a composition within a system of perspective, but cannot co-ordinate the elements within his representation; there is a rather confused mixture of layer composition and perspective composition. This pupil has some conception of what he is trying to do, but is inefficient in its execution. The less mature pupil executes his intentions efficiently, and produces a more satisfactory finished product. Both with the babies and the pupils, the less mature are the more competent, because they are more efficient. Examples of such distinctions are frequent in the classroom, the development of a more mature mode of operation being often accompanied by a loss of efficiency in its execution. Intelligence tests have, to date, failed to distinguish between the pupil who operates efficiently at a lower level of maturity and the pupil who attempts, sometimes unsuccessfully, a solution in terms of a more mature level of thought. This division of competence into a component of maturity and of efficiency is necessary before assessment of maturity can be made. Only the first steps have so far been taken to achieve this.

The other requirement for any assessment of a pupil's maturational level is a system of norms and variability for each age. We ask, what do we expect of the average eight-year-old, and what is the extent of the differences among eight-year-olds? Piaget did not report how far the children whom he observed were representative of their age or not; he used his observations as demonstrations of the mode of thought he was discussing. There have been investigations to ascertain how far Piaget's modes of thought are shown by all children, and what is the variability among children in the establishment of such modes. Table 1 gives the findings of one such inquiry, by Lovell and Ogilvie, on children aged 7+ to 11+ in an English junior school. The cognitive operation was the conservation of substance, as tested by Plasticine in a ball and a sausage shape.

TABLE 1[1]   *Percentages of Children aged 7–11 years showing Conservation of Quantity*

Class	No.	Non-conserving	Transition	Conserving
1st year	83	31	33	36
2nd year	65	20	12	68
3rd year	99	11	15	74
4th year	75	5	9	86

Here we see emerging the kind of information a teacher needs. At age seven to eight years (1st year) about one third of the pupils have attained the concept of conservation, one third have not, and one third are in a transitional stage. By the age of eleven years, 86 per cent of the pupils have attained the concept, but, and this is important for the teacher, 14 per cent have not. The variability among these children is very great indeed. The age of attainment of the concept of conservation of substance is spread over at least four school years, and how far down the age range the process goes is not known. It is such a range of age differences that Piaget's records do not reveal.

Weakness of Evidence about Cognitive Maturation

It is investigations like Lovell's and Ogilvie's that reveal the weakness of much of the evidence upon which schemes of maturation are founded. Piaget's is the most detailed of such schemes, but the rather complex theoretical structure of Piaget's system cannot

[1] Lovell, K., and E. Ogilvie: "A Study of the Conservation of Substance in the Junior School Child", *British Journal of Educational Psychology*, 1960, no. 30, pp. 100–118.

yet be accepted as based on adequate supporting evidence; this implies that a teacher accepting Piaget's statements as a sound basis for educational practice may find these statements inadequate or misleading.

The weaknesses of Piaget's system lie in four main aspects. The first is that most of his evidence is anecdotal; he supports his conclusions by quoting illustrative cases without any indication of how far the children's responses are representative. Proof by selected instances is not sufficient. Another weakness of Piaget's evidence is that much of what is claimed to be a pattern of the thought processes of children is not consistently or clearly manifest in their behaviour. Even in the experimental situations devised by Piaget to demonstrate a particular mode of thought, a considerable number of the responses of children are not clearly classifiable in Piaget's terms. In the experiments we described with the lemonade and the glasses, children frequently do not respond 'according to the book'. They have difficulty in accepting that the quantities in the glasses are equal; the difficulty appears to be a real one, the same as children encounter when asked to choose between two apparently equal pieces of cake. It is quite possible that the child's perception of the sizes does change, so that the other always appears that much bigger. The children also fuss over the few drops of liquid left adhering to the sides of the glass. Latterly Piaget's colleagues tended to use small beads instead of liquids.

A third difficulty is the impossibility of distinguishing between learned responses and those which reflect the child's maturational stage of cognitive structure. Children can learn rules and principles, the difference between the mature and less mature child being that, to the younger or less mature child, the rule or principle is part of the situation itself, to the more mature child the rule is the structure of a set of situations. In a game, the younger children think they must follow the known rules to play the game; the older children can modify rules so that the game can be played. But this difference of thought is not easy to detect, and the probing questions that are needed to clarify the child's attitude can themselves very easily influence the child's responses. There is some suspicion that Piaget's early finding that children tend to attribute life to moving objects may be the result of the reflexive verb in French; the door, for example, shuts itself.

The final difficulty in accepting Piaget's scheme is illustrated by Table 1 (p. 62), and by the brief outline below of the major sequences in development:

(1) Under seven: mostly sensori-motor development.
(2) Seven to twelve: developing concrete operations.
(3) About twelve: concrete operations established.
(4) Eleven to fourteen: developing formal operations.
(5) Fifteen plus: formal operations established.

The stages of development take about four or five years to pass through, and children can be at various points of development within the stages. The sweep is so broad as to be of little use as a basis for an educational method. The school periods of infants, primary, and secondary each roughly contain a major sequence, but more precision is necessary for both psychologist and teacher.

The value of Piaget's work has been to emphasize the difference in the modes of thought of pupils at different stages of development; it has also inspired an increasing volume of inquiry into the nature and development of these modes of thought. But this work is not yet completed and despite the detailed complexity of much of Piaget's theoretical discussion, the present policy for psychologist and teacher is best one of caution and patience.

MAIN PRINCIPLES OF MATURATION

We can conclude this discussion by stating somewhat categorically the broad principles which appear to apply to all aspects of maturation, though we cannot yet state precisely how these principles operate in much detail.

1. The first principle is that development is from molar to molecular. This means that earlier behaviour is more massive, generalized, and total than later behaviour. The young child grasps objects clumsily and massively, involving the whole body in the action; this is molar or mass behaviour. The older child picks up an object by using thumb and forefinger only; it is a more precise, articulated form of behaviour, limited to the single action; this we call molecular. In speech, the young child tries to produce the general sound of a word as he hears it. If the word is "cream", he says "eem", which is probably what he hears, then becomes increasingly precise in his articulation, shaping the word through "keem" to "kweem" to "cream". In language, the same

process can be observed. A child wanting to see over a wall says "Up". He is not trying to say "Lift me up"; the one word "up" is sufficient to express his meaning, for him it is an 'up' situation not yet analysed into component elements. He does not need more words; the situation is a single massive one, for which one word is adequate. It is not till later that more words are needed; by then the situation is perceived as having three elements, 'lift', 'me', and 'up', which require to be co-ordinated into a more precise, complex, and articulated statement. The child does not mature by adding additional items of behaviour like bricks; the development is rather that the massive, unformed behaviour becomes shaped, analysed, co-ordinated, and more precise.

2. The second principle is that maturation is irreversible. Though talking to infants we may say "up" we can no longer think of the situation as just one of 'upness'. We must think in adult terms and say that what the child means is, "Lift me up". The thinking and interpretations of children are a closed book to the adult; we can no longer see a classroom through the eyes of an infant. Our earlier modes of thought have been replaced by later modes, and we are as much prisoners of our modes of thought as the child is of his. We have fragments of memories, usually unreliable before the age of four. Adults were all very old, time could be very long, other people's houses had different smells, legs could become very tired, and the dark could be terrifying. The way to understand children's behaviour is not to try to recreate a child's experience, but to use our adult abilities of close and systematic observation of children's behaviour.

The principle of irreversibility has certain implications for education. The psychological processes of a twelve-year-old learning French are not the same as a French two-year-old learning French; the difference is that between the thinking and experience of a two-year-old and those of a twelve-year-old, and it is a very substantial difference. Psychologists use the term infantile regression for the behaviour of older children who find that the social and emotional demands made upon them are greater than they can meet, and who escape by regressing to the—to them—simpler and more protected world of the infant. Like Peter Pan, they do not want to grow up. Such regression may appear in a child who seeks to gain the attention of his parents by acting helpless, or by competing with a younger brother or sister for the mother's apparently lost affection and care. The behaviour of such children is not properly a regression to an earlier level of behaviour; the child is acting the role of a younger child as he sees it, and the difference between a seven-year-old acting the part of a four-year-old, and a real four-year-old, is not difficult to observe.

3. Maturation in children is not a uniform process. It is uniform neither for all children nor for any one child. We have already referred to the 'adolescent spurt' and to Lovell's and Ogilvie's investigation. Until, however, we have more exact methods of identifying what stage of maturation a child is at, and what is the extent of variation among children, we can do little more than state that differences do exist, but that we cannot, except possibly in physical growth, identify them very precisely. In general, there is some association between different sectors of children's development. Intelligence quotient and physique, for example, are positively associated; children above average in IQ tend to be above average in height and weight (see Chapter 7, p. 189).

4. The final principle concerns the relation between maturation and learning. The maturation of a pattern of behaviour is itself a motive for the exercise of that behaviour. This exercise necessarily involved learning, which not only leads to the establishment of the behaviour but to increased efficiency in its operation. A child who has developed the ability to walk persists in walking despite stumbles and tumbles, and learns how to walk more efficiently. Learning comes more readily if in step with maturational development, as is demonstrated by the co-twin experiment in climbing steps. The same principle almost certainly applies in school learning, though there the situation is complicated by the difficulty of establishing clearly the pupil's maturational stage, and by the fact that school learning is frequently a rather complex structure of various psychological processes going on at the same time. A careful study, still to be undertaken, of the relationship between children's games and their intellectual, social, and physical development would probably reveal the same relationship; the children begin to play particular games when they have developed the ability to play them.

If education is to be related to the interests and ability of pupils, then this relationship between maturation and learning is central to education. We examine it more fully in the next chapter.

3

Education, Maturation, and Learning

COMPONENTS IN THE SCHOOL SITUATION

In this chapter we examine some of the ways in which the contents of the previous chapters on learning and on maturation apply in school learning. A school is an institution in which learning takes place. Teaching is an aid to learning, and learning theory, however well founded, does not necessarily generate a teaching method. Learning can take place without teaching, and teaching can take place without learning. In early reading, for example, a teacher may be presenting the process of reading in terms of phonics, while the pupil may be learning to read by sight methods of word recognition.

We have in the school situation three major sets of structures and processes. There is the structure of the subject matter to be learned. There is the structure of the learning process itself, whether in terms of S-R or cognitive structure, or a mixture of these. There is finally the structure of the learner's thought processes, which we shall follow on the broad lines of Piaget's theory, which implies change in thought structure by maturation. Each of these is structured according to its own requirements and limitations, and functions accordingly. Let us examine each in turn.

Subject Matter—Formal Structure

The division of the content of school learning into 'subjects' is partly traditional and partly founded on good psychological principles. Though the classification of subjects may change from time to time, each major subject area does tend to represent a different cognitive structure in both content and mode of thought. The learning of the mother tongue involves different psychological processes from the later learning of a foreign language. The learning of an experimentally based science like chemistry calls for a kind of thinking and observation not required in mathematics. History and geography may be combined as social studies or environmental studies, but if carried beyond the anecdotal and purely factual level, they tend to separate. The geographer's interpretation of events is not the same as the historian's, and there is the difficulty that a lot of history can happen in very little geography. The scientific mode of thought can differ widely from the literary or aesthetic mode of thought. We can illustrate with the anecdote of the teacher of English who went off ill as his class were reading the speech, "The quality of mercy is not strained . . ." in *The Merchant of Venice*. He was temporarily replaced by a teacher of science. When a pupil asked if the word "strained" meant "stretched" or "filtered", the science teacher, true to his mode of thinking, replied that as the quality of mercy had not in fact been strained, the question did not arise.

The same basic psychological processes of learning, remembering, and thinking are common to all school 'subjects'. Though the ingredients are the same, the recipe is different for each subject, some involving much more routine learning, others involving much more thinking at a formal operations level. We believe, for instance, that pupils obtain some benefit from the reading of Shakespeare's plays, but we regard Einstein's theory of relativity as too difficult. Both represent a very high level of human achievement in different spheres of activity; but the psychological requirements in those two spheres are different.

No adequate analysis has yet been made of the psychological requirements of different disciplines, but in its very simplest terms a school subject consists of a number of items of information, organized into a particular structure of relationships, together with a method of extending these relationships. What we have to ask is whether the learning of these items of information involves the same kind of learning in all subjects—does the S-R formula, for example, apply to the learning of vocabulary as well as to chemical formulae or geographical facts? And does the learning of the structure of relationships involve another kind of learning, or are they learned the same way? And is the learning of either information or relationships related to the maturational level of the learner, or can we distinguish ingredients in the subject which can be learned at any age from those which require a more mature system of thinking? And are there differences between children, such that the learning of a particular mode of thought comes more easily to some than to others?

Subject Matter—Teaching Structure

There is also a further distinction to be made within school subjects. The structure of a school subject as such is in terms of adult modes of thought or, in Piaget's terms, formal operations. It has been recognized for a long time, about two hundred years or so, that the formal, logical development of a subject is not the most suitable way of presentation to children. The wind has to be tempered; and the process of tempering has been determined much more by educational dogmatism than by psychological knowledge. It probably still is, but as our psychological inquiries into how children learn and think are extended, it is to be hoped that what children are expected to learn will come ever closer to what children are able to learn.

The conflict between the logical structure of a subject and the psychological processes of children's learning is a real one. In arithmetic, for example, a pupil may easily enough learn the rules for a simple sum like $1+3+0 = 4$, but the simplest number relationships are the most difficult to explain. A number is a class of a class of concepts. What is the difference between a man and one man? What does adding mean, as distinct from knowing how to add? What does the equal sign mean? Obviously it does not mean 'the same as', for $1+3+0$ is clearly not the same as 4, because the two sides of the equation are different; $4 = 4$ is not an equation. Similarly with measurement. The two simplest shapes in common objects are the rectangle and the circle. But the diagonal of a rectangle cannot be measured exactly in the same units as the two sides. The root of two is reported to have driven Pythagoras to suicide; if the inhabitants of the infant classroom took their understanding of number as seriously as Pythagoras, they would follow his example. Fortunately they do not. But root two and pi are not matters commonly raised in the infant class, though they are basic to any 'understanding' of number and measurement. The more elementary the mathematical operation, the closer it is to the fundamental axioms of mathematics, and mathematics is formal operations par excellence.

˹ The conflict is usually side-stepped by the teacher, who relies on selected instances which avoid difficulty. Before remainders have been taught, division sums come out exactly. In history, for example, which is a study of how human social relationships evolve and change through time, the need for simplification results in the annual crop of howlers to which history tends to contribute more than its fair share. In some methods of teaching history the pupil may cover the same period more than once in his school life, such familiar figures as Canute, Columbus, and Cromwell appearing in increasingly complex contexts as the pupil's ability to understand personal and social relations increases with maturity and experience.

Learning Process—Operant Conditioning

It is the teaching structure of subject matter that the pupil encounters in school and we confine our discussion to the learning of that. There is also, as we have discussed, more than one kind of learning process. The classical conditioning pattern of learning has virtually no place in the schoolroom context. Skinner's scheme of operant conditioning, the shaping of behaviour, is more relevant. The basic pattern may be presented thus:

$$S—R_0—S_1—R_1$$

where S is the condition of the learner which sets the behaviour in motion. In the laboratory it is often hunger, but in school it may be desire for approval, or competition with others, or conformity to routine, or avoidance of boredom or punishment, or interest in developing schemes of thought. This condition S originates behaviour; the response R_0 of the organism, here the pupil, is to find ways of satisfying the needs of the condition S. At this point, S_1 is the presentation of a specific stimulus, the behaviour to be learned, such as a word whose meaning is to be learned, or an arithmetic relationship to be completed, or an article to be made. R_1 is the completion of the response, which acts as a reinforcer, and establishes the response as an element of learned behaviour. A pupil given the stimulus S_1, for example, $H_2O + SO_3$, gives the response H_2SO_4, which, if known to be correct, is thereby reinforced. The same pattern of learning can apply to number relations, mathematical formulae, historical and geographical facts, spelling, vocabulary, and so on. In fact, any kind of study which involves the giving of a prescribed response, whether verbal or otherwise, to a presented stimulus can be fitted into this pattern.

Before learning on this pattern can occur, certain conditions have to be fulfilled. First, the formula for operant conditioning falls into two parts. The first part, $S—R_0$, implies some form of directed activity by the learner. He is not passive, but the precise behaviour by which his activity will find satisfaction has not yet been established. A pupil seeks an approving response from his teacher, or wants to know the outcome of an experiment, or wants to pass an examination. To do this, the pupil must learn the appropriate specific forms of behaviour. Such general motives are sufficient to create a readiness to learn the required set of specific S-R units of behaviour. According to operant conditioning theory, there must be some kind of motivation to start the learning process. We discuss later whether this is necessarily a correct view.

The second condition for operant conditioning learning is that there must be reinforcement. This raises one of the fundamental questions in learning. There are two aspects of the question. One is, how is a pupil to know whether his response is correct or not? The other aspect concerns the unlearning of established responses. The first aspect requires us to distinguish between a response which satisfies the learner, and is therefore reinforced, and one which is correct in terms of subject matter. Ideally in education the response should be both correct and satisfying, but it does not always happen so. Herein is one of the gaps between the laboratory and the classroom. The experimental animal gains its food or its freedom, and the effective response is established. But a pupil working out a problem in arithmetic may add 8 and 5, and give the answer 11. He then goes on to the next problem, the completion of the first task having reinforced his response of 11. What is the solution in practice? It lies in the devising of teaching methods in which the pupil's error is self-evident or in which there is close supervision by the teacher, who can remedy error immediately it occurs. Skinner was fully aware of this difficulty, and has devised a solution called Programmed Learning, which we discuss more fully later. One feature of programmed learning is that correction of wrong responses occurs immediately. The traditional method of direct instruction also has the merit of the teacher, by questioning, being able to negatively reinforce undesired responses immediately, and to positively reinforce correct ones.

Where learning of the operant conditioning pattern is taking place, the practice of letting pupils discover and learn is probably the least effective.

The other solution to the difficulty is learning by self-correcting material or tasks. The Montessori material for infants is based on this principle, but its application throughout the school is limited. But there is one important part of school learning where the learning task is self-correcting, the learning of manual skills. The learning of such a skill, as we have seen, involves the establishing of a chain of S-R units, the successful acquisition of a skill depending on the establishment not only of the correct individual responses, but on the correct sequence of responses, where the response to one stimulus acts as the stimulus for the next response in the chain. The learner's behaviour is being 'shaped' more and more precisely, and he is aware of the immediate outcome of his responses in the shape of a dropped catch, a wrong note, an unsatisfactory line in drawing or a loose fitting in a model. All of these act as negative reinforcers for the wrong response, which becomes eliminated, and the recognition by the learner of an improved performance or the successful accomplishment of his task reinforces the effective set of responses. The S-R theory and practice of learning fits well with this kind of school learning, and the only additional reinforcement that may be needed is that when the learner is satisfied with a lower level of skill than the teacher requires.

The second aspect of reinforcement concerns the unlearning of established responses. Teachers are aware that part of their time has to be spent in unteaching, whether it is called getting rid of bad habits or clearing up wrong ideas. A child may learn to count successfully by using his fingers, and the behaviour becomes established. Another may learn science by demonstration or experiment, and be satisfied with the first solution reached; the practice of verifying will not be established. Another may learn, "six from three, you cannot", and find difficulty later in learning that $3 - 6 = -3$. The behaviour to be unlearned is frequently the outcome of the child's maturational level of behaviour and thinking. Though the cognitive structure of interpretation may change with age, specific responses do not necessarily change with it; S-R units are relatively stable.

How does S-R theory fit the classroom requirements of unlearning? According to theory, unlearning takes place in two ways, by extinction and by negative reinforcement. If a pigeon has learned to peck a bar to obtain food, and the food supply is stopped, the pigeon soon ceases to peck the bar. The response has been extinguished. If a pupil learns a skill like playing a musical instrument, but ceases to use the skill and obtain satisfaction from it, the skilled responses will gradually be lost. Similarly, specific responses to specific stimuli which are not maintained by reinforcement—for example, vocabulary in a foreign language—will also become extinguished. But the process of extinction is not a reliable one from the classroom point of view; it depends on the withdrawal of reinforcement, which is not wholly under the teacher's control; skills in particular seem resistant to extinction, for reasons which are not yet clear.

A more effective method of unlearning is negative reinforcement. This, as the name implies, is associating the response with an outcome not satisfying to the learner. Punishment of any sort is a negative reinforcer; punishment need not be severe—the disapproval of the teacher or the knowledge that the response is incorrect can be negative reinforcers. Negative reinforcement does not generate learning, and unlearning is only effective where a substitute acceptable response is available for the response being eliminated. The most effective application of the theory of reinforcement to learning practice is negative reinforcement of the undesired response, accompanied by positive reinforcement of the desired response, both responses satisfying the same need in the learner. The educational practice derived from this part of the theory is fairly obvious, but to be effective in the classroom it needs to be applied more precisely and systematically than is usually done. In practice, however, most of the responses learned by S-R learning in school do not require to be unlearned later.

Learning Process—Cognitive Structure

We have so far considered the process of learning in terms of the acquiring of S-R units of behaviour, and examined how far this mode of learning applies to the learning of certain elements of school subjects. But there are some components of subject matter to which the S-R learning pattern does not fit. There is the component of learning to organize and to develop in other contexts the specific items of behaviour learned. Facts without interpretation are as valueless as interpretations without facts. As we saw in Chapter 1, S-R learning theory does attempt to account for this sector of learning, but not very convincingly. The S-R interpretation is based on the processes of stimulus generalization and stimulus discrimination, but both these processes imply a system of classification which the S-R theory fails to explain, as, for example, in Harlow's experiment with the monkeys who learned to choose the middle object.

Such a system of classification is one example of what we have called a cognitive structure. The acquiring of such cognitive structures is directly related to maturation, and appears to be a form of learning virtually restricted to man and certain higher animals. This is the way a pupil learns to organize his experience and to extend his learning. A pupil learns to add 6 and 3 to give 9. This does not help him when presented with 4+2, as the responses have to be learned as independent S-R units. He proceeds to 6+3+4, in which previously learned S-R units are incorporated in a chain, but he has also learned the operation of 'carrying' to express the answer 13 in terms of tens and units. If he has acquired the necessary factual knowledge of other specific number relations, such as 7+6+4, he can then express the total, 17, in the same pattern of tens and units. A simple cognitive structure has been acquired, which can be applied to an indefinite number of other learned number combinations. It has been shown that children of about nine years old and upwards have little difficulty in learning number systems to the base of eight, two, twelve, and so on. The cognitive structures so acquired enable pupils to organize the number combinations they have learned, mainly by rote, in systems other than decimal. But it must be emphasized that a cognitive structure must have content, that it is an organization of behaviour, much of which has been learned in the form of S-R units. Outside of Wonderland, there are no grins without cats. As another example, consider a pupil learning Latin. He faces a twofold task. One is the learning of the vocabulary and the forms of the language. The other is learning the cognitive structure of thought characteristic of a highly inflected language. The learning of Latin vocabulary is not a very different process psychologically from learning French vocabulary, or geographical or scientific facts. Such learning will enable the pupil to advance only as far in the learning of Latin as he is permitted by the process of looking through a passage, picking out the nominative forms, finding the right verb, then searching for the accusative forms. To progress further the structure of thought has to be interpreted in Latin structure; 'arma virumque cano' is not 'arms the man-and sing-I.'

The processes whereby a pupil acquires and develops a system of cognitive structures is not yet clearly understood. There is a maturational component, which makes the fitting of the structure of subject matter to the structure of the pupil's level of thinking an uncertain task. Our lack of knowledge of how the pupil's thinking and interpretation of experience develops means that we have less control of the learning process than we have in the S-R learning pattern. We have already noted that the process of letting the pupil learn by the process of 'discovery' is unreliable and uncertain. Experiments and investigation by the pupil require to be so devised that the pupil cannot fail to 'discover' the correct or desired conclusion. A problem which the pupil cannot solve is of no assistance to learning; a problem in which the pupil reaches a wrong conclusion, in terms of subject structure, means another unlearning problem for the teacher. There is no doubt that pupils have to learn to organize and structure their experience correctly as part of the learning of a school subject. We are still uncertain about the teaching and learning techniques involved. The probability is that such learning will be found to require as much detailed and precise guidance as the learning of vocabulary, spelling, and factual information.

Where the subject structure is presented to a pupil whose systems of cognitive structures are either too immature or too inefficient for him to apprehend the subject structure some learning will take place, but it will be mainly on the S-R pattern. One difficulty is that efficient S-R learning, of a geometrical proposition, or a scientific definition and process, is very difficult to distinguish from 'understanding'. We put the word 'understanding' in inverted commas because it is the source of much educational confusion. If pupils have learned to find the right answer to a question or a problem, how do we distinguish the pupil who 'understands' from the one who does not? We have already given the psychologist's answer. We cannot. And what has still to be investigated is the effect on the pupil's learning of too much explanation—that is, the presenting to pupils of cognitive structures too complex and mature for them to acquire.

Learning as cognitive structure leaves unsolved virtually the same difficulties as we discussed for S-R learning. There is the distinction between the 'correct' structure educationally, and the satisfying structure to the pupil, whose standards may not be those of the teacher. The unlearning difficulty is present also, but in a somewhat different form. As a maturational change is in process during the pupil's school life, the cognitive structures learned are not so stable as those elements of behaviour acquired by the S-R learning process. So earlier systems of interpretation of experience may change, but how the changes are to be controlled by the teacher to coincide more closely with the structure of the subject is not known. The difficulty with learning in terms of cognitive structure is not that it is limited to certain sectors of learning, but it is so pervasive throughout all human learning that there is no firm handle for the teacher to take hold of. The more precise and particular the process and the content of learning, the more easily can the learning be directed.

Maturation: The Development of Thought Structures

The third component in the school situation, maturation, we have already discussed, with particular emphasis on Piaget's system of cognitive structure development. Those elements in the school subjects and the learning process which fit into S-R patterns are not significantly related to maturation. A younger child can learn the response 7, to $3+4$, in the same way as an older child learns the response 12 to 3×4, or a still older child learns 0·75 as response to $\frac{3}{4}$, or a yet older child learns 81 as the response to 3^4. In terms of S-R learning, the older child can acquire a larger repertoire of responses, but the process of acquiring them is not significantly changed with age.

The evidence obtained from Piaget's and similar investigations has established firmly that there are substantial differences in the quality of children's thinking at different ages. The mode of thought called concrete operations is not just an incomplete or undeveloped form of formal operations; it is relatively self-consistent and of a different pattern from the later mode of formal operations, and has its own logic. This difference is significant for education, especially for the relating of the structure of thought involved in school subjects to the process of learning cognitive structures and the maturational sequence of different cognitive structures. It has long been an accepted principle in education that the subject matter should be adapted to the level of the growing child's ability to learn, but the underlying assumption has tended to be that cognitive development is a continuous process, and that if the school learning tasks were presented in a simple form and taken slowly, the child's learning would steadily develop as he grew older. Piaget's findings have shown this concept to be inadequate as far as cognitive structure is concerned, and this has raised educational problems which we are just beginning to investigate.

To the educational questions which Piaget's studies have raised there are at present no clear answers. To keep our thinking clear, there are certain points which must not be lost sight of. The first is that the investigations of Piaget, Bruner, and others on the structure of the thinking processes of children were psychological inquiries. They did not arise from educational situations, nor were they aimed at answering educational questions. The second point is that the psychologist is concerned with evidence; that is, he cannot reach a conclusion which goes beyond the evidence available to him. When adequate information is available, the educational implications of the psychologists' findings can be investigated and tried out. Which leads us to the third point to keep in mind, that the psychologist's contribution to education is mainly to enable the teacher to distinguish what he does know about children from what he does not know. And the present position about the significance of Piaget's findings about children in relation to educational practice is that we do not know.

There are a number of questions which the teacher can legitimately ask. If primary-school pupils' structure of thought is in terms of concrete operations, later to develop, for most, into a system of formal operations, is there any justification for teaching such formally based subjects as mathematics and science to younger children? Or does extensive and satisfying learning by children at the concrete operations level lead to easier and more flexible learning at later stages in their developmental sequence? Would it be best in the earlier school years to present to children only such learning tasks as can be acquired by S-R processes, and leave interpretation till the child can acquire adult modes of thought about the subject matter? Is there justification for the teacher preventing certain learning which is acceptable to immature children, but will almost certainly have to be unlearned later? To each question the psychologist can as yet only give an incomplete answer. We do know that primary-school pupils can learn number combinations and rules which will enable them to solve some mathematical problems, and in the field of science they can acquire a wide range of information about the world around them in the form of what used to be called nature study. Also, in the sector of social and personal education we do prevent learning, with some degree of success, of various undesirable forms of behaviour like wiping the nose on the sleeve, swearing, greed, or unduly aggressive behaviour to others. But to the core of the teachers' questions there can only be one answer in the present state of our knowledge. We do not know. The practice of educational policy-makers of reforming school practices before there is adequate information of which practices are in need of reform and what the effects of reform are, leaves the teacher in somewhat of a dilemma. He cannot, especially if under pressure to adopt 'modern' or 'progressive' practices, stand still until the effects of such changes have been adequately investigated. The teacher who adopts new but unproved techniques in an exploratory manner, prepared to observe carefully the effects on the children's learning and prepared to continue and modify what seems effective, but also to abandon what creates difficulty, is adding to the information available, and supplementing the more precise investigations of the psychologist. The teacher who adopts new content and method as an act of faith is, to put it bluntly, obstructing the gathering of reliable information, and acting irresponsibly to the pupils in his care. Doctrinaire ignorance is not progress; acknowledged ignorance can be the beginning of progress.

WHERE TEACHING AND PSYCHOLOGY MEET

Piaget and cognitive structure, however, is not the whole of maturation, and our present ignorance of the educational significance of Piaget's findings does not imply that the applications to education of psychological findings on maturation and learning are wholly unknown. There are a number of points of contact between the psychologist's evidence and conclusions on the one hand and school practice on the other, and it is a few of these that we now examine in more detail. Our aim is to be specific and detailed, and to take certain topics as models of the kind of contributions the psychologist can make to educational practice. We consider in turn five such topics: Readiness, Late Developers, Motivation, Learning Techniques, and Programmed Learning. All involve the psychological processes of learning and maturation as related to educational practice.

READINESS TO LEARN TO READ

As an example of readiness we take reading readiness, mainly because it has been much more fully investigated than most other sectors of school learning. There are certain requirements in the structure of the reading process, and the relation of these to the pupil's maturational level and his ability to learn has been to a very large extent established, mainly by work done in the first quarter of this century. We proceed from an analysis of the process of reading to the corresponding analysis of the psychological development of the pupil. When the pupil has developed the ability to learn the operations involved in reading, he is said to be ready to read. The term tends to be confined to the first stages of reading, but there is no reason why we should not ask the same questions about the abilities of secondary-school pupils. When are they ready to study linguistics as distinct from learning to use a language? When are they ready to be introduced to the concepts involved in literary criticism? When can they begin to appreciate the essay as a literary form? There is a lack of precise information about the later stages of reading.

The Process of Reading

If we undertake a 'job analysis' of the first stages in reading, we find that reading is in the first instance a muscular and perceptual skill. The reader's eyes move in a series of orderly flicks along the horizontal line of print; a skilled reader makes about four pauses or fixations per line in reading material such as this. For about 95 per cent of the time the eyes are at rest, each fixation taking about two-fifths of a second. There are occasional backward movements or regressions, but these are few in a skilled reader, about one for each two or three lines read. The reader has also to organize his perceptual field into figure and ground, so that only the words being read, together with a few words ahead, are perceived as the figure. The remainder of the page is ground. The perceptual field has to be reorganized each time the reader's eyes fixate the line of print. Part of the skill of reading is to learn to recognize words or phrases from perceptual cues; not all of each word need be perceived, the reader learns to recognize words by their characteristic shapes. For example, 'xlgxbxx' is more easily recognized than 'axxexra', though of the word 'algebra' only three letters are presented in the first outline and four in the second. Other cues are certain common combinations of letters, like 'ation', the initial letters of the word, and the pattern of the upper half of the letters of the words. The learning of such cues is of the same nature as the learning of a skill. Further, the reader must learn the conventions of print in English and similar languages, where the letter is a symbol representing a spoken sound, and not as in Chinese the object or idea referred to.

Comprehension is a secondary function, dependent on the meaningfulness of the spoken language into which the symbols are translated. It is possible to say that we have read a passage, but cannot understand it; failure to comprehend the content of an article on biochemistry is not due to inability to read it; it is due to lack of knowledge of biochemistry, which is remedied by learning biochemistry, not by learning to read.

Reading Readiness

When is the pupil able to begin learning this skill called reading? First, he must have sufficient co-ordination of his eye muscles to be able to see the print by an orderly sequence of movements of both eyes. The muscular co-ordination of children under about four years old has not developed sufficiently for them to learn to make other than very massive and clumsy eye movements, not precise enough to read anything but the largest of print well spaced out. Most children reach the stage of physical maturity necessary to learn this skill between their fifth and sixth birthdays; some slow-maturing pupils may be later, but nearly all have reached the required level of maturation by the age of seven. Once the required level of maturational development has been reached, the rate of increase in skill by learning is fairly rapid at first; though with the slower-maturing children muscular fatigue due to learning an unaccustomed movement is always a possibility.

Another maturational component is the fact that around the age of six, the physical growth of some children may involve a slight temporary change in the shape of the eye-ball. This may become slightly distorted, so that the child has a tendency to long sight —that is, difficulty in bringing near objects, like words in a book, into clear focus. This also may lead to greater susceptibility to fatigue of the muscles of the lenses.

The next requirement is that the pupil should be able to organize his perceptual field to attend only to the group of words being read at the time. Less is known of the maturation of such perceptual ability, but it is known that the perceptual organization of younger children is of a broader and more massive nature than is required for reading; finer distinctions in the visual field are not systematically observed. The next stage is the ability to isolate single details with increasing precision; the third stage involves the ability to co-ordinate such details into a pattern within the more massive perception. This third stage is necessary before reading can be learned effectively. When it is attained by most children is uncertain, but it does seem that when a child is mature enough to co-ordinate eye movements, he is usually also mature enough to begin to learn to organize his visual and auditory fields. But children may need help in learning these perceptual skills. Large print, well spaced, is one such aid. Use of the finger to identify the visual area being attended to is another. Children learning by phonic methods often have a similar difficulty; the single sounds 'ka', 'uh', 'tuh', are not always easily co-ordinated to form the word "cat"; nor are the separate letters, c, a, t, always co-ordinated to make a recognizable single word pattern. Such pupils may be able to read letters or simple groups of letters, but have difficulty with longer words. This ability to form more complex perceptual patterns may develop late or develop slowly; perceptual immaturity can be a factor in delaying reading readiness.

Another major maturational factor in reading readiness is the pupil's ability to interpret the printed letters and words as symbols, not pictures. Many children between four and five years of age regard the letters p, q, b, and d as the same object in different positions. They can identify the letter, but fail to understand the significance of the different positions. A similar lack of maturity may lead young children to fail to appreciate the difference of the order of individual letters in a word, such that ate, eat, and tea may not be distinguished as separate words, the letters being the same. Another source of confusion, which may be due to immaturity or bad teaching, is shown in the pupil who recognizes the word "pig" because it has a curly tail, or the word "look" because it has two eyes, oo, to look with. This aspect of maturational development involving the appreciation of the symbolic nature of print coincides roughly with the first emergence of Piaget's concrete operational stage and of Bruner's symbolic representation. Whether there is a connection or not is uncertain; if there is, the psychological evidence would tend to support the view that the appropriate age to begin reading would be after the sixth birthday rather than the fifth.

There are certain other sectors of the child's maturational development which are sometimes related to reading readiness in educational practice, but for which there is no psychological evidence in support. Vocabulary development is one such. The evidence is that, other than in exceptional cases, the child's vocabulary and language structure are more than adequate for the simple requirements of the earlier readers. Nor is there any psychological evidence to suggest that the study of pictures bears any relationship to the process of learning to read.

The maturation of the various functions involved in the reading process does not occur at the same time in any one child, or at the same time in different pupils. Generally, these functions mature between the ages of five and seven years. But there is no single psychological function called reading ability, and no single learning operation called reading. Reading readiness is a phase of development, not a single point. As the psychological functions may mature at different points in the pupil's development, various attempts have been made to enable the learning of some of the components of reading to become quicker and easier for the pupil. Phonic methods, in the older form, present the pupil with a selected vocabulary where rules of phonic relations of letters and sounds may be directly applied—the big pig has a wig, or the cat sat on a mat; such material probably offends the teacher more than the pupil. The Initial Teaching Alphabet, or i.t.a., uses a more extensive vocabulary, but also extends the range of symbols to enable more direct correspondences between letters and sounds to be established. Another method, known as the reduced alphabet, concentrates on reducing the demands of visual discrimination on the young reader by using only one form of a letter shape which may appear as a different letter in different positions; the letters u and n do not both appear, as u is n upside down. So with b, d, p, and q. The excluded letters are introduced as reading skill develops. Other methods use colour as an aid in discriminating letter-sound responses.

It is not easy to sum up the vast amount of information available about the earlier stages of learning to read. There is perhaps one conclusion that can be drawn, that such methods as we have mentioned are all aids to easier learning after the psychological functions have matured; they are not a substitute for maturation. The evidence is that any advantage such selective methods have over what can be called the traditional or direct approach is due to the faster learning of children who have begun the process of learning to read; the slower-maturing children are virtually unaffected by such methods. We have emphasized that reading is not a single psychological function, but a complex of muscular, perceptual, and intellectual functions maturing at different points. We do not propose here to further complicate the picture by examining the different kinds and levels of learning processes involved in learning to read. Reference to Gragné's scheme outlined in Chapter 1 would suggest that the learning processes of operant conditioning, chaining, verbal association, multiple discrimination, concept learning, and principle learning are all involved to a greater or lesser degree in even the earliest steps in learning to read.

Nearly all school-children learn to read more or less well sooner or later. What then is the contribution of this extensive research to the teacher? The first answer is that it demonstrates that children are not taught to read; the teacher helps them to learn to read when they have developed the necessary maturity. This applies to nearly all other sectors of school learning. The second contribution is to draw attention to the differences between children in the development of readiness for reading or for any other school study. A third contribution is to demonstrate the complex nature of the processes involved in learning to read, such that a deficiency or delay in any one of them can create difficulty with the whole system of processes.

THE LATE DEVELOPER

We take this topic for fuller examination because there are children who are correctly so described, and others, also so described, who are not late developers. The later developer is only a late developer when he has developed. The rate at which children progress through the maturational sequence is not the same for all, so that at any given age there will be children who are more mature than others, and others less mature. By definition, about half will be below average for their age in any sector of maturity which can be assessed. If the rate of development for each child were uniform, then the slow-developing child would remain below average. If the pattern of development were one of spurts and rests, then a pupil's maturational standing among his contemporaries would change from time to time. We have to settle the question on the evidence available. In physical growth there is some evidence that development is predominantly uniform, but not wholly so. The adolescent spurt is the best known exception to uniformity. In cognitive, or intellectual, growth there is no corresponding evidence of spurts and rests. The main source of evidence comes at present from the study of intelligence-test findings. These tests do provide evidence about the maturational development of children, but, as we have seen, measure competence, of which intellectual maturity is one, but not the only, component. The evidence here is fairly consistent; the tendency for the pupil's IQ to vary is less strong than the tendency for the IQ to remain relatively constant. Table 2 gives the results of one American study of the changes in children's intellectual level over a period of twelve years. The same group of children were assessed at regular intervals throughout their school life, from the age of six to the age of eighteen. The findings are given in correlation coefficients. This measure is discussed more fully in a later chapter; here it suffices to say that a high correlation coefficient means a greater degree of correspondence, or constancy of standing, than a low coefficient, and a correlation coefficient of 0·75 represents a substantial amount of correspondence.

TABLE 2[1]   *Constancy of IQs of the same group of children for IQ at 10 years and 18 years*

Age in Years	Correlation with IQ at Age 10	Correlation with IQ at Age 18
6	0.76	0.61
7	0.78	0.71
8	0.88	0.70
9	0.90	0.76
10	(1.0)	0.70
12	0.87	0.76

As might be expected, the least agreement between the IQs is that between those of the children at age six and at age eighteen. But the whole trend of the table is to indicate that a pupil of high intelligence tends to remain so, and similarly for pupils of low intelligence and average intelligence. When interpreted further in terms of late developers, the evidence supports the conclusion that the later developer tends to remain backward, and the early developer to retain his advantage; the late developer who 'makes up' for his late start is the exception. This finding is in general agreement with common observation within the school. Further, the slow learner who later blossoms is only one of a number of kinds of pupils who constitute the exceptions. There is the average learner who becomes above-average, and the quick learner who becomes quicker. And there is the other side of the coin, the corresponding set of pupils whose progress is down the scale, not upwards. A more precise assessment of maturational growth as such has not yet been devised, but it would not be at all surprising if the features reflected in the IQ assessments were equally evident in cognitive maturation too, the rate of maturations remaining relatively the same for each pupil.

MOTIVATION

It has traditionally been assumed that some form of motivation is necessary to initiate and sustain learning. This has led to a way of thinking about learning which regards the learning process and the motive for learning as two independent variables. It has

[1] Honzik, M. P., J. W. Macfarlane, and L. Allen, *Journal of Experimental Education*, 1948, no. 17.

been the custom, almost the ritual, in laboratory learning experiments to provide an incentive for the animal's behaviour, by starving the animal and providing food as a reward, or by giving an electric shock as a punishment to be avoided. From this approach have come many studies measuring the relationship between the strength of the motive and the effectiveness of the learning. There have also been studies of the effects of rewards, punishments, competition, and knowledge of results on the learning of school-children. There is no doubt that incentives do often lead to more efficiency in learning; paying the pupils seems to be one of the most effective but least used; but the question is whether such incentives are necessary for all learning, or whether the findings are relevant only to certain aspects of learning.

There are two ways of resolving the question. One is to assume that all learning is dependent on motivation and whenever learning is observed, to seek to establish the motive. This has not proved to be very profitable; it is not always possible to identify a motive, and often the motive assigned may be so general as to be of little meaning. The alternative is to investigate the possibility that there are some situations where learning may take place without any identifiable motive, and so distinguish between those instances of learning where motivation seems to be necessary, and those where it is not.

Attention has been recently drawn to various aspects of experimental work on learning which had previously been ignored as not fitting into the traditional view. Thorndike reported that the fish was found unnecessary to motivate some of his cats to find their way out of the puzzle box. Harlow found no difference between the learning of monkeys who were well fed and those who were hungry. Rats learn a maze and monkeys learn to manipulate simple puzzles without reward or punishment. Children acquire information for which they have no apparent need, and show in play a persistence of learning activity often greater than is evoked by incentives. Doubts about the necessity of motivation are strengthened by some experiments by Guthrie, who found that repetition, as such, resulted in learning, no reinforcement being required. He concluded that contiguity can be sufficient condition for some learning, such that if act A were followed by act B, the later occurrence of act A would tend to be followed by B. A final consideration is that strong motivation or need does not aid learning; it tends often to interfere with effective learning. Mild anxiety encourages learning, but severe anxiety inhibits learning.

Rewards and Punishments

The outcome of these considerations about motivation is that there is no direct point-to-point connection between the processes of learning on the one hand and a system of motives on the other. We have seen that there are levels of complexity in the learning process, from elementary S-R conditioning to the learning of concepts and cognitive structures. So too we can recognize a system of motivation, from fairly precisely defined incentives, to more broadly operative systems of motives which for want of a better term we shall call activity. This system tends to coincide generally with the level of the learning processes, but not exactly so.

Incentives consist of rewards and punishments which are devised to direct the learning of specific forms of behaviour. The reward is attained when a definite form of behaviour has been learned. If the obtaining of a reward equals successful learning, then learning finishes when the reward is attained. Punishment is also directly associated with particular behaviour; if the punishment is effective, the learning again ends. The incentives of reward and punishment therefore do not generate learning; what they can do effectively is direct the learning into prescribed paths. Within their limits incentives are effective and are a part of classroom practice. Praise, prizes, marks, or privileges are all rewards which lead to more effective learning, and reproof, denial of privilege, poor marks, or physical discomfort are punishments which can effectively prevent undesirable forms of behaviour being acquired. The limitations of incentives to direct learning are, however, fairly clear. To be effective, a reward must have some value for the learner, the nature of the learning task must be known to the learner, who must also know when it is completed. And the reward must follow closely upon the successful completion of the task, and as far as that particular item of behaviour is concerned the learning comes to an end. The main arguments against the use of rewards in school practice is that they draw children's attention to differences in ability between pupils, and that children may learn not to learn without rewards. There is not enough evidence to support or refute these views, so the side-effects of rewards must remain a matter for speculation only.

Punishments are not just the opposite of rewards. To be effective, punishment must meet the same set of conditions as for rewards, but the main difference is that though punishment may prevent a particular pattern of behaviour becoming established, it does not remove the motive for that behaviour. In addition, punishment may itself create a learning situation of an unwanted kind. A child wants to go on playing at bedtime, or an adolescent stays out late against parents' instructions. The offender resists parental authority and is punished. The child, or the adolescent, is liable to acquire a fear or anxiety associated with his aggressive behaviour; that is, he becomes afraid of being aggressive. On the other hand he has learned that without being aggressive he will not get what he wants, and his parents have demonstrated by their punishment that aggressive behaviour can be effective. A conflict develops, from which he may learn for himself the technique of punishing as a means of dealing with a difficult situation. There can also be rather deep-rooted personality factors involved in punishment, which are associated with feelings of aggression and guilt. These are deep waters, but these emotional undertones often render rational application and discussion of the incentive of punishment rather difficult. School prizes as rewards do not engender the same emotional and moral heat as corporal punishment, which incidentally is not usually considered by pupils to be the least desirable kind of punishment.

Motives

The broad distinction we have made between incentives and motives is that incentives are part of a situation set up by someone other than the learner himself, and are intended to direct the learner's immediate behaviour by encouraging or preventing the learning of specific sectors of behaviour. A motive, on the other hand, is a need or drive originating in the learner himself, which the learner satisfies by learning the appropriate behaviour. A boy is given a bicycle for doing well at school. The bicycle is an incentive to school learning, but he also desires the esteem of being a skilled cyclist. This is a motive for learning to ride a bicycle. Or a girl wants to become a nurse. This is a motive for studying for the necessary entrance qualifications.

The range of motives is as wide as the range of human needs. There have been various attempts to bring order into the complex of motives initiating learning; as an example of a system of motives which is comprehensive enough to cover most kinds of motivation and yet precise enough to be useful, we take that of Maslow. He does not claim that the system is directly related to learning, or that each class of motive operates independently. He calls it a hierarchy, as the basic motives must be satisfied before the higher-level motives are effective. He proposes five levels of motivation or needs:

1. The physiological needs are fundamental. These are needs for food, liquid, sleep, and so on. They function on the principle of homeostasis, the body's need to keep functioning in a state of balance. Too little liquid disturbs the balance of the bodily functions, and the need is accompanied by the experience of thirst, which leads us to redress the balance of drinking. Such needs play little part in school learning, except that in so far as a pupil is hungry, thirsty, sleepy, cold, hot, or needing to empty bladder, bowels, or stomach, that pupil's needs over-ride any other motives for learning. This applies whether the pupil's needs are of physiological or psychological origin. A pupil with a need to empty his bladder as an emotional response has as strong a need as one who has drunk not wisely but too well.

2. Safety needs are the next level. These involve the motives of avoiding danger or physical pain, and of being secure to go about one's business. Pupils may find much of their security in routine, which protects against the unknown and the threatening. If the routine involves learning, then the need to conform to the security of the routine can be a motive for learning. From a secure base adventures may be undertaken, but if security is lacking, fear and anxiety prevail.

3. When physiological and security needs are satisfied, there emerges a need for affection and acceptance by other persons. These Maslow calls the 'love needs'. These needs are the main motives underlying the learning of social behaviour, and may, as we have seen, be linked with incentives in particular situations. Failure to satisfy these needs can lead to maladjustment and emotional distress.

4. The 'esteem needs' are next. A child needs not only to be loved but to be respected by others, and to have his achievements recognized not only by others but by himself. The pupil's need for self-esteem in the home and in the school is usually based on a realistic

assessment of his achievements. The possibility of attaining his goal is a motive for learning; failure may lead to escape into fantasy to satisfy the need for esteem.

5. The final need is for self-actualization. This is rather vaguely defined by Maslow, and is more clearly developed by Carl Rogers in his theory of personality, which we discuss in a later chapter. It means that we have a need to be someone, to have our distinctive characteristics and to realize in behaviour our potentialities. These potentialities may lead to learning in various sectors of behaviour—the artist must paint, the athlete must excel, the sociable man find his company, and the reformer his injustices. It is the need to be what we can be, to be an individual different in some way from others.

This system of motivation implies that different pupils will be responsive to different motives for learning. Desire for affection and security may be a motive for one pupil; for another pupil who feels secure and loved the need for esteem will be stronger. Acceptance as a member of a group will satisfy the first, and his level of competitive aspiration will be low, and not effective as a learning motive. For the other, with a higher level of aspiration, the stronger motive will be to excel and be first in the class. Or the two motives may be combined, where a pupil's acceptance by his teacher or parents may depend on his academic performance, success leading to security and to at least temporary esteem.

Activity as Motivation

It does not follow that as these needs are satisfied, learning ceases to take place. If learning depended wholly on motives and incentives this would be so. But there are conditions where learning occurs without being linked to any system of motives. There is Bruner's suggestion that we learn to avoid later learning. The whole process of maturation implies a continuous reorganizing of experience, and of adapting and extending behaviour, which means learning. The child expects his world to have order and system, he needs it for security, and he is continuously learning to organize his experience and behaviour in structures which relate to the world he lives in. Such exploration, experiment, and adjustment seem to be necessary activities, distinct from formal occasions of learning. Well-fed rats explore a maze spontaneously. Chimpanzees who have used a stick to obtain bananas proceed to find other uses for the stick. Children play beyond the point of fatigue. To deprive a human being of the opportunity for mental or physical activity creates distress; we cannot stop thinking, imagining, and organizing experience and behaviour. This general activity crystallizes into more specific situations which involve motivation for learning. Cognitive dissonance, the lack of correspondence between the expected and the observed structure, is one. The Gestalt phenomenon of closure is another. It has been shown that uncompleted learning tasks tend to be remembered better than completed; the inference is that they have been learned more effectively; the further inference is that the incompleteness is acting as a motivation to keep the learning process alive. Once more, a completed operation ends learning.

LEARNING TO LEARN

Learning, like any other behaviour, may be performed with various degrees of skill and efficiency. Perhaps not enough attention is paid by teachers to this aspect of school work, and the help given to the pupil to acquire skills in learning is often less than that devoted to teaching the skills of reading, mathematics, languages, science, and so on. There have been a number of investigations into the learning of learning. Ausubel investigated the effects of what he called 'advance organizers'. In practice an advance organizer consists of an introduction to the material to be learned, concentrating on the basic concepts or general principles, in short, the conceptual cognitive structure. In one experiment students were required to learn the properties of carbon steel. One group was given an advance organizer of the kind mentioned, a parallel group were given a more factual historical introduction. The first group not only learned more effectively, but remembered better. This and similar inquiries would suggest that introduction to the conceptual structure of the subject matter is an aid to later learning.

Another example of learning techniques is known as SQ3R. The letters stand for:

Survey: the process of gaining an understanding of the structure of what is to be learned. In a book, the chapter-headings or table of contents give an indication of such structure. This is an elementary form of advance organizer.

Question: the devising of questions which arise out of the survey. Thus, the chapter-headings may be rephrased as questions.
Read: the reading of the material in an attempt to answer the questions raised. This often involves the reconstruction of the questions.
Recite: the attempt to answer the questions after the subject has been studied, or the book read. This should be done as far as possible without reference to the original material. Lengthy answers are not necessary, but adequate ones should be noted.
Review: the revision of the previous steps, which may have to be repeated till the answers to the revised questions are thoroughly known.

This system, devised by F. P. Robinson, is but one of several such aids to learning. Their aim is to provide a technique of learning which the learner can acquire, and so perform more effectively the operation of learning. Study, however, of how we learn to learn is still at a somewhat elementary stage.

PROGRAMMED LEARNING

Finally we examine a technique of learning which is directly derived from a theory of learning. Programmed learning is an attempt to apply the theory of operant conditioning in a practical learning situation. This technique was originated by Pressey, who used a form of programmed instruction for training U.S. Army recruits in the First World War. It was not adopted as an educational practice till B. F. Skinner developed it as an application of his theory of operant conditioning. The technique is now being explored and its properties are becoming known. One finding, for example, is that teaching machines are not as necessary for programmed learning as was once thought, and a programmed text is as efficient in most situations.

The basic teaching machine is a box in which a roll containing a number of frames, or unit steps of learning, can be exposed, one frame at a time. The learner reads the frame, selects what he believes to be the correct response to the statement or question in the frame, and responds by writing or pressing a button. There must be an active response of some sort. The learner then uncovers the correct response, and if his own response is correct, he proceeds to the next frame. In what are called linear programmes the items, or contents of the frame, are so devised as to evoke the correct response in nearly all cases; in about 95 per cent of the frames the learners should give the correct responses. The learner can be helped to give the correct response by prompts or cues. Formal cues may consist of the initial letter of the response word, or a verbal reference to the wording of the frame item; for example, the statement in the frame may read: "The point at which a stimulus elicits a response is called the threshold". The response is to complete the sentence: "The point at which the response is elicited is the . . .". Formal cues can help the learner in the earlier stages of a programme to acquire the techniques of programmed learning, but in general thematic cues are to be preferred. Thematic cues are derived from the content of the programme and the development of the theme. In the other main type of programme, the branching programme, the learner is offered several possible responses from which to select the correct one. If he selects the correct response, he goes on to the next frame. If he selects the wrong response, he is led on to a short branch or series of frames in which his error is explained, and he is then returned to the main sequence of frames. There are teaching machines of various degrees of sophistication, using films, or tape recordings of foreign languages, but the principle is the same for all. In programmed texts, the basic principle is the same; the programme is set out in book form, with a paper slip as a mask for covering the correct answers. Evidence to date suggests that unless the material specially needs presentation by machine the text is just as effective.

In the construction of a programme, there are certain working principles to be followed. As an illustration of programmed learning we present some of them in the form of a very short linear programme. A slip of paper should be used to mask both the answer to the frame being read, and the following frames. Responses to each frame should be jotted down on a separate sheet before lowering the mask to uncover the next frame.

1. The subject matter of a programme is divided into a series of unit steps, each step being called a frame. There are therefore as many unit steps as there are . . . . . . in the programme.

(frames)

2. Each frame contains a stimulus statement and the response. There are therefore two components in each . . . . . .

(frame)

3. One component is the s . . . . s . . . .
(stimulus statement)

4. The other component is the r . . . .
(response)

5. The learner should be able to give the correct response for each frame. Therefore the stimulus statement should be simple and clear. If the stimulus statement is not . . . . . . and . . . . . , the learner may give the wrong response.
(simple: clear)

6. A wrong response may become established, and the correction may not be effective, so it is important that the . . . . . response should be the correct one.
(first)

7. Too frequent wrong responses may discourage the learner. The effect of easy frames is to . . . . the learner.
(encourage)

8. Another effect of too many wrong responses is to delay the learner's progress. Getting the response correct the first time makes learning progress more q . . . .
(quickly)

9. One method of ensuring correct responses is chaining. This means relating the contents of each frame to those of the preceding and f . . . . frames.
(following)

10. By chaining, the learner is helped to follow the development of the subject, and to anticipate the next response. He is therefore more likely to make a . . . . response.
(correct)

This very condensed specimen of a programmed text is only intended to demonstrate the method of presentation in programmed form. We have possibly overloaded the selection with formal cues and, in a short extract, no attempt has been made to overcome one of the difficulties in programme construction, the transition from one topic to another. Also, a longer programme would normally contain a number of revision frames, together with short 'unit' tests which the learner undertakes to assess his progress.

By working through a programme a teacher is able to decide whether the content is suitable for his purpose, and to judge the correctness of the responses the pupil is to learn. But the teacher is not able to assess how effective the programme is as an aid to learning. This can only be done by trying out the programme on representative samples of pupils, and assessing its effectiveness by comparing the scores on a pre-test, given before they commence the programme, and a post-test, given after the programme has been completed. Both pre-test and post-test are on the contents of the programme; attitude questionnaires can also be given to assess the extent to which pupils find the programme interesting, useful, or boring. High scores on the pre-test indicate that the pupils may not need the programme; they are already well informed on the content.

A further general rule of thumb is to estimate pupils' learning time at about one minute per frame, with of course individual differences between pupils. On the other hand, the total construction time for a tested and completed programmed text is of the order of three or four hours per frame. The construction of an extensive programme is not, therefore, a task to be undertaken lightly. Nevertheless, it is a very useful exercise for a teacher to recast a part of his curriculum in programme form.

Since programmed learning technique is founded on Skinner's theories of 'shaping' behaviour by operant conditioning, we should be able to examine in some detail the mechanisms of learning involved. The initial assumption is that the learner must have some motivation to learn; a completely indifferent learner will not learn. The learner's behaviour, which is composed of series of S-R units, is directed into the desired sequence by the application of reinforcement (positive more than negative), and extinction. The learner is presented with a stimulus statement, and makes an active response. If this response is correct, the response acts as its own positive reinforcement, and the learner has taken one step towards learning. Hence the emphasis on correct responses. If the response is wrong, the failure acts as a negative reinforcer, tending to eliminate that response, which is replaced by the correct response supplied in the form of the printed response. In linear programmes no wrong responses are presented to the learner. Other responses which may be irrelevant are not called for, and thus extinguished, and the learner is kept firmly on the sequence required by the programme and prevented from straying into irrelevance. By building up a series of reinforced correct responses the desired pattern of behaviour is established. Relationships between sequences of responses are established by stimulus generalization, whereby the same responses are established for different stimuli; for example an arithmetic programme could have the same response of 7 to such statements as $2+5$, $5+2$, $4+3$, and $3+4$. Distinctions are established by the process of stimulus discrimination; in the same arithmetic programme we could find different responses being established to the stimulus statements $5+2$, $5-2$, 5×2, and so on. Correctness of response is just as necessary to reinforce generalization and discrimination; error is not used as an aid in programmed learning.

How effective is Programmed Learning?

It is only recently that programmed learning has been introduced into school practice, and not extensively at that, so any evaluation of its effectiveness must be provisional. It is necessary to keep in mind that programmed learning is a method of instruction; it is not a substitute for a teacher, nor a method of testing what has been learned. It has been shown quite clearly that learning does take place with programmed instruction. Especially in further technical and commercial education and in some aspects of primary-school work, the programmed text or teaching machine appear to be as effective as other methods of teaching. Programmes appear to be particularly suitable for the teaching of routine material, not because explanation cannot be handled by programming techniques, but because there is less disagreement about factual knowledge than about its interpretation.

In general, programmes take a little longer to cover the same ground than the more traditional methods of presentation by the teacher, but in the long run the greater thoroughness of the programme method may balance the difference by requiring less revision time. Indeed, some programmes show greater retention of the content after a few months than immediately after the completion of the programme. What characteristics of a programme are associated with delayed retention are not yet known. Another feature of programmed learning is that the learner proceeds at his own pace. This is educationally sound, but may raise difficulties in classroom organization which more traditional methods may overcome by ignoring differences in learning speeds. It is desirable in practice to have some supplementary activities available for early finishers. It is also possible in programmed texts for the pupil to 'cheat' by looking at the responses in advance. This is overcome to some extent in the more elaborate teaching machines, but in texts it has been found that the pupil's failure to complete the tests incorporated in a good programme will soon discourage the pupil from this practice. Some pupils may not immediately appreciate that the pupil who cheats only cheats himself; but evidence is accumulating that 'cheating' is not a persistent feature of programmed learning. It tends to be confined to some pupils in the earlier stages of learning how to use a programme. Some pupils also report that they found programmes boring and long-winded. This can be true; it can also be true of teachers. The real difficulty, however, lies in assessing whether a somewhat lengthy and detailed treatment is necessary for adequate learning, or whether it is poor programme construction.

In addition to enabling the learner to progress at his own pace, and ensuring more thorough and systematic learning, the programme has the advantage of relieving the teacher of the routine tasks of teaching subject matter which essentially involves concentration by the pupils on learning it. In addition, a properly constructed programme provides, in the form of pre-tests and post-tests, a much more precise measure of the pupil's progress than is available in normal teaching practice, where pre-testing is seldom to be observed. The ultimate contribution of programmed learning techniques to education may not necessarily be in the provision of yet another weapon in the teacher's armoury, but in the intimate association between teaching practice and a clearly formulated learning theory, such that the clarification of practice by its formulation in theoretical terms results in more precise control and direction of the pupil's learning.

4

Attending, Remembering, and Forgetting

In the chapter on learning, the perceptive reader may have noted that we begged several rather fundamental questions. We assumed the existence of a stimulus in the discussion of S-R learning, but did not discuss how a stimulus was identified. Can any event in the physical environment (including the learner's body) constitute a stimulus, or can we only define a stimulus as an event which produces a response? The basic assumption of S-R theory is that there are two independent systems of events, those that occur in the physical world around us, usually called the environment, and those that we call behaviour. The inquiries of S-R psychologists are directed to the ways in which these two systems of events become linked to each other, the relations between the physical stimulus event and the behavioural response event. This does not seem to be adequate, as the learner can only respond to events he is aware of. A very high pitched note, for instance, cannot be a stimulus to a human learner when it is above the range of his hearing, but the same note can be a stimulus to a dog and to a bat. We know it is a stimulus only because the dog and bat can respond to it. The process of selection and organization of physical events is what we call attending.

Nor in the discussion of learning did we distinguish between the rat which pressed a bar and obtained food, and the rat which had *learned* to press a bar to obtain food. Could the ape, who used boxes to obtain fruit, but could not repeat the behaviour, be said to have learned how to get the fruit, or not? Or had it learned and then forgotten? All psychological definitions of learning imply a modification of behaviour to a change in environment, and a tendency for the modified behaviour to be repeated when the same environmental change takes place on a later occasion. Some of the more rigorous psychologists go little further than that. In Guthrie's theory of contiguity, for example, the observation that if event A is followed by event B, the repetition of event A tends to be followed by event B, is taken as evidence that learning has occurred. Learning is assessed by the increasing probability that event A (a stimulus) will be followed by event B (a response). Perhaps this does Guthrie less than justice, but it is the essence of his approach. Other psychologists introduce more interpretation and explanation of what happens in the learner between the first response and the later ones. But all psychological investigations of learning have to examine the processes by which the disposition to respond in the same way to the same stimulus is retained between the first and later occasions. This disposition for the acquired response to be repeated we call remembering. The psychologist then proceeds, in his usual way, to examine the conditions under which behaviour is retained or forgotten, and investigates, for example, the question whether forgetting is simply the absence of remembering, or whether there are two different positive processes, one of remembering and another of forgetting, each operating under its own set of conditions.

Part of the difficulty is the want of words. The teacher can distinguish between the pupil who is not attending, the pupil who is learning, the pupil who remembers, and the pupil who forgets. The psychologist's difficulty is that these four processes are part of one process, for which there is no name. Learning necessarily involves attending, and necessarily involves some remembering. The pupil who does not attend cannot learn, and the pupil who has learned must in some way remember, but not necessarily in the teacher's use of the word remembering, which usually means explicit reproduction of the original learned behaviour. We have therefore to discuss attending and remembering in the context of a total learning process.

ATTENDING

Attending implies selection and organization of external events. The physical world around us is buzzing furiously with all sorts of energy changes, from whose onslaught we are protected by the selective limitations of our sense organs. We can attend to those wavelengths of electro-magnetic radiation which we respond to as light. We are unaware of radiations of shorter wavelength. Slightly longer wavelengths we respond to as radiant heat; still longer wavelengths we are again unaware of, fortunately perhaps, because these carry all the radio programmes. The physical events we can attend to are selected for us by the properties of our sense organs, and any defect like colour-blindness still further restricts the range of attention, and therefore of learning and remembering. To adapt our behaviour to the overwhelming chaos of the world around us, we must organize it, so that there is an orderliness in it which can make sense to us. This further organizing function of attention depends on three main factors. One is maturation, in which the pattern of our interpretation changes as we grow older. In the drawings of younger children the perceived differences in the sizes of distant houses are not attended to; their attention selects the fact that the houses are known to be of the same size.

A second factor is previous learning. The rat who has learned to press a bar to obtain food looks for the bar when placed in another cage. In cognitive structure learning, we can illustrate by another experiment by Harlow on monkeys. He put a grape under one of two containers according to a consistent rule: for instance, always the left one, or always the smaller one. In due course the monkeys learned to make the correct selection. The containers were changed, and the monkeys again learned, this time more rapidly. After a few such changes the monkeys were able to learn to make the correct selections comparatively easily and quickly. Harlow describes the monkeys as having acquired learning sets; they had acquired a disposition to look for the rule, and were organizing their attending activity in accordance with this acquired set or disposition.

The third factor is motivation, which we use broadly to include interest, attitudes, personality structure, and emotional state at the time. People with grievances are prone to interpret events into the pattern of their attitude, and attend readily to those events which justify their complaints. Those in a state of anxiety attend to events that are perceived as threats; their responses are different from those of a secure person in the same situation. The selective influence of interest is illustrated by a rather striking experiment. A cat had electrodes attached to the short length of nerve which connects the ear to the brain. When a musical note was sounded, the passage of impulses along the nerve could be observed and recorded. A jar containing mice was placed in front of the cat. The cat's behaviour indicated close attention to the mice; when the note was sounded, the cat made no sign of response to it. What was unexpected was that there was no passage of impulses along the nerve. Whether this happens in human beings is unknown, but it is possible that the pupil who was attending to some other matter of interest and says he did not hear the teacher's question may indeed be telling the literal truth.

Attention in the Classroom

The teacher's use of the term 'attention' is not quite the same as the psychologist's. To the teacher, the pupil who is daydreaming is not attending; to the psychologist, he is attending, but is not selecting that sector of his experience involving current class activity. The organization of attention is most easily considered in terms of figure and ground. The figure is attended to, the ground experiences are not. The pupil who is listening to noises outside the classroom selects that particular set of components of his experience and co-ordinates them into a meaningful figure or pattern, running footsteps in the corridor, or a van drawing up outside the school. The classroom activities, the teacher's voice, or the pupil's exercise, form the relatively unorganized and unstructured ground. The pupil turns his attention to the teacher's lesson by reorganizing the pattern of his experience; what was the ground now becomes the figure. For the teacher, the pupil is now attending; for the psychologist, he was attending all the time, but the pattern of selection of his experience has been changed. The selective function of attention can be fairly easily demonstrated by taking a tape recording of classroom proceedings for some minutes. As we noted in Chapter 1, the tape recorder does not select, noises from different sources are equally prominent, and if more than one person speaks at the same time the result is confusion.

What characterizes the selected sector of experience is a greater clarity and meaningfulness. The component in our experience which acts as a stimulus in S-R learning is perceived as a separate and meaningful element in our environment. It does not act as a stimulus till it is attended to. In the same way the creation of a cognitive structure of our experience is a function of attention. The connection between awareness or consciousness and the process of attention is regularly demonstrated when we fall asleep.

To sleep, we try to eliminate attending. The room is in a uniform darkness, and quiet; we avoid extremes of heat and cold, and in a relaxed bodily condition we allow the clear and orderly structure of our experience to disintegrate into disconnected fragments. As long as we count sheep we do not sleep, for we are attending. We lose count and drift into sleep. Anything that we attend to, which organizes our experience, tends to wake us up; the awareness that our feet are cold, or that the alarm is ringing, means we are attending to a meaningful pattern of experience, and we wake. Psychologically, therefore, the only state of inattention is unconsciousness.

Conditions of Attention

The teacher is concerned with eliciting and maintaining a desired organization of experience by the pupil. One condition which directs attention is change. Attending appears to involve a scanning function, by which there is a continuously varying awareness of different aspects of our environment. In vision, for example, we cannot see for more than a second or two if our eyes are not moving; the cells in the retina become very rapidly fatigued. Though we are not aware of it, our eyes are in a state of high frequency vibration, about fifty very small movements per second; it appears that it is by this continual quivering movement that we are able to perceive the outlines of objects. Accompanying this is a flicking movement of the eyes, so that our eyes are scanning the visual field in a series of rapid flicks, called saccades. If for example we try to fixate the dot at the end of this sentence, we find it impossible to keep our eyes from moving, and the fixation can only be maintained by a corresponding series of return movements. Figures showing reversible perspective illustrate the scanning function in the context of perceptual organization. The figure on page 29 is perceived either with the centre fold pointing to us or away from us. Once again we cannot maintain any unchanging structure, and the figure fluctuates in spite of our efforts to prevent change. There is also evidence from the distress caused by sensory deprivation. One source of this distress is the conflict between the actively changing organization of our attention in our conscious state and the uniformity of experience caused by deprivation.

What seems to be happening is that the active function of attention is to create change; our awareness is never static, and we scan and restructure our experience continuously. If the environment changes, then we can attend; if the environment is unchanging, we need to impose change upon it. Monotony is the enemy of attention, and if a lesson or other class activity becomes monotonous, either at the sensory level of tone of voice or at the level of development of the cognitive structure, then this function of attention involving the need for change virtually forces us to transfer our attention to other aspects of our experience. It is common experience that in monotonous tasks like learning vocabulary lists or the like, it becomes increasingly difficult to prevent our attention from wandering. It is rather pointless, therefore, to discuss topics such as the span of attention. Young children may pursue a varying activity for a long period, older children may be unable to attend to a monotonous task for more than a short period.

Another condition strongly affecting attention is bodily condition. Pain, hunger, and other forms of bodily discomfort tend to direct attention to themselves; it is difficult to cease to attend to a toothache and go to sleep, or attend to other activities like reading or music. Excessive emotional experience, like fear or anger, also tends to monopolize our attention. These physical and emotional conditions appear to override the more usual functions of attention we have just been discussing; though interesting psychologically, they are of marginal educational interest. Pupils in pain, or emotionally disturbed, are unlikely to learn easily, but they are a small minority in the normal classroom; in fact, they should not be there.

Another condition affecting classroom attention is the pupil's attitude. We have already mentioned Harlow's 'learning sets', but the use of the term 'set' extends beyond this. The instruction to a runner to 'get set' indicates what the psychological term set means. It is the adopting of an attitude of anticipation of a signal for a known form of behaviour; the expectation that a given stimulus will be presented tends to produce easily the learned response. Set is usually accompanied by the taking up of a particular physical posture in readiness to respond, and attention is almost wholly directed to the anticipated stimulus. A dog waiting for a biscuit to be tossed to it, a pupil taking out his pencil and work-book, or a class being told to sit up and listen, are all examples of set. The bodily attitude of the pupil, and indeed the lay-out of the classroom, can influence attention. Interest is another aspect of the pupil's attitude. This implies the pupil has a system of knowledge, motivation, and thinking about an activity, and obtains satisfaction by developing such a structure. The establishment of interest is one of the teacher's main concerns.

Attention and Learning

Much of what can be said about attention has already been discussed in other contexts. The 'doctrine of interest' in education is several centuries old; we described Herbart's version of it, and much of the discussion of Piaget's sequence of cognitive development can be translated into changing sequences of selective attention by children. Show a film to children of different ages and ask them to report; it is often difficult to recognize it as the same film. There is also a close connection between attention and motivation in learning. The condition of change in attention is what we referred to as the natural activity of the learner as a motive in learning. The effect of bodily discomfort on attention is expressed in Maslow's hierarchy of motives in terms of the basic physiological needs. If these needs are not satisfied, they dominate attention, and other motives for learning do not operate.

We have taken attention as the first phase in the attending-learning-remembering process. It follows that what is not attended to will not be learned or remembered. In the school situation a considerable amount of what is called forgetting can be attributed to the pupil not having attended in the first instance. The classroom practice of revision has a part to play here. Revision serves several purposes in the learning process. It can play an effective part in maintaining the responses necessary in learning a skill; it is also effective when used as an aid to the systematic organization of responses already learned. It appears to be relatively ineffective in establishing responses where a motive for learning is lacking; repetition as such does not create learning. It has been shown that pupils who work through arithmetical exercises without knowledge of their results, or without comment on their work, show no improvement; those who know their results or receive praise or blame do show progress in learning. This, however, applies to individual pupils; class revision has an additional function. It is unlikely that all pupils were attending all the time, and what is to some pupils repetition may to others be the first presentation, and to all there may be some element in the revision which was not attended to previously. What pupils learn is not so readily forgotten as classroom experience might suggest. Much of what is 'forgotten' was never learned.

REMEMBERING—CONSERVING

The first phase of remembering we call conservation. A distinction can be made between immediate and delayed recall. Immediate memory involves the total reproduction of the learned behaviour in the order in which it was learned. In that sense it may be called photographic. But immediate memory only operates when there is no other set of experiences between the learning and the reinstatement. If there is some intervening experience between the learning and the reinstatement of the behaviour, then we can compare the behaviour learned with the behaviour reinstated, and differences between the two patterns of behaviour can be attributed to what happened during the phase of conservation. From such comparisons we find that in fact there appears to be a process of organization, involving selection, rejection, and often distortion, which occurs during the conserving phase, and is very similar to that in the process of attending.

Conserving

It is necessary to be clear in our thinking about what is being conserved. Ordinary language suggests that memories are stored like cards in a box, and phrases like "keeping in mind" and "store of memories" reflect this rather naïve way of thinking. Memories are not things, nor the mind, whatever it may be, a container for keeping them in. What are conserved are dispositions to behave in a particular way, and dispositions can only be inferred from the observation of behaviour. Nor can we separate ourselves from our memories; dispositions are specific characteristics of the total functioning of the individual. Learning is a modification of behaviour, and memory may be defined as a disposition for that modification to be repeated when a later stimulus situation is perceived as being similar to the original one. If we are presented with the line, "A little learning is a dang'rous thing," and we respond with, "Drink deep, or taste not the Pierian spring," our ability to produce the desired response indicates that the response had at one time been learned, and that the disposition to make the same response has been conserved as a component in our total behaviour pattern. If our response were, "Something about drinking from some sort of spring", the disposition is still conserved, but has become modified during the conservation phase. We may also 'feel that we ought to know it'; the recognition that the stimulus situation has been presented before indicates once more that a disposition has been retained, but in a much modified pattern.

As with learning, remembering can be very broadly divided into two kinds. We have to account for the fact that we can remember a very large number of isolated responses, either in the form of factual information or of skilled motor responses. Primary-school pupils, especially boys, seem to be particularly good at this. It is also possible, without too much difficulty, to learn and remember most of seven or eight hundred paired words such as house–animal, travel–cup, and so on, so that when we are presented with the first of the pair, we can reinstate the second. This kind of remembering is parallel to learning in S-R units; the other kind of remembering is parallel to learning of cognitive structure.

Aids to Remembering

A certain amount of remembering required in the classroom is of this first kind, the ability to reproduce specific responses to specific stimuli. There are various teaching devices for assisting this kind of remembering. One is overlearning. It has been shown that if rote learning is continued beyond the point at which the task is first successfully completed, reinstatement is more complete. The evidence also is that the periods of overlearning, which include drill and revision, are best spaced at increasingly greater intervals from the occasion of the original learning. Arithmetical relations and tables, and spelling, are examples of school subjects where overlearning is effective; but overlearning has its limits, as too much may conflict with the pupil's ability to attend. Another device is the mnemonic. There are various styles of mnemonic; one is a simple and systematic set of signs for a more complex system of rules or facts. BOMDAS, for example, gives the order of operation of more complex arithmetical expressions, 'brackets, of, multiply, divide, add, subtract'. BOMDAS and its twin DOMBAS are easier to remember than ROYGBV, the colours of the spectrum.

This is scarcely a mnemonic, as it lacks the features of system, apparent meaningfulness, and pronounceability. Another type of mnemonic depends on the use of accidental associations between letters; stalactites (with a 'c') come from the ceiling, but stalagmites (with a 'g') grow from the ground.

Another common type of mnemonic is that where the response is systematized by rhyme and metre, which is known to be retained more easily than connected prose, and still more easily than disconnected words or phrases. Examples are:

> In fourteen hundred and ninety-two
> Columbus sailed the ocean blue,
>
> Joshua son of Nun and Caleb the son of Jephunneh
> Were the only two
> Who ever got through
> To the land of milk and honey,
>
> How I wish I could determine
> In circle round
> The exact relation Aristotle found.

This last gives, by the number of letters in each word, the value of pi to thirteen decimal places. Aristotle's name has nine letters, but unfortunately he did not evaluate pi; perhaps it should be Lindemann. The feature of the mnemonic is that an S-R unit is embedded in a cognitive structure which is relatively simple and memorable; the mnemonic has the advantages of both worlds. It serves a humble but useful part as a teaching aid. Perhaps the best tribute to their effectiveness is the number of former pupils whose only memory of Latin syntax is a mnemonic verse about the use of the subjunctive.

Another device for aiding the remembering of rote material is fading. This device, like programmed learning, is due to B. F. Skinner, and operates as follows:

1. Fading means first presenting the whole response. The response is then presented again with certain parts of the content left out. This process is repeated, with more and more left out, till the learner is able to reproduce the whole response without the help of cues or prompts.

2. Fading means ..... presenting the ..... response. The .... is then .... again with certain ..... of the .... left out. This process .. .. with .... and

.... left out, till the .... is able to .... the whole
response without the .... of .... or ....

3. ...... means .... the ..... response.
The .... again with ....
.... out. This .... with ...
and ...., till .... to .... the
whole .... the .... of ....

4.

The fading here may have been too rapid but, after a few such
repetitions, the whole passage can be remembered word for word.
It is a particularly effective way of learning verse, but there are other
applications.

Cognitive Structures

The processes of remembering we have been discussing are
concerned mainly with the conservation of isolated responses
learned as S-R units. There is also the remembering of schemes of
relationships or cognitive structures. These cognitive structures
appear to be more liable to modification during the period of
conservation than do the unitary S-R dispositions, which tend
either to be conserved, or to be forgotten. What tends to be conserved in cognitive structure is the meaningful pattern, and what
is not very quickly incorporated into such a pattern will soon be
forgotten. Thus the conservation of such dispositions appears in
the end to depend more on the interpretation, in terms of cognitive
structure, of the original experience than upon the content of the
original learning. It can almost be said that we remember what
we know rather than what we learned. This feature is frequently
illustrated in studies of the psychology of testimony. A witness of a
street accident, in which one car pulls out to pass a standing bus,
and collides with another car out of sight of the witness, will
frequently remember seeing the collision, because he knows how
it must have happened.

The British psychologist F. C. Bartlett performed a series of
simple but illuminating experiments on this topic. He presented a
series of simple geometrical drawings to two groups of subjects.

Each group was given a different explanation of what the drawing meant, and at a later stage they were asked to reproduce the drawings. In all cases the reproductions of the same drawing by the two groups were easily distinguishable in terms of what the group has been told the drawing represented. Here is one illustration of the kind of result Bartlett obtained. The original drawing is in the centre.

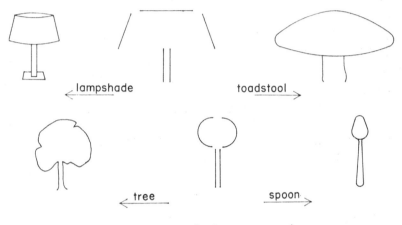

Fig. 3

The witness of the accident and Bartlett's subjects both demonstrate how the original experience is modified to fit a particular cognitive structure. There is a general tendency in these cognitive structures, which are organized as figure and ground, for the figure to become increasingly simple, such that irrelevant and dissonant components are forgotten; the feature of closure is also evident, where events which should have occurred, but did not, are remembered to make a consistent pattern, or gaps are filled in as in Bartlett's figures; the pattern of the cognitive structure being conserved is also modified to fit the broader cognitive system of the individual, such that if we think of ourselves as financially astute, it is easy to forget or to distort the recollection of the occasions when we were not. The extreme case of such modification of cognitive structure during conservation is forgetting. This is probably the explanation of our failure to remember events of our earlier years, as our cognitive structures mature into such different modes that the original learning structure now has no place in our systems of interpretation.

The educational implications of these changes during conservation are wide-reaching but not precise, and the general principles of aiding retention are well known. New structures to be learned are best explicitly related to existing structures. Initially, forgetting is rapid, and revision is necessary first at an early stage in the conservation and later at increasingly large intervals of time. There are few short cuts, and the pupil who can reinstate the components in a systematic way is more efficient than one who remembers more detail, but in a less orderly and meaningful structure. Selective forgetting is the mark of effective conservation, and a comprehensive memory is not always the best kind of memory. The positive relationship between high intelligence and effective remembering is most easily explained by the fact that the intelligent pupil is retaining a more complex and extensive system of cognitive structures, and therefore needs to conserve more to maintain such structures.

REMEMBERING—REINSTATING

Of the two phases of remembering, reinstatement is the one which provides the basis for observation. We can only observe the original learned behaviour, and later the reinstated behaviour; the intervening phase of conserving is studied by inference, not direct observation. A distinction can be made between two modes of reinstatement, reproduction and recognition. Reproduction is the reinstatement of the original response on later presentation of the original stimulus. Thus a pupil, asked what is the Latin verb "to love", responds "amare"; this is reproduction. If the pupil were presented with the words, *stare, monere, amare,* and *venire,* and identified *amare* as the required response, that would be recognition. The distinction is of no great importance; it depends to some extent on what cues are available to the pupil which kind of response is made. We mention it, however, as the distinction forms the basis of two different types of examination question. The open-ended type of question requires reproduction; the more objective multiple choice or matching type of question requires recognition, but does not exclude reproduction. There is no virtue in one type as against the other; it is a matter of suitability for the kind of assessment the examiner is looking for.

Conditions of Reinstatement

We have noted that remembering is best thought of in terms of dispositions to behave in a particular way. In the reinstating phase we ask what are the conditions under which these dispositions to respond are most readily elicited. Essentially, the condition for reinstatement is the presentation of the original stimulus. The isolated responses we have discussed are stimulus-bound. If the S-R disposition has been conserved, the presentation of S will evoke the response R. If no response, or the wrong response, is evoked, there is little that can be done except to begin the process of relearning, and, if necessary, unlearning. The reinstatement of behaviour reflecting a cognitive system is a more complex matter, as when we are presented with a problem and have to remember how to solve it, or are presented with an isolated stimulus and have to reinstate the system of which it is a component. This is a common educational situation.

Logically there are two elements in the process of reinstatement. The first is the recognition of the nature of the stimulus, the apprehending that it requires a particular set of responses. The other is the reinstatement of the appropriate responses. There is a failure of remembering if we recognize a geometrical theorem, but cannot recall the proof, or recognize a foreign word or phrase, but forget its meaning. This was the trouble with Köhler's ape, who recognized the box as a means of obtaining bananas, but could not reinstate the appropriate behaviour. Logically the two elements can be separated, but whether they are psychologically distinct is not so certain. When pupils are set a test on material previously learned, and are instructed to answer all the items they know, or probably know, there is left a set of items for which the pupils are unable to reinstate any response. If they are then instructed to guess the response, there is found a positive correlation between the proportion of items answered correctly as known and those guessed correctly. Those with most knowledge tend to guess more correctly than those who have learned less, which leads to the inference that the recognition of the stimulus and the reinstatement of the response are not wholly independent. The S-R disposition is a single unit, and the reinstatement of a response can lead to the identification of the stimulus; for example, "*amare*—to love" could be "to love—*amare*".

Effective reinstatement is therefore aided by explicitly relating the stimulus to the response in the original learning process, such that the stimulus will be learned in terms of the response. This means not only teaching pupils how to solve problems, but equally teaching them how to recognize problems that can be so solved. For example:

(*a*) Six men build a wall in six days. How long for one man to build the same wall?

(*b*) Six cats catch six rats in six days. How long for one cat to catch the same number of rats?

(*c*) Six ships cross the Atlantic in six days. How long for one ship to cross?

A pupil who has learned the system of responses called 'proportion sums' may easily apply the same set of responses to each of the three stimulus situations. His reinstatement of the cognitive system learned is perfectly adequate. His failure to reach correct solutions cannot be blamed on failure to reinstate; we must again beware of attributing failure in remembering to imperfect reinstatement, when the failure lies in the conditions of the original learning.

Reinstatement, therefore, depends on the presentation of a stimulus situation in a form recognizable as that of the original learning situation. Further, the reinstated behaviour pattern must have some relevance to the individual's current behaviour at the time of reinstatement; there needs to be a reason or motive for remembering. The system of motives we discussed in connection with the learning process is equally relevant to reinstatement, and needs no further elaboration. The learning motivation itself need not be reinstated, but reinstatement is activated by the same range of motivation as learning. Another aid to reinstatement is prompting. This is the process of presenting part of the response to be reinstated, in order to elicit the remaining components of the chain or structure. Again, this is a well-known educational practice, the value of which is doubtful. There is no evidence to support the view that a response elicited from a pupil by a series of skilful promptings is more firmly established in later behaviour than one which is directly presented to the pupil. Unless the process of prompting can be demonstrated to have some relevance to the pupil's learning, it is an unnecessary display of the teacher's skill.

Suggestion

There is a further factor influencing reinstatement which merits fuller discussion. This is suggestion. In the earlier years of this century, much attention was paid by psychologists to the explanation of behaviour in terms of instincts. Lists of instincts—fear, sex, pugnacity, and so on—were produced; William McDougall listed about twenty instincts, Freud based his psychological interpretations on two basic instincts. The doctrine of instincts is no longer acceptable, as it raised more difficulties than it resolved, though it must be admitted that, having discarded instincts, the psychologists are still looking for a substitute system of interpretation of behaviour. Allied to the instincts were a group of what were then known as 'general reactive tendencies': namely, play, imitation, sympathy, and suggestion. Play and imitation mean much the same as in ordinary English usage. Sympathy was defined as the tendency to experience the emotions and feelings of another person on perceiving their expression in the behaviour of other persons. Sympathy has been offered as the explanation of our emotional response to acting, music, and other forms of art; the weakness of the explanation is that it goes no further than that, and gives little help in explaining the conditions under which such responses take place, or for predicting our behaviour in any given circumstances. Do we laugh or weep at the death of Little Nell?

The concept of suggestion, however, has stood the test of time better than the others, chiefly because it has been found useful in the fields of social psychology, of the psychology of testimony, and in the clinical psychology of hypnosis and hysteria. Suggestion is defined as the tendency to adopt uncritically the attitudes and schemes of thought of other persons. Translated into the psychological terms we have been using, it is a process by which cognitive structures are adopted without their being co-ordinated into the individual's existing system of cognitive structures. The lack of co-ordination or integration into larger systems is what is meant by the term uncritically. A cognitive structure adopted uncritically remains as an independent element in the person's total system of cognitive structures.

Hypnosis demonstrates the operation of suggestion in an extreme and often spectacular form, but other instances are common enough in our daily lives. Comments about sick cats made to someone facing up to a plate of macaroni cheese can put them off the eating of it. They are aware, in terms of their total system of cognitive structure, that the dish consists of macaroni and cheese, but have accepted uncritically the independent system of ideas which renders them unable to eat it. People vary in their degrees of suggestibility. Consider once more the man who is standing on the pavement beside which a bus has drawn up. He observes a car drawing out to pass the bus and another approaching from the opposite direction. He hears a crash, hurries round the back of the bus and sees the wrecked cars. Later, as a witness, he is quite likely to testify that he remembers seeing the two cars collide, which he could not have done through the body of the bus. The witness has accepted the suggestion that there must have been a collision, and has reinstated as a fact something he did not observe. Here we have the uncritical acceptance of a remembered event; the witness reinstated what he knew, not what he observed, and his cognitive structure of inference is independent of his cognitive structure of observation.

Most of what is learned in school, and out of it, has been affected by suggestion. We accept facts without verifying by observation, and systems of ideas without testing their validity. Pupils do not accept that the moon is made of green cheese, because they have been told it is not, and later accept as proof the fact that green cheese is incompatible with a system of ideas about physics which they have learned equally uncritically. They accept the system of ideas involving the earth as a sphere, though daily observation would lead to the conclusion that it is flat. Examples can be multiplied indefinitely; if all learning were dependent on direct observation and inference, life would be intolerable, and knowledge scanty.

In the context of the topic of reinstatement, we have already introduced the condition of suggestion in Bartlett's experiments. The geometrical figure was reinstated differently by the two groups in accordance with the suggestions offered to them. In a well known demonstration, called the 'Aussage' experiment, pupils are shown a picture of, for example, a farm kitchen. After a few minutes, the picture is removed and the pupils required to reinstate their observations. Questions are asked, which can be neutral, "Was there a dog in the picture?" or containing a suggestion, "Was the dog black or white?" There is no dog in the picture, but a high proportion of pupils will give an answer to the second question which suggests there was a dog. The element of suggestion may not be immediately obvious. The Danish psychologist, Katz, performed a simple experiment on what he called 'dazzle'. Here are four columns of addition. In A, B, and C, the addition is simple addition of units. In D exactly the same arithmetical processes are performed on three-figure numbers.

A	B	C	D
7	2	4	724
3	6	9	369
2	5	7	257
7	2	8	728
4	3	9	439
2	3	—	——
—	—	37	2517
25	21	—	——
—	—		

One group of pupils was given A, B, and C to add up one after the other. The total time and error was recorded. Another carefully matched group was given D to add up, and time and error recorded. The finding was that D was a more difficult operation than A+B+C. The reinstatement requirements for the responses for both groups was precisely the same; the difference in performance was apparently due to the suggestion, contained in the form of the presentation, that D was a more difficult kind of sum, the pupils taking longer and making more errors.

It is virtually impossible to eliminate the effects of suggestion on recall. The wording of an examination question, the context of the situation involving reinstatement, the prompts given by a teacher, all contain some element of suggestion.

FORGETTING

In view of all the hazards of attending, conserving, and reinstating, we may begin to wonder how pupils manage to remember anything at all. In fact they do remember a remarkable amount;

the question of interest to psychologists is why pupils fail to remember what they have learned. There are psychologists who consider that nothing learned can be forgotten, and if we knew more about the conditions of reinstatement, all learned behaviour could be reinstated. This is perhaps an extreme view, but it has been proposed seriously by more than one psychologist as a necessary assumption in the study of remembering and forgetting. It can never, of course, be proved by direct observation. Forgetting, which is failure to reinstate the learned response when the original stimulus is presented again, takes different forms. There may be failure to reinstate a response, there may be only partial reinstatement, there may be reinstatement of a response to a different stimulus, or there may be elicited a new response, the remembering of something that never happened. The variety of ways in which forgetting can be observed makes us suspect that more than one process of forgetting may be operating. More rigorous investigation confirms this suspicion, and psychological theories of forgetting are of three main types, fading, repression, and interference. We do not need to choose between these processes; there is more than one way of forgetting.

Fading

Fading is the classical explanation of forgetting, but it is supported by more recent evidence from learning theory and neurological investigations. The basic principle of fading is that responses which are not elicited tend to disappear from our repertoire. The S-R feature of extinction through lack of reinforcement implies fading. On the neurological side, it has been demonstrated that the resistance of the synapse to the transmission of a nervous impulse is reduced by frequent use, and spontaneously increases with disuse. The synapse is the junction of two neurones, or nerve cells, and in the extremely complex system of nerve connections necessary for even the simplest behavioural response, the nervous impulses will flow most freely along these pathways where the synapse resistance is lowest. Disuse tends to reconstitute the original pattern of nervous activity, and the learned pattern fades out. Fading is probably a necessary process for effective behaviour. We need to clear the decks, as it were, for further learning to take place, and one of the functions of forgetting is to aid learning. Fading is a sufficient explanation for much of our forgetting; what it fails to explain adequately is false or distorted remembering.

Repression

The repression theory was first fully developed by Freud, as part of his general theory of personality. The organized, mainly conscious, personality system called the ego tends to reject emotionally unpleasant memories; it prevents their reinstatement in the conscious personality. By definition we are not aware of this repression, we only experience it as forgetting. If the repression is complete we are not aware even of having had the experience; if it is partial, then we are aware of an inability to reinstate. We forget to pay debts when the person to whom we owe them is available, later we remember. We forget names, places, and incidents for no reason obvious to us. Repression operates to protect our present experience from emotionally disturbing remembering. There is no doubt that some forgetting is the result of repression, but how much cannot easily be assessed. In school practice, the probability is that it is comparatively little. The repression theory can adequately account for complete forgetting, but it also offers a reasonable explanation of false remembering, in that a distorted and more acceptable version of our original experience may be remembered where the true version is unacceptable.

Interference

This explanation of forgetting takes several forms, but all have in common the proposition that only a limited amount of reinstatement can take place in our behaviour on any occasion. We have learned much more than we can reinstate, we cannot recapitulate all our previous behaviour and experience, and therefore there is, as it were, competition for the restricted channels of reinstatement available. One aspect of their theory is the forgetting associated with the maturation of cognitive structures; as earlier structures are developed into later structures, the learned content of the earlier structures is either organized into the new structure, or suppressed and therefore forgotten. The same effect follows upon the learning of new cognitive structures; when there is an amalgamation of such systems into a more comprehensive scheme of thought, elements of the component structures may become isolated from the major structure, and either remembered as single

S-R units, or forgotten as incompatible with the new structure. Another interpretation of the interference theory is that there is no forgetting of learned responses, but only reinstatement of wrong responses. This implies a failure of the ideal situation of a one-to-one connection between the original stimulus and the reinstated response. For a number of reasons, not clearly specified, the lines can get crossed, and the result is apparent forgetting. Again, this is not a sufficient explanation of all failure to remember accurately, but it probably accounts for some occasions of forgetting. Finally, another explanation stresses the limited number of responses which can be organized into coherent and effective behaviour patterns. Like machines, we can only store a limited number of dispositions, and therefore the learning of a new set of responses involves the corresponding unlearning of other sets of responses. The later learning displaces the earlier learning, and forgetting is the outcome.

Conclusion

All the explanations we have outlined are adequate for different aspects of forgetting, and none is a sufficient explanation for all forgetting. We have not pursued their implications into educational practice, because the critical information is still lacking. That information is the identification of the psychological process involved in any given forgetting, and the knowledge of the conditions under which the various kinds of forgetting processes operate. Psychologically, selective forgetting is as necessary a part of education as learning. At present the only techniques of forgetting available to us are the S-R processes of extinction and negative reinforcement. When our knowledge and techniques become more extensive, then we can begin to teach pupils how to forget appropriately; the direct approach of telling pupils to forget is as effective as telling them to think of anything they like, except an elephant.

5

Thinking

Man has been defined as a thinking animal, homo sapiens. As such, the process of thinking is involved in nearly all aspects of his behaviour, and we have already touched upon the topic of thinking in our previous discussions. We noted the difficulties of S-R theories of learning in explaining the more complex levels of learning, which involve thinking; the use of sign language is a feature of thought. Piaget's scheme of cognitive maturation is essentially a description of the development of different kinds of thinking processes in children; in a later chapter on intelligence we shall be considering how we identify and measure differences in competence in thinking among pupils. Perhaps we can most usefully consider thinking as an extension of the process of attending. Attention means selection and organization. Thinking is a further process of ordering our experience and behaviour, the construction of rules according to which we learn to respond more easily and effectively to changes in our environment. Thinking entails the systematic ordering of our experience and behaviour. When we do not perceive order, thinking begins, to create order.

Thinking has always proved to be a difficult process for the psychologist to come to grips with, as the process of thought cannot be directly observed, but only inferred from behaviour. We can, however, make a broad distinction between two types of thinking, which we shall call rational thinking and emotive thinking. The latter includes the types of thinking we call imagination, aesthetic thinking, and part at least of the thinking we do in ordering our personal and social relationships. The nature of this thinking process, and the conditions under which our thinking operates in those spheres of our activity, have been far from adequately explored. Education in the aesthetic appreciation of literature, music, and art may be an important component in any school curriculum, but the solid evidence and effective guidance which can be provided by psychological inquiry is negligibly small; educational practice still rests on intuition and dogma. The other type of thinking, rational thinking, is that which conforms to the external requirements of a system of logic. In its fully developed form this thinking is a process of formal relations, but we have seen from Piaget's studies that children's rational thinking conforms to somewhat different logical systems as they develop their attempts to order their experience. Rational thinking is that which characterizes scientific and mathematical studies, but in any operation of thinking we normally use both the rational and emotive modes of thought. We have our hunches, our 'wishful thinking', and our prejudices, even in science and mathematics. The educational problem in science and mathematics, at least for older pupils who have achieved formal relations, does not seem to lie in the learning of the logical rules against which the outcomes of rational thinking can be checked. The main difficulty appears to be in the learning of how to separate the two modes of thought, how to operate in a rational system independently of emotive thinking. To many pupils this does not come easily, and in the present lack of adequate psychological information we can offer them little help. Perhaps this is why some pupils find mathematics and physical science such difficult subjects, and so different from others in the school curriculum. And will 'integration' of subject studies resolve or increase this difficulty?

How we study Thinking

Towards the end of the last century various studies in thinking were undertaken by German psychologists, such as Lotze, who investigated the 'relating activity' of the mind, and Ach, who inquired whether 'imageless thought' was possible. They depended for their evidence on introspection, and as it is very difficult to think and observe how we think at the same time, their investigations could not proceed very far. More recently, as psychological methods of inquiry have become more sophisticated, and with the advent of electronic computing devices, there has been a revival of interest in the thought processes, and progress is beginning to be made. These investigations have been almost entirely limited to rational thinking, but even here there is still a long way to go.

How, then, do we begin to examine the processes of rational thinking? First we must ask what kinds of observations we can make. Introspection is not very satisfactory, though such evidence cannot wholly be discarded. More direct observation of behaviour is necessary, and Piaget and Bruner have indicated how inferences about the structure and functioning of the thinking processes can be made from systematic observation of behaviour. A parallel approach is through the study of language, wherein the structure of language is taken to reflect the structure of thought. Animals do not talk, because they have nothing to say that requires language, and the differences between the language of younger and older children expresses differences in their thinking processes. We have also suggested that children's drawings reflect the pattern of their thinking. Another approach is being made through the study of machines which can reproduce the behaviour attributed in humans to thought. Such machines can be used as models and analogies for testing explanations of human thinking. When a machine solves a problem, we know how it did it; do humans solve the same problem in the same way? Whether we say the machine thinks or not is a matter of definition.

The first step is the usual one of defining the process of thinking. We first distinguish between the logical and psychological structure of thinking. Logic is a set of rules which, if followed, will lead to a conclusion that is accepted as valid. But it is well known that our thinking does not proceed step by step in a logical pattern. We tend to anticipate the conclusion, and employ logic to check the results of our thinking. The psychologist's interest in logic is not so much on the light it throws on the process of thinking, but on why we accept logical conclusions as so final and correct.

All men are mortal

Socrates was a man

∴ Socrates was mortal

We cannot deny the conclusion, given the premises.

What is a Concept?

The other distinction we need to make is between the operation of thinking, and the content of thought. We call the structures on which we operate in thinking, ideas, thoughts, or concepts, and

5

we have already discussed concept learning. What is a concept? The earlier German investigations into thinking were concerned with the distinction between percepts, images, and concepts. We can begin with our immediate awareness of our surroundings, which is organized in figure and ground. This book is perceived as an object distinct from the rest of our immediate experience, with properties of weight, shape, texture, and so on. That awareness of the book as an object is a percept. Remove the book, and we can reinstate the percept and describe its properties. The reinstated percept is an image. Can we take the next step? We have percepts and images of a number of different objects which have characteristics in common which enable us to call them books. What is the nature of our experience when we think of a book, which is not any particular book? This is the point at which the early German inquiries broke down. The evidence, based on introspective reports, showed that some persons claimed to identify concepts in their thinking, but had difficulty in describing them, while others reported only general or diagrammatic imagery. The methods of inquiry available did not enable any further investigation to be made. There was also the logical difficulty of whether the percept of a particular book did not imply a concept which enabled the individual to recognize it as a book.

Though thinking was not a topic of major interest to the psychological behaviourists, a further attack on the nature of concepts was made in the context of S-R theory. The explanation was in terms of stimulus generalization and stimulus discrimination. The S-R attempt to explain a concept as a classification of stimuli broke down on Harlow's experiment with the monkeys, who learned to select the middle one of three stimuli to which they had learned no response whatever. And what Harlow's monkeys did with some difficulty is done easily by children. A child who can count is able to count many objects to which he has learned no response.

Both lines of inquiry into the nature of concepts have proved unprofitable; but the fact remains that we can solve geometrical problems about triangles, and can identify the middle one of objects entirely new to us. The more recent inquiries have concentrated on the operational aspect of thinking rather than on the content of thought. The question asked is how do we set about this activity called thinking?

THE OPERATIONAL STUDY OF THINKING

Plans

The two main lines of attack are in terms of plans and strategies, and of information processing. We take first the explanation offered by Miller, Galanter, and Pribam. They regard thinking as basically a process of making decisions. The thinker does not know what the ultimate solution to his problem is going to be, though he may have decided that there is a limited number of possible solutions. As he proceeds with his thinking, he makes a series of decisions. He cannot at any point be sure that his decision is the correct one, as he does not know the road to the correct solution. What he has to guide his thinking is a set of rules, according to which he can make a decision at each step in the process of thinking. These rules are applied in units called TOTEs, which function in four stages. First, there is a test to establish the difference between the present state of affairs and the desired solution. Second, there is the putting into operation of behaviour which it is considered will reduce this difference. Third, there is a test to ascertain what differences, if any, still remain. Fourth, there is an exit to a solution, or to the next TOTE (Test, Operate, Test, Exit). The progress of thought is governed by a Plan, which is a system of TOTEs.

Thinking is explained as operating in a series of TOTE units. TOTEs may be linked together such that the second test from one unit provides a first test for the next. Or TOTEs may operate in pyramid fashion, where the sequence of TOTEs may be patterned according to a master Plan. To illustrate how the plan operates in practice, let us analyse into TOTE units Piaget's problem of finding the mixture of liquids to give a yellow liquid. TOTEs imply formal operations. Pupil first sets up Test 1, tries liquid A with liquid B. Operate by mixing A and B. Test 2 shows no colour change, so operate again. He then repeats by mixing all other pairs of liquids, reaching no solution. The next step is to try a higher-level TOTE; test he has used all possible pairs; operate by checking his procedure; test shows still no solution. He can then try another level of TOTE. Test that it may be a mixture of three liquids; operate by trying mixtures of three, test by observing that $A + C + E$ gives yellow, and exit, with solution. A higher-level TOTE may be employed to ascertain that the solution is unique.

A still higher level TOTE may be used to verify that the solution is not accidental, by repeating the whole experiment, test that the solution may be accidental, operate by repeating, test that the same result is observed, and exit. And still another TOTE may be operated to establish how many repetitions are necessary to eliminate the possibility of accidental error. The TOTE is therefore considered as the elementary unit of the thinking process, in much the same way as the S-R unit has been presented as the basic unit of the learning process. S-R units have not proved to be an adequate explanation of all our learning and have only a limited application to the thinking process. The TOTE unit is best considered at present as supplementing the S-R contribution, but the conditions under which TOTE units operate have still to be investigated. At present, the TOTE remains a descriptive theory, with considerable possibilities for educational application in the future.

Strategies

A somewhat more intensive investigation of how our thinking operates has been made by Bruner, Austin, and Goodnow. Where Miller uses plans, Bruner uses strategies, but the basic approach is the same. A typical Bruner experiment was to take eighty-one cards, each with four different characteristics—colour, shape of figure, number of figures, and number of borders. By combining these characteristics it was possible to obtain 225 'concepts', such as all red with two borders, all black with one cross, and so on. The experimenter decided on a concept—red with two figures, for example—and showed the eighty-one cards to the subject, informing him whether the card represented the concept or not. The subject's task was to identify the concept. The methods of thinking used by the different thinkers in the experiment were analysed and classified into the different kinds of strategies used.

Bruner found that all strategies had a common basic pattern, not unlike a TOTE. The first step was to check the hypothesis, that the card represented the concept, against the information given by the experimenter that it did, or did not. The second step was the retaining or revision of the hypothesis. The third step was the revision of the hypothesis in the case of error. This process continued as the series of cards was presented. The procedure is not unlike school learning. The experimenter knows the concept he wishes his subjects to attain, the teacher knows the structure of thought he wants his pupils to acquire. The subjects of the experiment have to proceed from ignorance to identification of the concept on information given by the experimenter; the pupils have to acquire the structure of thought with guidance from the teacher.

Analysis of the subject's processes of thought showed that more than one kind of strategy could be used. What Bruner called the reception strategies were of two main kinds, the focussing and the scanning. The focussing strategy was the most commonly used. Suppose the concept were [two figures, one border]. For clarity we put the concepts in square brackets. The first card to which the experimenter says "Yes" is, say, No. 6.

Card 6. Two triangles, red, one border. This is the first positive instance and the subject takes that as his first hypothesis: namely, [two triangles, red, one border].

Card 7. One circle, black, one border. The experimenter says "No", this being a negative instance. This confirms the subject's hypothesis, and he does not change it.

Card 8. Two circles, black, one border. This is a positive instance [two figures, one border] but it contradicts the subject's first hypothesis [two triangles, red, one border]. He selects what is common to the two positive instances, Cards 6 and 8, [two figures, one border] and this becomes his new hypothesis. In this simple and short example it is the correct concept, and later cards will confirm it.

The ideal focussing strategy may be summed up in five rules:

(1) Select the first positive instance as the hypothesis.
(2) In confirming positive instances, retain the hypothesis.
(3) In confirming negative instances, retain the hypothesis.
(4) In contradicting positive instances, change the hypothesis to what the previous hypothesis and the new positive instance have in common.
(5) In contradicting negative instances, review memory of previous instances, as there has been an error.

There are varieties of the focussing strategy; the one we have described is conservative focussing. It is safe, methodical, but slow. An alternative is focus gambling, in which the subject tries to make changes in his hypothesis for more than one characteristic of the cards at the same time. This is not illustrated in our single example, but Piaget's experiment with the yellow liquid can be recast in the pattern of both types of focussing strategy. There will be only one positive instance.

The other main type of reception strategy is the scanning strategy. We give the basic rules:

(1) Select one characteristic of the first positive instance, and use this as the first part of the hypothesis.
(2) In confirming positive instances, retain hypothesis.
(3) In confirming negative instances, retain hypothesis.
(4) In contradicting positive instances, change hypothesis to make it consistent with previous instances, which means a review of the previous instances.
(5) In contradicting negative instances, change as in (4).

The scanning strategy also has two varieties, simultaneous scanning, where the subject tries to keep all possible combinations of the characteristics under review all the time, and successive scanning, where the subject takes only one characteristic at a time. This latter closely resembles a trial and error procedure.

Strategies employed in other kinds of problem situations were also investigated by Bruner and his colleagues, and were reported in *A Study in Thinking* in 1956. In selection strategies, the subject has all the cards laid out in front of him, he is given one which represents the concept, and has to select the other cards representing the same concept, with only 'yes' or 'no' information from the experimenter. Studies are also proceeding into the strategies used when a problem has only a most probable solution, not a certain one.

The subjects of Bruner's experiments were intelligent and adult, so formal operations prevailed. How children at earlier stages of cognitive development would have tackled the problems has not been fully investigated. It has also to be kept in mind that Bruner's strategies are ideal strategies; the subjects did make mistakes. The most favoured strategy was focussing rather than scanning, and the rule giving the greatest difficulty was that dealing with the contradicting negative; the least troublesome was the confirming positive instance. The implication is that it is easier to comprehend a concept in terms of what it is, rather than what it is not.

Another interesting feature about these inquiries is that they reveal individual differences among thinkers. About two thirds focus, and one third scan, and they tend to do so consistently. Some are reluctant to change hypotheses, others change more frequently than necessary. Some proceed by the safe but slow method of conservative focussing, others gamble on their first hypothesis being correct. Some solve the problem item by item, others try to apprehend the whole scheme as one operation. Whether these differences represent differences in personality and temperament has not been established; probably they do, and selection of a rational methodical approach in preference to an intuitive one may well be one aspect of a different personality structure. A teacher in a secondary-school class may find pupils employing different strategies to the same presentation; some may be focussers, others scanners.

MACHINE THINKING

We can study thinking not only in terms of a model derived from the study of human behaviour as Miller, Bruner, and Piaget have done, but also in terms of a model derived from the operation of a machine. A thinking machine is one which passes what is called Turing's Test; the test is, "In a particular set of problems, is there a way by which the performance of the machine can be distinguished from that of a human being?" If the answer is "No", then either the machine is thinking, or the human being is not. It is possible to design, if not always to construct, machines which will solve mathematical problems, machines which will scan and mark essays on a prescribed marking scheme, machines which can learn from experience by reviewing their previous activities, selecting an appropriate solution, and applying it to a current problem, and machines which, by feedback of correct and wrong responses, can learn to conduct their thinking more efficiently. Once again, these activities are not unlike those of a school classroom; the prospect of such machines coming into extensive use, like the motor-car or telephone, leaves us wondering how much it will be necessary for the pupil of the future to learn to do himself. We still depend on animals and plants for our food, but learning to hunt and raise crops is no longer part of our education.

The relevance of the machine thinking to the study of human thinking lies in the fact that if a machine can reach the same solution from the same information as a human can, the processes used by the machine can be analysed and used as a model against which human thinking processes can be compared. The machine processes and the human processes may not be the same, but the machine model guides us as to what to look for.

Algorithms

There are two basic methods of information processing, algorithms and heuristics. An algorithm is a method of search which is bound to produce a solution, or definitely establish that no solution exists. Heuristics is a method which is designed to have a reasonable chance of producing a solution in a reasonable time. The algorithm is best thought of in the form of a tree, which takes the form of a branching series of TOTEs, not unlike some parlour games. We think of a number, say 23. The line of search would be, "Is it even?" (Yes or no), then "Is it one figure?" (Yes or no), "Is it two figures?" (Yes or no), "Is it less than 50?" (Yes or no), and so on. This can be laid out as a branching scheme, in which a series of decisions taken at each fork would lead to the ultimate solution. Chemical analysis can be set out in the same way:

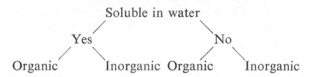

Soluble in water

Yes   No

Organic   Inorganic Organic   Inorganic

and so on. If the properties of the substance are known it will ultimately be identified. A similar device has been suggested to clarify the completion of official returns by the public.

The process is that of taking a 'decision path' from the stem of the tree to the branch which is the required solution. The process can be complex and intolerably long, and may be an almost indefinite series of trial and error. In this respect it does not serve as a model for human thinking, but within smaller systems some of our thinking does conform to the algorithm pattern. We want to travel from A to B by rail, and have to make connections through C or D. Reference to a timetable enables us to select the best route from various possible and impossible connections. The teacher who asks the pupil, "Is the subject singular or plural?", "Is the tense past or present?" is guiding the pupil through an algorithm.

There are several features of human thinking which prevent us from accepting the algorithm as a complete model. One is a possible block by a well established S-R response at one of the forks, or nodes. A previously quoted example illustrates this. The pupil who has learned "six from three, you cannot" is unable to proceed along certain paths of an algorithm, not through logical error, but because the previously established response is blocking the progress of his thinking. The imposition of English language structures upon foreign languages can provide other instances. Further, the algorithm system assumes that adequate information is available for each TOTE decision to be made. The amount of information available depends on the capacity of the machine; similarly the capacity of the human thinker cannot be extended beyond a certain point. It has been shown that too much information supplied to a human thinker reduces the efficiency of his thinking; there appears to be an optimum amount of information which a human can process. Miller suggests that the number of items of information a human being can handle as a system is "seven plus or minus two". A 'bit' of information is defined as that needed to make a 'yes' or 'no' decision at any point in the algorithm tree, so that about three or four 'bits' are required to organize seven items into an algorithm, thus:

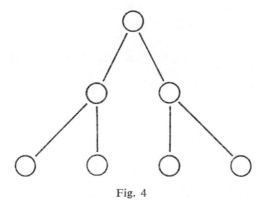

Fig. 4

This would suggest that human ability to think in algorithms is limited to smaller systems, whose conclusions may be co-ordinated into other systems of similar extent. The educational practice of taking a topic step by step in manageable sections reflects this apparent limitation of human capacity.

Heuristics

The heuristic system is operated by supplying the machine with a set of rules which are applied in the appropriate context. Thus a machine for solving geometrical problems would be supplied with the pattern of Pythagoras' theorem, the theorem about the sum of the interior angles, and so on. The machine is so set that when a triangle comes into the problem, it is connected up with the triangle theorems, and if further it involves a right-angled triangle, it selects Pythagoras. A small number of such ready-made systems increased the machine's speed of solution considerably. Not all problems could be solved, but those which were solved were completed much more rapidly than by algorithm. The machine could also be educated, in the sense that it could record solutions to previous problems and use these as rules for future problems. In fact, this proved to be less efficient than the supplying of ready-made rules.

The resemblance of the machine's operation to some human thinking is close. The purpose of teaching geometrical theorems is not far removed from the feeding of theorems into a machine. It is also inefficient and time-wasting to expect pupils to solve such problems from first principles when a limited number of ready-made solutions are available and can be applied to most contingencies. Similarly, a teacher diagnosing a pupil's reading difficulty does not proceed by algorithm, but rather has in mind a limited number of possible sources of difficulty. By observation and TOTE the teacher reaches a pattern of information which coincides with one of the possible causes, long-sightedness for example; his knowledge of the signs and symptoms of long-sightedness then directs the teacher's further observations.

The heuristic method we have been discussing is not the same heuristic method of teaching advocated by Armstrong some sixty years ago. The essence of Armstrong's heuristic method was to teach science by the methods by which scientific investigations were conducted. If applied literally, the approach was the algorithm; the method has never been extensively adopted because of the uncertainty of the pupil ever reaching a solution at all, and the time it consumed.

LANGUAGE AND THINKING

Language is a complex and curious psychological phenomenon, which serves many purposes in our behaviour. We need some kind of language to think with, and some kind of language to communicate with. Within these uses there are still complexities. Thinking requires words to act as signs in identifying classes of experience, and to enable us to identify relations between these classes. But there are systems of signs other than words, which serve the same function, such as mathematical symbols, road signs, electricians' symbols, and artistic conventions like perspective. We have distinguished between the signal and the sign use of language, but there are other distinctions. Language is used not only as the vehicle for rational thought, but for social, emotional, and aesthetic experience as well. Nor is language limited to representing our thinking. Vygotsky and Luria have produced evidence that children use language to control their behaviour and direct their thinking. To children, the language response is part of the behaviour response, and when behaviour is internalized in the form of thinking, language is used to control thinking.

Bruner, in a Piaget-type experiment on conservation with beakers of water, found that children who stated verbally what they expected to find (the tops only of the beakers were visible), showed more conservation than those who witnessed the actual operation. He suggested that the use of language encouraged symbolic thinking rather than the less mature iconic representation. The psychologists' difficulty is obvious: how do we distinguish between language functioning to direct thought and language as an expression of the thinking processes?

Language also serves the purpose of communication, but again it is not limited to the communication of rational thinking processes. It serves as a means of establishing a social relationship, so that children wishing to gain the approval of an adult by identifying themselves with the adult's attitudes and expectations will adopt adult forms of language. And how far the conventions and structure of any particular language, necessary for communication between its speakers, affect the structure and operation of thinking is still uncertain. Do Germans think in a pattern which piles up all the operative words, the verbs, at the end of their utterances, or is this just the result of the conventions of the language they use? And how did the Greeks and Romans ever manage to think at all? Again the psychologist's difficulty is obvious: how do we distinguish between the processes of thinking and the conventions of the language we use to think with?

What at first sight might appear to be a very powerful method for the study of thinking has proved to be not very profitable. Much has been done on the development of language in children, and these studies have their value in demonstrating the increasing complexity of children's thought structures. Unfortunately, they give little information about how children's thinking operates. Even Piaget's inquiries, which distinguish processes like formal or concrete operations, are not very informative about the way these operations function. He is more concerned with the logical properties of these operations than how they function in psychological terms.

Another aspect of language study which might throw some light on the process of thinking is linguistics. It has been recognized for some time that the formal categories of traditional grammar are not adequate to explain all the ways in which language functions. Whether the present inquiries into the function and structure of language will result in a more flexible and realistic system of classification of language function, which will enable us to use language more directly as a means of identifying the thinking process it embodies, has still to be seen. We must wait till the linguistic fog clears.

Though most of the conclusions reached from the study of language and thinking tend to be negative though not valueless from the psychological point of view, there are some conclusions of positive interest to the teacher. One is that any form of deficiency in language can result in less effective thinking. An eleven-year-old pupil of average ability can today perform arithmetical operations beyond the powers of any of the Classical Greek mathematicians, except possibly Archimedes. Not that the pupil has greater intellectual ability than Pythagoras, Euclid, and the others, but he has a mathematical language of Arabic numbers and an Indian zero, which is so much more powerful and flexible than anything the Greeks had. Another finding is that language does not necessarily follow comprehension and thinking. The learning of the appropriate language, even in advance of comprehension, can aid, if not actually create, the corresponding pattern of thinking. The language form can be transferred from rote learning to an instrument of thinking. We have already pointed out the value in appropriate circumstances of pupils 'saying' an operation.

CONCLUSION

The psychological study of thinking is still in its early stages and it is as necessary to be clear about what we do not know as what we do know. We lack information about the relationship between developmental stages and the strategies of thinking. How far are efficient systems of thinking operated by younger children, and how far are their thinking processes of a different quality? In what ways do they modify or distort ideal strategies? How many different systems of thinking do we use, and under what conditions? What happens to our thinking processes under emotional stress? Do they just become less efficient, or does the pattern change qualitatively? Most of the information we have is about rational thinking, but how many other lines of thinking are there, and how do they mingle? What factors other than logical requirements direct the processes of our thinking, and do these differ between children and adults? What are the difficulties and obstructions that prevent us thinking clearly and easily? How much is thinking dependent on the amount of information we have available? What are the individual differences in modes of thinking? And how do we learn to think, and acquire strategies? Is it the same as learning a skill? And how far are all pupils able to reach the level of formal thinking?

When such questions are answered, teaching practice may be extensively modified, but probably not revolutionized, as teaching practice cannot for very long depart too far from basic psychological facts. We aim at teaching children how to think, but as yet we do not know how to do it. In the absence of well-established psychological evidence to guide him, the teacher's attitude is best one of some scepticism to any educational reform based on one aspect of one sector of a very wide area of human behaviour, together with an increased sharpness of his own observations and inferences.

6

Measurement in Education

A school class is being set an examination in arithmetic and in English composition. The teacher has drawn up a set of twenty questions (usually exactly twenty, seldom nineteen or twenty-three) in arithmetic, and given a topic for the composition. At the end of the prescribed times, the pupils' papers are collected, and commonly the teacher marks them 'out of' twenty, or fifty, or a hundred, and a mark is recorded for each pupil. School examinations, especially written examinations, are not as old as we may sometimes think, but they have already acquired an element of ritual. There are certain magic numbers, such as 100, than which no pupil gets more, and 0, than which no pupil gets less, and 50, which traditionally separates the sheep from the goats. Examinations are given at the end of the term, rather than at the beginning, when the information could often be of more use to the teacher. Time limits are set, such that speed and correctness of work are not easily separated, and the use of such aids as multiplication tables and dictionaries tend to be regarded as slightly improper. Examination rituals tend not only to obscure the essential process of measurement, which is fundamentally a simple one, but can also obstruct efficient measurement. Let us look carefully into what is happening in a school examination, to find the basic principles of measurement.

Sectors, Dimensions, and Scales

The basis of psychological and educational measurement is the observation of differences of behaviour. The first step, therefore, is to define as clearly as possible the sector of behaviour that is being measured. This sector may be arithmetic, or more precisely, the multiplication of decimal fractions; or it may be speed of comprehension in reading; or the stability of social relationships between members of a class; or the variability of a pupil's emotional moods; or attitudes to school or employment. All of these cannot be assessed together, or indeed in the same way, but each can be assessed. No one person can ever know all about another; the teacher, the mother, the younger brother, the older sister, and the woman next door all observe and assess different sectors of a child's behaviour from different points of view, and each, with equal justification, may make different assessments of this behaviour. Also, at this point it can be stressed that the name given to a test is not an adequate definition of the sector of behaviour being assessed. The only adequate definition is the content of the test itself; two tests of, say, social maturity may not each be assessing the same sectors of behaviour. Names can be misleading.

The teacher or the psychologist, therefore, is observing differences in certain aspects or sectors of children's behaviour. As distinct from description, measurement also requires a dimension and a scale. For the want of a better word, we use dimension in the limited sense of indicating what a high or low score means. In a test marked for errors, a high score means a poor performance, and a low score a good one. An intelligence test could become a test of stupidity by reversing the dimension. Other measures are not so obvious. Extreme emotional unresponsiveness is no more desirable than extreme variability of mood, but in an assessment of variability of mood a dimension is needed to indicate whether a high or a low score means much or little variability of mood.

The simplest scale of assessment is that of 'is' or 'is not'. In arithmetic an answer can be given one point if correct, no points if wrong. The same scale can be used in spelling, or in factual examinations in history or geography. It also appears in attitude and personality assessments, where the pupil is asked such questions as "Do you think homework is necessary?" or "Do you ever dream of falling from high places?" This can be called a two-point scale. The two-point scale can be used very extensively, and is, in fact, a way of measuring what are often rather pompously described as the 'imponderables' in education. If any difference between persons can be observed, it can be assessed on a two-point scale at the least. If one set of pupils are claimed as possessing 'responsibility', or 'initiative', or 'character', and so on, and another set are not, then a measurement is being made, on a two-point scale. The difficulty with such assessment is not the measurement; it is the definition of the sector of behaviour being measured.

To return to arithmetic, if twenty questions set were each
marked on a two-point scale, the possible total of marks could
range from 0 to 20, the total mark being obtained by addition of
twenty separate scores each on a two-point scale. This is not the
same as that used when an English composition is marked on a
scale of 0 to 20, which, since zero is included, is a twenty-one-point
scale. Here the marker is assessing finer degrees of differences in the
pupil's behaviour; the total mark is not obtained by the addition
of separate scales, but represents the placing of the pupil on a
single scale. Often the two procedures are combined. In an attitude test, five items, each on a four-point scale, can give a possible
total of twenty points. Two matters of practical interest arise out
of this discussion. In the attitude scale, and in similar kinds of
assessment, a four-point scale is preferable to either a three-point
or five-point scale, as it prevents pupils seeking refuge in the noncommittal categories of 'average' or 'medium'. The average is
not a kind of pupil; it is a point on a scale. The other point is
that when the total score is the sum of a number of short scales,
such as two-point, it is possible for a pupil to obtain the maximum
possible score. On a twenty-point scale, as may be used for essays,
the teacher is usually unwilling to give the maximum possible
mark, as this is considered to imply a perfect performance. This
is why pupils in school can get 'full marks' in certain subjects, but
scarcely ever in others.

Units of Educational Measurement

There is no system of educational or psychological units com-
parable to litres, grams, metres, or volts. What the teacher or
tester is doing is observing differences in certain sectors of behaviour and recording those differences on a scale. The only possible
units are steps of just noticeable differences, or j.n.d.s as they are
called in experimental psychology. If, in a set of English essays,
the teacher can only distinguish ten steps of difference, then the
scale of marks can only be from 0 to 9. The marks may appear
as 5 to 14 on a twenty-point scale, but the upper and lower five-
point intervals are not used, and are unnecessary. The scale used
is a ten-point, not a twenty-point, scale. Similarly, if the marker
is confined to a ten-point scale, and can distinguish twenty degrees
of difference in the essays, then each point on the ten-point scale
represents two intervals or steps of noticeable difference. Whether

these intervals or steps are in any sense equal or not there is no means of knowing; there are no independent units to measure them against, and it does not matter in any case.

The scale may be thought of as the language in which the marker expresses his observation of these differences. In Table 3, a piece of work by five pupils, A, B, C, D, and E, is being assessed by six different markers, I to VI.

TABLE 3
Marker

Pupil	I	II	III	IV	V	VI
A	10	A −	A	Ex	100	20
B	9	B +	B	VG +	90	19
C	9	B +	B	VG +	90	19
D	7	B −	D	VG −	70	17
E	5	C	F	G	50	15

Each of the six markers has reached exactly the same judgement, but they have expressed these judgements in different scales. They are all agreed that—

(1) The order is A, BC, D, and E.
(2) B and C are equal.
(3) The difference between D and BC is twice the difference between A and BC.
(4) The difference between D and E is the same as that between BC and D.

What they have done is to express the differences in different languages. Some more learned examiners may use Greek.

From Table 3 we can derive certain rules for converting from one scale to another. Briefly these are:

(1) There is no real difference between number and letter scales. If the difference between marks of B and D represents two noticeable intervals of difference, then the difference can equally be expressed as that between, say, 7 and 5 marks.

(2) If each mark on any scale is multiplied or divided by the same number, the judgement remains unchanged, only the language being altered. The scale of Marker V is ten times that of Marker I.

(3) If the same number is added to or subtracted from each mark on any scale, the judgement is unchanged. Scale VI is Scale I plus 10.

(4) In converting from one scale to another the order and the relative size of the intervals between marks should remain unchanged. There is one exception to this, conversion to a 'normally distributed' scale, but this is discussed later, as it applies mainly to a large population of children, not to a relatively small group like a school class.

There are two matters of practice in educational measurement which require comment. The first is that of the 'pass' mark. There are two ways of establishing the 'pass' mark. One which can be used with a small number of pupils is for the marker to decide that a certain piece of work is the least satisfactory he can accept. The mark given to this piece of work becomes the pass mark. All lower marks are 'fail'. The other method, used in the more extensive regional or national examinations, is to pass much the same proportion of pupils each year. This may appear arbitrary and possibly unjust, but it is probable that a more consistent standard is maintained by a percentage than would be maintained by an attempt to establish whether a borderline candidate has done better or worse work than one marked a year ago, on different questions and probably by different examiners.

Where a pass mark, say 50, is prescribed, it is not possible, whatever method is used, for a marker to guarantee that his prescribed pass mark will agree exactly with either his judgement of the quality of the work, or the required percentage. In such circumstances, the procedure is to convert the marker's first scale to one which meets this requirement, using the rules set out above.

The other point of practical application is that, with the increasing use of punched-card systems and computers, it is increasingly necessary to distinguish between assessment scales and code numbers. The main difference is that code numbers as such have no dimension. Groups of occupations, such as professional and skilled manual workers, may be given code numbers, but unless there is some basis of assessment, such as average income or length of training or ascribed status, these numbers are descriptive labels, and the order of the code numbers can be changed at will. On the other hand, size of family or number of hobbies are assessments. It is therefore proper to say that the average size of the family of a set of pupils is 2·3, or that the average number of hobbies is 3·4, but it is not proper to say that the average father's occupation is 3·7, unless the father's occupations are assessed on a defined sector, with a dimension and on a scale.

THE BASIC MEASURES IN EDUCATION

There are four basic measures commonly used in education. These are measures of central tendency (of which the average is one), of dispersion, of significance, and of correspondence. We are not here concerned with the methods of computing these measures, but rather with the applications and interpretations of them. We are considering educational statistics as a method of classifying large amounts of information in such a way that the main relationships among all our information become clearer.

Measures of Central Tendency

If one group of pupils is taught arithmetic using concrete material, and another by paper and pencil, we would be interested in comparing their final attainment. Every pupil in the one group cannot be compared with every pupil in the other group; what is needed is one score which would best represent the performance of a group as a whole. This score is a measure of central tendency, usually called an average. There are three averages in common use. The mode, which is the most frequently occurring score, is seldom used in educational work; in any case there may be more than one mode. The median is the middle score of the group, where the scores are arranged in order according to the dimension. The actual values of all the scores are not used, only the rank order; half the pupils in the group will be above the median score, and half below. The arithmetic mean, commonly called the average, is the score obtained by pooling all the scores of the group, and dividing this total of scores equally among all the pupils in the group. The arithmetic mean depends on the value of the scores, so that, unlike the median, a few either very high or very low scores, but not both, can make a substantial difference to the value of the arithmetic mean.

Measures of Dispersion

When a pupil brings home a report card with the entries, "English 60, mathematics 70", the information is meaningless. We require first to know the average of the class. If the median for English is 48 marks, and that for mathematics is 65, we now know the pupil is above average for the class in both subjects. We still do not know how much above average. What is needed is a measure of dispersion, which will measure the amount or extent of the difference between scores. If the scores are closely grouped over a small range, the dispersion is small; if they are spread over a wide range, the dispersion is large. There are two systems of measuring dispersion, one based on the median, the other on the arithmetic mean.

If, as for the median, the scores are ranked in order, it is possible to obtain for each pupil in the group a percentile score. This is the pupil's position in the rank order, expressed as a percentage. Thus the 20 percentile score is that which divides the lower 20 per cent of the pupils from the upper 80 per cent. Similarly, a pupil with a percentile score of 75 scores higher than 75 per cent of the group, but lower than 25 per cent. The median, therefore, is the 50 percentile score. The 25 percentile is called the lower quartile, and the 75 percentile is the upper quartile. The difference between these two marks is the interquartile range; and half that difference is the semi-interquartile range, which is the measure of dispersion used in this system. To return to the report card, the information that the semi-interquartile range in English is 12 enables us to establish the pupil's percentile rank in English. The median mark of 48 in English, plus the semi-interquartile range of 12, gives the 75 percentile mark as 60, which is what the pupil obtained. He has therefore obtained a percentile score of 75 in English. In mathematics the median is 65, and if we knew that the semi-interquartile range for mathematics was 6, the 75 percentile score would be 71. The pupil has obtained a mark of 70, just below the 75 percentile score, so despite his higher mark in mathematics, the pupil has done slightly better in English. We also see that the marks in English were more widely spread than those in mathematics.

The semi-interquartile range is probably the more useful measure for small groups like school classes; it is easily calculated and is accurate enough. But for most other assessments the standard deviation is used. This measure is obtained by finding the difference between each mark and the arithmetic mean, squaring each difference, adding them up, and dividing this total by the number of scores. This gives the variance of the set of scores. To return this to the same scale as the original scores, we take the square root of the variance. This is the standard deviation, which is commonly represented either by the Greek letter sigma σ, or by SD. If the value of SD is large, the scores are widely dispersed; if small, the scores are clustered closely around the arithmetic mean.

We have already described the scale as the language of a marker's assessments. A scale is best defined in terms of its mean and standard deviation. Referring back to Table 3, we find by calculation that Marker I is using a scale of mean 8 and SD$\sqrt{3\cdot2}$, or 1·79; Marker V is using a scale of mean 80 and SD 17·9; Marker VI is using mean 18 and SD 1·79. This is only an illustrative model; five scores scarcely need such precise measurement. Intelligence quotients are expressed on a scale of mean 100, with SD commonly 15; another commonly used scale is mean 50 and SD 10. The basic scale to which all others can be converted is mean of zero and SD of one, but as it involves both negative numbers and decimal points it is liable to clerical error, and is not frequently used in practice.

The 'Normal' Distribution

There is one scale which is extensively used in educational assessment, particularly when large numbers of pupils are involved. This is known as the Normal Distribution scale. The normal distribution is found frequently in biological measurement. The height of an adult population, for instance, is found to approach very closely to a normal distribution, as are the leaf lengths in plants and so on. Most educational and psychological assessments are not directly concerned with biological differences as such, but the normal distribution is a very useful one to use, and does not offend the common observation that extreme scores are much less frequent than average ones. Another application of the normal distribution in education measurement is in tests of significance. If a group of pupils were given an objective test, and instructed to answer the items by tossing a penny or rolling dice, differences between their scores would be a matter of pure chance. Their scores, however, would be normally distributed, and the scale could be calculated. This enables us to set up a standard of chance scores, with which the observed scores can be compared, and an assessment made of the extent to which differences in the observed scores could be attributed to chance. Further, if scores are expressed in a normal distribution, conversion of standard deviation scales to percentile scales is simple.

Though the mathematical properties of the normal distribution are not simple, it is relatively easy to construct a normal distribution by using Pascal's Triangle:

$$1$$
$$1 \quad 1$$
$$1 \quad 2 \quad 1$$
$$1 \quad 3 \quad 3 \quad 1$$
$$1 \quad 4 \quad 6 \quad 4 \quad 1$$

The next line is 1, (1+4), (4+6), (6+4), (4+1), 1. This gives us thirty-two scores normally distributed over six points. Each line of Pascal's Triangle is a normal distribution, and if the process is continued indefinitely we obtain the smooth curve shown in Fig. 5:

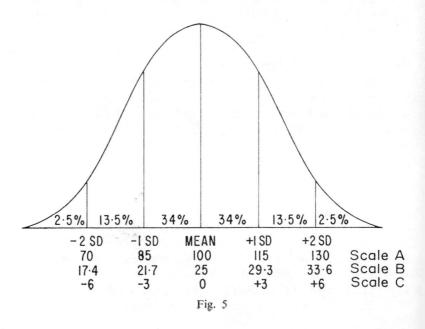

Fig. 5

Reference to Fig. 5 shows that in a normal distribution approximately 68 per cent of the scores will lie between the mean and plus or minus one SD; that 84 per cent of the scores lie below the mean plus one SD, the mean plus one SD being therefore the 84 percentile mark. Reference to the appropriate tables is needed to find intermediate values.

Since this form of distribution is frequently used in education and psychology, a certain caution is needed in its interpretation. If we take a population of children of the same age, we find the distribution of height is very close to a normal one. Were we to take the same population of children, and give them an intelligence test, we would not expect to find their test scores normally distributed. Since there are no units like inches or centimetres in which intelligence is measured, we convert the scores to a normal distribution, expressing them in IQs, so that there is a common scale of IQ on which the scores from various different intelligence tests can be expressed. With an SD of 15 points of IQ, this gives scale A in Fig. 5.

If, however, we assessed the same population of children on the degree of emotional maladjustment, we could expect to find that the majority of the pupils were not maladjusted, that a small proportion of them were mildly maladjusted, and that a still smaller proportion were seriously maladjusted. Here there is no justification for converting the assessments to a normally distributed scale.

Nor would it be expected that the scores of a small group, such as a school class, would be normally distributed, even in measures like height, as the class is not necessarily representative of a whole population. Finally, in so far as the distribution of scores departs from 'normal' the conversion of SD to percentile becomes less precise.

Measures of Significance

The third-year pupils in a secondary school are divided at random into two groups, such that any pupil has as much chance of being in one group as in the other. One group learns chemistry from a programmed text, the other by class teaching. At the end of the course, both groups are tested, and the programmed text group obtains a higher mean score than the other. Does this mean that the programmed learning is more effective, or that the difference could be accidental, due possibly to more of the abler pupils having by chance got into the programmed group? This is one of the questions that measures of significance are used to answer. A definite "yes" or "no" cannot be given; the measures of significance only give the probability that the observed results could be due to chance.

The statistical treatment of significance, which is based on the principle that chance effects, or 'error' as it is technically called, are normally distributed, is too complex to discuss here. But the working rule is that a difference is said to be statistically significant if it is unlikely to be due to chance. The degree of significance is usually expressed by the letter p, such that if p is equal to or less than 0·05, the probability of the difference being due to chance is less than 1 in 20. If p is less than 0·01, the probability of a chance difference is less than 1 in 100.

The statistical significance of such differences depends on the number of pupils assessed, the standard deviation of their scores, and the amount of the difference. With a small number of pupils, only large differences are usually statistically significant. On the other hand, intelligence-test scores from a large number of pupils, say 100,000 or more, show a significant difference in mean scores for each day of age. The difference is very small and of no educational significance, but as it is statistically significant it is unlikely to have occurred by chance. To be educationally significant a difference has generally to be both large and statistically significant.

Another application of statistical significance is concerned with what is known as 'standard error'. For example, a pupil obtains an IQ of 107 in a group intelligence test. How precise is this assessment? If we take the value of ±3 as the standard error of the IQ, which is a value typical of a group intelligence test, we can refer to scale C of Fig. 5 to estimate the significance of the observed IQ. In scale C, we take 107 IQ as the zero point, so that a range of ±3 gives us an IQ range of 104–110. We see from Fig. 5 that another measure of the pupil's IQ would probably lie within the range 104–110 IQ in 68 occasions out of 100; the chances that a second measure would lie outside that range are 32 in 100. If we apply a stricter standard, and use twice the standard error, we find that the chances of another measure of the pupil's IQ lying outside the range 107 ± 6 (that is, 101–113 IQ) are 5 in 100; in other words the chance of an observed IQ of 107 exceeding 113 or being less than 101 is $p = 0.05$. We discuss the meaning of 'reliability' later, but the group intelligence test is one of the most reliable measuring devices we have; many tests, and most examinations, are less reliable, so an examination mark of 60 may, with a probability of $p = 0.05$, be anywhere between 48 and 72, assuming a not unlikely standard error of 6 marks.

The conclusion is two-fold. No educational or psychological measure is precise and final. On the other hand, where there is a probability of 1 in 20 that a difference may occur by chance, there is also a probability of 19 in 20 that it may not. Being over-cautious in interpretation can be as misleading as being too ready to take assessments at their face value.

Measures of Correspondence

When we ask whether pupils who are good at reading are also good at writing, or whether there is any relation between intelligence and personal characteristics, we need a measure of the degree of correspondence between the two sets of assessments. The correlation coefficient is such a measure; some form of the letter r is used to indicate it.

The correlation coefficient derived from the median and semi-interquartile-range system is calculated by the formula

$$\rho = 1 - \frac{6\Sigma d^2}{n(n^2-1)}$$

where 'ρ', the Greek letter *rho*, is the correlation coefficient, 'Σ' means the sum of, d is the difference between the pupil's rank order in the two sets of assessments, and n is the number of pupils. This formula is sufficiently exact and convenient for small numbers of pupils, say fewer than fifty, but is unsuitable for more extensive and precise inquiries.

Another and more widely used formula for the correlation coefficient r is

$$r = \frac{\Sigma(xy)}{\sqrt{\Sigma(x^2)\,\Sigma(y^2)}}$$

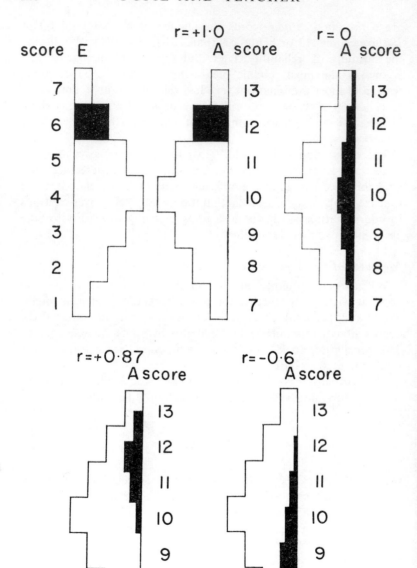

Fig. 6

where x and y are the SD scores on the two assessments, each set measured from its own arithmetic mean. This is known as the product-moment formula, and there are various methods of simplifying the calculations.

The correlation coefficient is a ratio and not a quantity, and the formula is such that if the correspondence between the two sets of scores is perfect, $r = +1$; if there is no correspondence, $r = 0$; if the correspondence is perfectly inverse, $r = -1$. In Table 3 (p. 137) the correlation between the assessments of Markers V and VI is $r = +1$. In Table 5 (p. 151) the correlation between the marks X and Y is $r = -1$.

In practice the correlation coefficient is nearly always a fraction, but it must be emphasized very strongly that a coefficient of $r = +0.8$ does not mean twice as much correspondence as a coefficient of $r = +0.4$. It is not as simple as that. In Fig. 6 we show the distribution of scores from 1 to 7 obtained by a set of pupils in an English test, E. In an arithmetic test, A, the scores of the same pupils are distributed on a scale of 7 to 13. Let us consider the four relationships illustrated in Fig. 6, $r = +1$, $r = 0$, $r = +0.87$, and $r = -0.6$. The diagrams in Fig. 6 are illustrative and not necessarily mathematically precise.

(1) $r = +1$. Here the correspondence is perfect, so that all pupils scoring 6 in test E obtain the corresponding mark in A, which is 12. Similarly all pupils scoring 5 in E, will score 11 in A, and so on. Knowing a pupil's score in E, we can predict exactly his score in A, and conversely. For any given score in E, there is no spread of the corresponding scores in A.

(2) $r = 0$. Since there is no correspondence between the scores in E and A, a pupil with any given score in E may have any score in A. The pupils scoring 6 in E have their scores distributed over the whole range of A. The same applies to all other scores in E, these building up the total distribution of A.

(3) $r = +0.87$. Here there is some correspondence; the pupils scoring 6 in E will tend to be above average in A, but their scores will be distributed over 50 per cent of the total distribution of A; ideally, the description of these A scores is symmetrical.

(4) $r = -0.6$. Here the degree of correspondence is less and is negative. The pupils scoring 6 in E will tend to be below average in A; their marks will be spread symmetrically over 80 per cent of the total distribution of marks in A.

The relationship between the value of the correlation coefficient and the proportion of the distribution is not self-evident. If we call the group of pupils obtaining the same score in one set of marks an 'array', then for any array in E we can calculate the dispersion of their marks in A as a percentage of the total dispersion of A by using the formula $\sqrt{(1-r^2)} \times 100$. Multiplication by 100 is to express as a percentage what is essentially a fraction of the standard deviation. Table 4 gives, for various values of r, the dispersion of marks in A as a percentage of the total dispersion of A, for each array in E.

TABLE 4

Showing, for any array in E, various values of r, the distribution of scores in A as percentages of the distribution of all scores in A.

$r =$	0	0·4	0·5	0·6	0·8	0·87	0·98	1·0
% of SD of all A	100	92	87	80	58	50	20	0

It is noteworthy that, for any array in E, a correlation of as high as $r = 0·87$ is required before the dispersion of the corresponding marks in A are reduced to 50 per cent of the dispersion of all marks in A. Also, the difference in the closeness of correspondence between $r = 0$ and $r = 0·6$ (namely, 20 per cent reduction of total dispersion) is exactly equal to that between $r = 0·98$ and $r = 1·0$. It is only with very high correlation coefficients that there is a close correspondence between marks gained in E and A.

To complete the picture, the dispersion of marks in A can be expressed directly in terms of the standard deviation of A. Thus, if the SD of all marks in A were 8, and $r = 0·5$, the actual standard deviation of marks in A for any array in E would be $8 \times 0·87$, which is approximately 7. This applies whether the correlation coefficient is positive or negative; it should also be noted that whatever applies to an array in E will apply conversely to an array in A.

Regression

Besides being able to calculate the dispersion of scores in A for any array in E, we can also calculate the mean score in A for the same array. This is comparatively easy. In our example, where $r = +0 \cdot 87$, the pupils scoring 6 in E are 2 marks above the mean of E. Their average mark in A will be $0 \cdot 87$ times 2 marks above the mean of A, that is $11 \cdot 7$. The calculation is simple because here the standard deviations of E and A are the same. If they are not, the general principle is that for an array in E, which is, say, x standard deviations from the mean of E, then the average mark in A for this array will be r times x standard deviations of A from the mean of A. For example, the correlation between scores on an English and arithmetic test is $r = +0 \cdot 8$. The mean of the English test scores is 70, with SD $= 5$, and the mean of the arithmetic test scores is 40, with SD $= 12$. Pupils scoring 75 on the English test are one SD above the mean, so the average score of these pupils in the arithmetic test will be $12 \times 0 \cdot 8$ above the arithmetic test mean of 40, namely $49 \cdot 6$. Where $r = 0$, then the average score in arithmetic of all arrays in English would be 40, as x SD times $0 = 0$ and $40 + 0 = 40$.

As perfect correspondence is virtually never found in educational measurement, it follows that a pupil who scores above or below the mean in one assessment will tend to have a score nearer the mean in another assessment. Not every pupil will score nearer the mean on the second assessment, but those who do not do so are the exceptions rather than the rule. This process is known as Regression to the Mean. It was first formulated by Sir Francis Galton, and is of fundamental importance in educational and psychological assessment. The way this process of regression operates may be briefly and rather formally stated as follows:

(1) For the same set of pupils, let there be two assessments, x and y, and let each assessment be expressed on a scale of its own mean and standard deviation. Let the correlation coefficient between the two assessments be r.

(2) If r is high, then for any array in x the dispersion of their scores in y will be relatively small; if r is low, the dispersion of their scores in y will be large.

(3) If r is high, then for any array in x the mean score in y will be close to that in x, but nearer the mean of y; as the value of r becomes less, the mean score in y, for any array in x, will move closer to the mean of all y scores.

(4) Whatever estimate of the score in y is made for an array in x, the same estimate can be made in x for an array in y.

We discuss examples of how regression operates in practice in the next section.

THE BASIC MEASURES IN PRACTICE

The measures of central tendency, dispersion, significance, and correspondence, whose properties we have been discussing, are not confined to formal statistical treatment of assessment; they are involved whenever any kind of assessment or judgement is made. Whenever a class teacher finds the class average for an examination or test, the interpretation of the result involves the properties of the arithmetic mean. When one class is said to be a little better than another in mathematics, there is the question whether the difference is significant or not; and when a pupil whose earlier work in English was good begins to do less well, there is the question whether this is regression due to low correlation between the earlier and later assessment, or whether it represents a real lowering of level of attainment. We take each of the four basic measures in turn and indicate how they operate in some common school situations, and how they can be used in interpreting the findings of educational and psychological research.

Central Tendency

This needs little comment, except to repeat that in the arithmetic mean the presence of a few scores at one extreme can either raise or lower the mean quite considerably in a small group, such as a school class.

Dispersion

The standard deviation of a set of assessments measures the extent of the differences between the behaviour of the pupils being assessed. It is frequently observed, for instance, that the SD of IQ among boys is greater than that among girls. There is, therefore, a larger proportion of very dull boys than very dull girls, and a larger proportion of very bright boys than very bright girls. As a consequence there is a slightly higher proportion of average girls than average boys. Here the boys and the girls are being assessed on the same scale; on the other hand, if the SD of English marks for a class is smaller than that of the arithmetic marks for the same class, no such conclusion can be drawn, as the scales in which the two sets of marks are being expressed are not necessarily the same. A common scale, standardized on a representative population for both English and arithmetic, would be needed before a direct comparison could be made.

Another application of standard deviation is in 'weighting'. At the end of a session, the marks in various subjects for a class are added together to give each pupil a total or composite class mark. Each subject does not necessarily have equal weight in determining the order of the composite mark. The rule is that the subject with the highest SD will have greatest influence on the final order. An extreme case is illustrated in Table 5 where the marks in the subject X and Y are correlated $r = -1\cdot0$, so that were they equally weighted, the two marks would cancel each other out in the total, and each pupil would receive the same mark.

TABLE 5   *Weighting of Marks*

Pupil	X	Y	(X + Y)	Y_2	(X + Y_2)
A	80	60	140	10	90
B	70	62	132	20	90
C	60	64	124	30	90
D	50	66	116	40	90
E	40	68	108	50	90
F	30	70	100	60	90
G	20	72	92	70	90
—	—	—	—	—	—
Mean =	50	66	116	40	90
SD =	20	4	16	20	0

In Table 5, the pupils A–G have in subject X a mean of 50 and SD of 20. Though the mean in Y is higher, its SD of 4 is lower. The result is that the order of the composite mark (X + Y) is that of X. In Y_2 the mean is lower than that of X, but the SD of Y_2 is the same as that of X. The marks in X and Y_2 therefore are equally weighted; since the correlation is $r = -1\cdot0$, the two sets of marks cancel each other. The effect of the SD on the composite mark is not so obvious when the correlation between the pairs of marks is high and positive, but it still operates; it also operates when there are several sets of marks being combined. It follows that marks can be combined with each mark having equal weight only when the standard deviations of the sets of marks are the same.

Significance

To estimate the significance of any measure or difference between measures involves statistical techniques beyond the scope of this book. We only repeat here the caution that statistical significance and psychological or educational significance are not necessarily the same.

Correspondence

In more precise research in education and psychology there has been a tendency to replace the method of correlation by analysis of variance. This method of analysis of variance, which is not discussed here, has the advantages that statistical significance can be more accurately calculated, and that more than two sets of assessments can be compared. On the other hand, the correlation method is limited to two sets of assessments, and though its statistical significance is not so precise, knowledge of the value of the correlation coefficient often enables interpretation to go beyond the purely statistical significance of analysis of variance.

The correlation coefficient only gives the extent of the correspondence between two assessments. It does not indicate how or why they are related. The observed correlation may be due to chance; the classical instance of this is a correlation of the order of $r = +0.7$ between the membership of a North American trade union and the death rate in the Indian state of Hyderabad, over a period of some years. Or the two assessments may be related through a third common variable. If we take all the children in a primary school and measure the size of their feet and their attainment in arithmetic, we would expect a positive correlation. The common variable would be the age of the pupil. In fact, it is difficult to find instances where the one variable is the direct cause of the other. What the nature of the relationship between assessments is cannot be discovered from the correlation coefficient itself, but from study of the experimental design of the inquiry.

Regression to the mean, which is one aspect of correlation, operates whenever two sets of assessments are compared. We shall examine five such situations.

(1) *Remedial teaching.* The reading attainment of a group of pupils is assessed, and the poorest 10 per cent of the pupils selected for remedial teaching. After a period of time the pupils' reading

attainment is again assessed; we can predict that their reading would tend to show improvement. The selected 10 per cent of poor readers are an array in the first assessment; as a result of regression we would expect their average score in the second assessment to be nearer the mean of the whole group—that is, higher. The real improvement due to remedial work is not shown by higher level of attainment, but by the excess of their attainment over what would be estimated as due to regression to the mean.

(2) *Selection.* If the upper quarter, by ability, of the pupils in a primary school were selected for an academic course in a secondary school, and these pupils were assessed after a period in the secondary school, it would be found that those whose assessment in the primary school was highest had not maintained their relative position in the secondary school, and those whose assessment was lowest would have tended to improve their position in the group. Both arrays are regressing to the mean of their secondary-school group. If we now consider the array just below the 75 percentile in the primary assessment, who, we will assume, have been allocated to less exacting academic courses in the secondary school, we would expect to find that they too had regressed towards the mean of their own secondary school group, or, in other words, had moved downwards in their relative class positions. This tendency for those just above the selection border-line to improve their relative position, and for those just below to regress to the mean of their group, can be adequately accounted for in terms of the correlation between the primary and secondary assessments. The degree of regression depends on the value of the correlation coefficient between the two sets of assessments.

(3) *Assessing progress.* The idea of assessing not only a pupil's level of attainment but also his rate of progress is an attractive one, but full of pitfalls. If a series of assessments of attainment correlate very highly with each other, then there is clearly very little difference between the pupils in respect of their rate of progress. Whatever the rate of progress, it is being made uniformly by all pupils. If there are differences among pupils in their relative rates of progress, the correlation between the assessments will be lower, and regression effects will appear. It is obvious that the pupil in the best position to obtain a good 'progress' mark is the one who begins at the foot of the class, and the least well placed, the one beginning at the top of the class. This may easily lead

to the paradoxical situation that the pupils who are in the array at the top of the class have to progress in order to remain in the same position, and those at the foot of the class could improve their position without progressing.

(4) *Teaching methods.* Regression may also lead to unjustified conclusions about the effects of teaching methods. The attainment in arithmetic of a group of pupils is assessed, and a new method of teaching tried out. The pupils are then assessed again. It appears that the poorest pupils have made relative progress, and the best pupils have slipped down the class order. It would be wrong to conclude that the new method is of greater benefit to the less able pupils than to the more able, at least until the regression effect has been allowed for.

(5) *Combining and comparing marks.* A group of pupils are assessed for English and arithmetic, each on a scale such that 10 per cent of the pupils score over, say, 80 marks in each subject. When the two assessments are added to give a composite mark, the proportion of pupils with a composite mark of 160 will be less than 10 per cent, unless the correlation between English and arithmetic is $r = +1\cdot0$. In fact, the lower the correlation co-efficient, the lower will the proportion be. The same applies equally to successive assessments in the same subject.

A similar effect of regression is observed when we compare pupils' IQs with their attainment in school subjects. The correlation coefficient between IQ and English in a population of the same age is of the order of $r = +0\cdot8$. Therefore pupils with very low IQs will tend to appear as relatively better in English, and may be labelled 'over-achievers'. Similarly, the array of pupils with very low attainments will have relatively higher IQs, and may be labelled 'under-achievers'. This again is regression to the mean, though, of course, other factors may also be operating in some cases.

Conclusion

The justification for stressing the properties of these various measures is that statistical classification of information is an aid to clearer understanding of the patterns of trends and relationships. The classification can range in sophistication from a teacher's judgement to precisely designed research, but in all cases some understanding of the process of classification is necessary to the understanding of the conclusions reached. Failure to comprehend the ideas of significance and regression, particularly, can lead to misinterpretation of the information available, which can in turn lead to educational efforts being wrongly directed.

WHAT IS A GOOD ASSESSMENT?

We have already defined the terms 'sector' and 'scale'. What we have not done is to examine the ways in which differences of pupils' behaviour may be most effectively assessed, so that the scale of assessments corresponds closely to the observed differences in behaviour. Educational assessments may be of various degrees of precision, from a teacher's observation that one pupil is a fast learner and another slow, or that one pupil is assertive and another shy, to a carefully constructed and standardized test of intelligence. But whatever the degree of precision, there are four basic requirements which any assessment must fulfil before it can be acted on with confidence. These are validity, reliability, objectivity, and standardization.

Validity

The purpose of any kind of educational assessment is to enable the appropriate educational action to be taken. If the results of an examination, for example, are not used by the teacher as some kind of guide to teaching procedure, there is no point in giving it. An educational assessment is like a medical diagnosis; the diagnosis indicates the treatment, and the outcome of the treatment is in turn assessed to establish how effective it has been. The extent to which the action taken as a result of the information from an assessment turns out to be the correct action is known as the predictive validity of the assessment. If a class were divided into two groups for more and less academic work, on the basis of an intelligence test, and it was later found that the grouping had been substantially correct, then the intelligence test has high predictive validity. On the other hand, should teachers, whose attitude as assessed by a questionnaire is shown as permissive, tend to act in the classroom in an authoritarian manner, then to that extent the attitude questionnaire has low predictive validity. It cannot therefore be said that an assessment is valid or not valid. The assessment may be valid for one purpose and not for another. A test of mechanical aptitude may have high predictive validity for a theoretical understanding of mechanics, but a low predictive validity for practical work. There is a further qualification. An assessment is only valid to a greater or lesser degree, which in practice is measured by the correlation of the original or test assessment with the criterion, which is an independent assessment of the sector of behaviour the test assessment is meant to predict.

Another kind of validity is content validity. Here the question asked is whether a test of attainment, for example, is an adequate assessment of the sector of knowledge or skills being measured. A test of ability in problems in arithmetic may have low content validity if the assessment depends to any considerable degree on the pupils' ability to read, or on their ability to compute readily in terms of mechanical arithmetic. Similarly, the content validity of an assessment of pupils' reading ability will be low if the assessment is limited to word recognition only.

Another common example of low content validity is known as the 'halo' effect. A pupil may have an alert and attractive manner; there is a tendency for teachers to rate such pupils more highly in attainment than the facts justify. Often, too, a pupil who is very weak in certain school subjects is rated lower than he deserves in other aspects of behaviour.

There is no objective method of estimating the content validity of an assessment in the way we can estimate the predictive validity by correlation of test with criterion. To ensure content validity, the sector of behaviour being assessed should be carefully defined and analysed, and a representative sample of the sector selected for assessment purposes.

The other kinds of validity require only brief mention. Curricular validity is an aspect of content validity. A test of French may have high content validity but be unsuitable for advanced students; it could, however, have high curricular validity if the content were appropriate to the particular area of French covered by an introductory course.

Construct validity refers to the agreement between assessment of behaviour and a theoretical scheme or structure. We may on theoretical grounds define two types of personality, introverts and extroverts. If an assessment of personality characteristics can be constructed which will distinguish between these two types, on the basis of our definition of these types, then the assessment has high construct validity.

Concurrent validity is found by a comparison of assessment with the attainment of the pupils at the time of assessment. Thus a test of typing aptitude would have high concurrent validity if the scores on the test corresponded closely with the present level of typing ability of the students tested. Concurrent validity, however, is normally estimated only where a proper estimate of predictive validity is not possible.

The need for validity of an assessment is obvious. All that need be said is that in so far as an assessment is not valid, it is not worth making.

Reliability

When it is used in connection with an assessment the term 'reliability' has a technical meaning. One way of looking at it is to consider an unreliable test as one of low content validity; much of what is being assessed is chance. But it is probably easier to consider reliability separately from validity, though the relationship is that an unreliable test cannot be valid, except by accident, and a reliable test may or may not be valid. An assessment is reliable if the scores obtained on any one occasion can be taken as representative of the scores which would be obtained on any other occasion. If an assessment is made, and then made again, the reliability of the assessment is most simply expressed in terms of the correlation coefficient between the two sets of assessments; this is the basic measure of reliability, known as test–retest reliability. For a satisfactory assessment the reliability coefficient should be high; for a group intelligence test the figure is about $r = +0.97$, for secondary-school examinations a value of $r = +0.7$ is above average.

The statistical significance of a test score is directly related to the reliability of the test. Taking a test with reliability coefficient $r = +0.96$, and with a standard deviation of scores of 15, we can use the formula for the standard error of a score, SD times $\sqrt{1-r}$. Inserting the relevant figures in the formula, we get the value of the standard error as three points of score. This is Scale C on Fig. 5, which we have already discussed (p. 142). The chances are 68 in 100 that a pupil's mark on such a test would be within $+3$ and -3 of his recorded score, if the test could be repeated under the same conditions. In actual fact, a test cannot be repeated under the same conditions, but the standard error is a measure of the preciseness of any given test score. This preciseness, as we see, depends on the reliability; the lower the reliability coefficient, the less precise or accurate the assessment is.

The main source of unreliability in an assessment is chance. If a pupil obtains a high score with luck on one occasion, it is unlikely that his luck would hold on other occasions; in other words, his score is not a representative one. One way to ensure maximum reliability is to make the assessment as thorough as possible, which means that the chance of an unrepresentative sample of the pupil's behaviour being assessed is reduced. A vocabulary test of ten words is less representative of the pupil's vocabulary than a test of one hundred words. A short, 'snapshot' test is seldom if ever reliable. The other way of ensuring maximum reliability is to construct the test so that as few marks as possible can be obtained by guesswork, by either the pupil or the marker. How this is best done is discussed in the next section. The importance of reliability is best emphasized by repeating that in so far as a test is unreliable, it is not valid.

Objectivity

In Table 6 are given the marks, on a seven-point scale, awarded to six English essays, A–F, by fifty teachers. The essays were a representative selection by eleven-year-olds, and no detailed marking instructions were given.

TABLE 6   *Marks assigned to each of six essays by fifty teachers marking independently of each other.*

| | Mark assigned | | | | | | |
Essay	Ex	VG	G+	G	G−	Fair	Unsat
A	—	2	14	17	10	7	—
B	5	12	21	8	4	—	—
C	1	3	7	14	12	9	4
D	8	14	10	10	6	2	—
E	—	2	4	20	13	8	3
F	—	—	1	7	19	15	8

Though there is a certain broad agreement among the fifty markers, essay B for example being considered better than essay F, the extent of difference of opinion among the markers is very wide indeed. The pupil who wrote essay C would have had an assessment of 'Excellent' had he been marked by one examiner, and precisely the same essay would have been assessed as failing by another four examiners. There is no means of knowing, even after the essay has been marked by fifty teachers, what the standing of C's essay is. Is it 'Excellent' or is it 'Unsatisfactory'? The assessment depends as much on who marks it as on the quality of the essay.

If, however, the test or examination is so constructed that the same performance will get the same mark or placing on the scale, then the assessment is said to be objective. Assessments may fail to be objective in two main ways. One is that there may be differences in the selection of content material for a test or examination. The effect of those differences can be reduced, though not wholly eliminated, by attention to the content validity of the test. The other source of lack of objectivity is in the marking. This can be done by constructing the test in such a way that for any item there is only one correct answer. How this is done is discussed later.

The need for objectivity is as vital to dependable assessment as is the need for validity and reliability. It is for this reason that psychological and educational investigations, as well as an increasing number of national examinations in the U.S.A., Britain, and elsewhere, are conducted in such a way that objective measurement is possible. To attain objectivity the examiner's range of methods of assessment may be somewhat restricted, but such restriction is undoubtedly preferable to the situation illustrated in Table 6. Had these essays been assessed by only one marker the extent of disagreement would not have been revealed. Table 6 deserves very careful consideration as its implications are fundamental. These implications are not theoretical only—decisions affecting a pupil's educational future often rest on very insecure foundations.

Standardization

The word 'standard' which is contained in Standardization is derived from 'standard deviation', and does not imply any standard of pass or fail. We have in fact already discussed the basic form of standardization when we stated that a scale is defined by its mean and dispersion. A class test, which has a mean of 70 and a standard deviation of 5, is standardized for that class. In other words, the standardization of a test is the defining of the scale on which the scores are expressed. Such a class test, however, is only standardized for the particular class to which it is given. It is quite possible that pupils who are below average in arithmetic in a class are nevertheless above average when compared with a representative population of pupils of the same age. The only way a teacher can find out if this is so is to give the class an arithmetic test which has been standardized on such a representative population. This is the usual use of the term 'standardized'. Here the scores of the representative population are converted to a normal distribution, generally with a mean of 100 and a standard deviation of 15. Scale A in Fig. 5 (p. 142) is such a scale, and as the distribution is 'normal', scores or quotients can be interpreted accordingly. Most standardized tests contain an age allowance. This means that a ten-year-old with a certain score may be average for his age; an eleven-year-old with the same score would then be below average for his age, and therefore obtain a lower standard score or quotient.

Another method of standardization is by age. The principle is simple enough. A test of reading is given to a representative sample of children of various ages. It is found that the average score for eight-year-olds is sixteen. Any pupil, of whatever age, who scores sixteen on the test is said to have a reading age of eight years. For younger pupils particularly, standardization by age, though less precise, is more meaningful and is adequate enough.

The standardization of tests of personality, attitude, and temperament often gives rise to difficulties. There is no good reason to suppose that personal characteristics such as a tendency to anxiety, or schizophrenia (a mental illness involving loss of contact with external realities), are normally distributed in the population. This kind of assessment is justified by its concurrent validity—that is, the extent to which the information given by the test agrees with the information obtained from clinical examination of patients known to be suffering from such mental illness. If such patients, on the assessment used, give positive responses to, say, 30 per cent of the items in the assessment, then the standardization consists of the information that anyone giving more than 30 per cent positive responses is probably suffering from the condition in question, and those with fewer than 30 per cent positive responses are not. This is, in effect, standardization on a two-point scale, but finer distinctions can often be used. Another type of personality assessment is the projective test. The Rorschach test, in which a person is presented with a set of printed inkblots and asked to say what he perceives, is a typical projective test. The test is scored according to a detailed and specialized scheme, in which are counted the number of interpretations involving the whole blot, or parts of it, and references to persons, animals, colour, movement, and so on. The standardization consists of a guide to the frequency of these references, so that it is possible to say that in a given case there was more than average reference to animals or colour, for example. Interpretation in terms of personality is a matter of validity.

There are many sectors of behaviour of interest to the educational psychologist and the teacher in which there are no standardized forms of assessment. Some projective tests which consist of asking the child to tell about a series of pictures, or to complete a story, are so inadequately standardized that it is not possible to say whether the child's responses are typical or not and, still less, to what degree they may be exceptional. There are no adequately standardized assessments of sectors such as social maturity. We just do not know what range of differences in this sector of behaviour is typical of pupils of various ages. Another sector of behaviour, important in young children learning to read, is their perceptual abilities. Again we do not know what to expect from a five-year-old in the way of auditory or visual discrimination, or perceptual speed. How many five-year-olds are in fact able to discriminate between 'saw' and 'was', or between 'house' and 'horse'? Most of them, about half of them, or only a few of them?

No assessment at all is probably less misleading than an inadequately standardized assessment. If the way an assessment is standardized is known, then the result can be interpreted. For example, if a backward fifteen-year-old has a reading age of ten years, this could on one standardization give him a reading quotient of 67, which looks bad; but if the test is age standardized, it means he has the reading ability of an average ten-year-old, which is by no means illiterate.

METHODS OF ASSESSMENT

If the teacher is a golfer, he carries a bag of clubs from which he selects the one most suitable for the shot he wants to make. He does not use a putter from the tee or from a bunker, not because it is against the rules, but because it is not efficient. In a similar way an educator has at his disposal an armoury of different kinds of assessing instruments, and various techniques for using them. The intelligence test is the form of assessment which has been most carefully studied and developed. Though some questions of validity are still under investigation, the techniques for ensuring reliability, objectivity, and standardization are by now well established. It would seem obvious that such techniques could profitably be applied to other forms of assessment, particularly to school examinations and tests. There is, however, considerable resistance to the use of what are known as objective tests in education. The sources of this resistance have not been investigated as they lie within that rather neglected branch of educational psychology which is concerned with the teacher rather than the pupil.

Objective Examinations

The arguments against extensive use of objective methods of examining are usually twofold. The first is that the objective examination, as contrasted with the essay type, does not give the pupil an opportunity to express himself freely and adequately. There is substance in this statement, especially in the literary subjects, but its relevance to assessment is doubtful. The pupils who wrote the essays in Table 6 had the opportunity to express themselves freely, but the table also shows how little confidence we can have in any single assessment. It is also questionable how far the traditional practice in school, college, and university examinations is in fact enabling candidates to express their views clearly and adequately. To state the case in its strongest terms, if a pupil is required to discuss freely a topic prescribed to him without notice, within a prescribed limit of time, for an audience or examiner who already knows much more about the topic than the pupil does, and in the knowledge that his educational future may depend on the result, we have created a situation which is as unfavourable to free and original expression as it is possible to imagine.

The other main argument against the objective examination is that marks can be obtained by guesswork. This is again correct, but it also applies to other kinds of examination. There is no reason to suppose that a pupil who is uncertain of the nature of a Mediterranean climate is not going to make a guess at it in a discussion, just as much as in an objective test. Further, with an objective examination we can estimate the effects of guesswork, or chance, much more precisely than in other types of examination. Take an objective examination of a hundred items, with four possible answers offered for each item. By chance alone the pupil will obtain one correct answer in four, so that the expected total score would be twenty-five. The effects of chance are normally distributed, so that scores obtained by chance will be normally distributed about the mean, in this case twenty-five. The SD of the distribution is given by the formula $\sqrt{npq}$, where n is the number of items, p the probability of a correct answer, and q the probability of a wrong answer. In this case $n = 100$, $p = 0 \cdot 25$ and $q = 0 \cdot 75$. This gives an SD of 4·3, and the distribution of scores by pure chance is set out as Scale B in Fig. 5 (p. 142). This is interpreted in the usual way—for example, the chances are 2·5 in 100 that a score of more than 33·6 would be obtained on the test by pure guesswork. It should, however, be kept in mind that there is no clear distinction between guessing and knowing; there are only degrees of certainty, and these are present to the same extent in any kind of assessment. It should also be noted that the scores calculated above cannot be used as a 'correction' for guessing. This correction would only apply when all pupils answer all questions by guessing only.

How far can any assessment be made objective? As an exercise in construct validity as well as objectivity, let us try an outline of an objective test in English composition. We set out to test objectively the various components which are the basis of assessment in English composition.

Correctness of grammar and usage, punctuation, and spelling are tested easily enough. Appropriateness of vocabulary could be assessed by tests such as this: "(startled by, noticing, distracted by, listening to) a menacing growl, he turned and was faced by an angry tiger (waving, flagellating, lashing, wagging) its tail furiously".

Style could be assessed in a similar way, by passages like the following:

A. What pleasure is there to compare with travelling? How delightful it is to journey alone! Much as I enjoy the warmth and gaiety of social gatherings, in the Great Outdoors, Nature is my best companion. In such company, can anyone feel alone?

B. One of the pleasantest things in the world is going on a journey; but I like to go by myself. I can enjoy society in a room; but out of doors, nature is company enough for me. I am then never less alone than when alone.

C. I like travelling; but I like to go by myself. I like the company of other people, but when I am out of doors, nature is my companion. I do not feel alone then.

Passage A is rather rhetorical, B is by William Hazlitt, and C is rather pedestrian.

Control of sentence structure could be assessed by tests like this:

1. Despite the increasing cold, we decided to continue our journey.
2. We decided to continue our journey
   (a) as the cold was increasing
   (b) to spite the increasing cold
   (c) though the cold was increasing
   (d) if the cold increased.

Originality and creativeness could be assessed by some of the more objective tests of 'creativity' discussed in the next chapter.

We do not claim either that the above items are perfect or that the test is the finished article, but it is technically possible to construct an objective test in the way outlined above. If examiners are given full freedom of judgement in the marking of written English we get the impossible situation shown in Table 6. The introduction of agreed marking schemes limits the examiners' discretion, and is the first small step to greater objectivity. If the method of assessment we have outlined is adopted, the examiners' judgement is transferred from the marking of the test to its construction. The examination can then be constructed to a known 'recipe' which can if necessary be varied, or weighted, to give maximum validity for the purpose for which the results are to be used. From the point of view of assessment, there is little doubt that the objective technique is an improvement on traditional methods; the practical difficulty will be in the reluctance of teachers to teach written English in a manner which they know will not be directly examinable.

Other Types of Examination

Other kinds of school examinations have not been investigated very thoroughly. Practical tests are required in certain subjects, such as art, domestic science, or technical subjects. The difficulties in art are the same as those in English composition. Similarly an examiner faced with fifty steak dumplings, resulting from a cookery test, may have the same difficulty of maintaining a consistent standard of assessment throughout as one faced with a set of essays on "The Future of Space Travel" or discussions on the failure of the League of Nations. Trade tests, used to assess the competence of apprentices, usually consist of a prescribed piece of practical work, with a list of points in the execution of the task which are to be observed and rated. Such tests can attain a fairly high level of objectivity, and the extension of this method from technical to other subjects should not be too difficult.

Another method of assessment, of whose efficiency little is known, is the oral examination. In spoken French, for example, the use of tape recordings is one step towards objectivity, but the assessment of such recordings is still subject to personal differences of opinion. Perhaps a set of graded recordings for comparison could be a further step to greater objectivity. The nearest approach to an oral or viva voce examination in any subject is the interview. This has been studied in connection with selection for the Armed Forces and the Civil Service particularly, and the general findings are fairly clear. The interview is not a particularly valid method of assessment, and there is little relationship between the interviewer's confidence in his judgement and the correctness of his judgement. It has been shown that the structured interview, which is like a trade test, with a standard set of points to be covered and an agreed rating scale, is both more valid and more objective than the unstructured interview, where the interviewer's intuitive judgement plays a large part in the assessment. The technique of oral examining will probably develop along similar lines.

Other Kinds of Assessment

There are other kinds of tests of value to the teacher. Diagnostic tests are designed to analyse a pupil's performance in a school subject, revealing both his strengths and his weaknesses. Diagnostic tests are constructed by first analysing the subject content into its component parts, and separate graded attainment tests made for each component. For example, in elementary arithmetic there would be tests of the operations of addition, subtraction, multiplication, division, and knowledge of the basic tables. These separate tests begin at a more elementary level than most teachers would usually do; the addition test would include items such as "$2+3 = ?$" Known areas of difficulty, such as use of zero and the process of carrying, would appear at the appropriate place in the graded tests. From scores on a diagnostic test the teacher can often obtain a profile of the pupil's competence in arithmetic, such that it may be evident that a pupil's difficulty in division may arise from a weakness in subtraction, or that his inability to do money sums may be due to ignorance of the twelve times table or the use of decimal points. If the pupil's difficulty is not detected early, a wide-spread weakness in arithmetic may develop, which should also be revealed in the diagnostic test. There is no reason why a teacher should not construct his own diagnostic test, either for use with a new class or as a guide to remedial teaching. To be of value to the teacher a diagnostic test must be thorough, and this means time.

Another group of tests are aptitude tests. Intelligence tests when used for educational selection are being used as aptitude tests for academic education. The aptitude test aims at assessing a pupil's suitability for certain future educational activities. There are, for example, tests of mechanical aptitude, clerical aptitude, mathematical aptitude, and so on. None of these tests has very high validity, and in general the negative conclusion that a pupil lacks aptitude for a particular study or vocation is more valid than the positive conclusion. Readiness tests are a form of aptitude test. Reading readiness, for example, is assessed in terms of the pupil's vocabulary, his ability to understand spoken instructions, to distinguish between visual patterns, and so on. Though useful as guiding the teacher's observations, the validity of such tests is again not very high.

The two remaining groups of tests are discussed in the appropriate chapters, intelligence tests in Chapter 7 and personality tests in Chapter 8.

CONCLUSION

"Whatever exists must exist in some quantity, and if it exists in some quantity, it can be measured." Though we have confined our discussion of measurements to the more immediate educational aspects, the scientific study of psychology depends on there being available to the psychologist some methods of measuring differences in observed behaviour. It is by such measurements that we can reach conclusions about the rate and effectiveness of learning by different methods and in different conditions. Statements about the sequence and progress of maturation are equally dependent on such assessments of behaviour. And, as we shall see, differences in intelligence and personality among pupils also necessarily involve a system of measurement. In education it is rather pointless for a teacher to set himself certain aims, but to have no means of assessing how far these aims are being achieved, whether they are the development of 'character' or the ability to solve quadratic equations. There are no 'imponderables' in education and there is no mystery about psychological measurement. The assessments may be of different degrees of precision; if a teacher observes that one boy is more timid than the others, this implies a scale of timidity of behaviour. There is no difficulty in the assessment; the obstacle is the definition of the sector of behaviour being assessed. An 'imponderable' is that which has not been clearly defined.

Intelligence

HOW DO WE DEFINE INTELLIGENCE?

No teacher can be very long with a class of children before he notices that some learn more easily than others, and are intellectually more active and alert. These children, he says, are the more intelligent ones. This judgement is often made easily and confidently, but when asked to define more exactly what this intelligence is that distinguishes one pupil from another, the teacher finds difficulty in expressing the idea in words. Nevertheless, the concept of intelligence is a useful and relevant one in educational practice. How does the psychologist view it?

The psychologist meets the not unusual difficulty arising out of common language usage. To him, differences in intelligence are differences in ways of behaving, so he finds the use of the noun 'intelligence' misleading; he thinks rather in terms of the adverb 'intelligently' as a description of behaviour. Also, as with learning, what can be a single concept in educational practice may turn out to be psychologically complex. We have already discussed some of the lines of psychological thinking and inquiry which converge upon the educational concept of intelligence. The intelligent pupil is the one who learns easily, quickly, and effectively. How is this related to the different kinds of learning processes going on in a classroom situation? Is the more intelligent pupil the one who relies mainly on cognitive structure learning, or does efficiency in establishing a wide repertoire of S-R behaviour units indicate a high level of intelligence? And to what extent are more mature pupils necessarily more intelligent? We noted that intellectual competence, which is almost the same as intelligence, was a blend of efficiency and maturity—but that efficiency and maturity did not necessarily go hand in hand. And how far is remembering a component of intelligent behaviour?

Can a pupil who forgets readily be properly described as intelligent? Thinking too is closely related to the common concept of intelligence, but how far can we distinguish between different styles of thinking, like focussing and scanning, as indicating different degrees of intelligence? Is the conservative focusser—methodical, slow, but surer in reaching a solution—to be considered as more intelligent than the gambling focusser, who may reach his solution more quickly and easily, but is more liable to find himself following a false trail? Psychologically, this concept of differences in intelligence is not a simple one, but since the idea of intelligence arose in an educational context, we shall begin with the attempts that have been made to define intelligence as a single function, and explore some of the lines along which more precise psychological inquiries lead us.

Some Formal Definitions of Intelligence

A. Binet, the Frenchman who was the pioneer of intelligence testing, wrote, "To judge well, to understand well, to reason well, these are the essentials of intelligence." The American L. M. Terman, who developed Binet's tests into the most widely used series of intelligence tests, wrote, "An individual is intelligent in proportion as he is able to carry on abstract thinking." These are but two attempts to define intelligence. There are many others, nearly all of which include at least three sectors of behaviour: the ability to think in abstract terms, the ability to learn, and the ability to cope with new situations. Even this was not found to be adequate. Another American, L. L. Thurstone, stated that, "Intelligence is the capacity to make focal impulses at their unfinished early stage of formation." He is contrasting considered intelligent behaviour with direct impulsive behaviour, holding that the intelligent person can inhibit his impulses, and stop to assess the situation before taking action. Other psychologists have pointed out the importance of memory and knowledge in intelligent behaviour.

All these points are relevant to a definition of intelligence, but to combine them all into one formal definition of intelligence would lead to a definition which is either too complicated or too vague to be of much help to anyone, particularly the teacher.

Defining Intelligence Operationally

In recent years, attention has been turned from what intelligence is, to what intelligence does. If we can agree about which ways of behaving are intelligent, we do not need to define too precisely what intelligence is, any more than it is necessary to define precisely the nature of chemical energy before we can learn to drive a car. What, then, is a teacher looking for when he is judging how intelligent his pupils are? Ability to learn quickly and accurately is one thing; but it is not the ability to learn just anything. Some kinds of behaviour are considered to involve intelligence more than others. If we take, as an example, a written composition by a pupil in a school class, we can look at the various components in the composition. Here is one possible analysis:

     *(i) Extent and appropriateness of vocabulary
     (ii) Correctness of spelling
    *(iii) Complexity of sentence structure
    (iv) Clearness and neatness of handwriting
    *(v) Organization of content

A teacher estimating the intelligence of his pupil would pay more attention to the items marked * than to the others. A pupil can be judged intelligent, but yet be a poor speller. A dull pupil may also be poor at spelling, but it is not because of his spelling that he is considered dull. On the other hand, it could not be easily said that a pupil is intelligent, but has a poor and limited vocabulary, cannot express himself except in very simple sentences, and cannot organize his thinking. Similar distinctions can be made in other school subjects, for instance in arithmetic between problem solving and rote learning of tables. The distinction can be extended to other activities. In games, chess is considered more intellectual than tiddly-winks, and contract bridge than snap! Occupations can also be ranked roughly according to their intellectual level. The significant result of such inquiries is the very substantial amount of agreement that is found. Though they find difficulty in defining exactly what is common to the various kinds of activity involving intelligence, most teachers agree very closely with each other in pointing out those aspects of school work which best reveal whether a pupil is intelligent or not.

ASSESSING INTELLIGENCE

It is because there is this agreement that it is possible to construct tests of intelligence. The questions set in an intelligence test require the pupil to do much the same kind of thinking as he does in those aspects of school work which are agreed to reveal differences of intelligence. Items on handwriting and spelling, for example, do not appear in intelligence tests. A few examples of the kind of items commonly appearing in intelligence tests will illustrate the point.

Analogies

1. Wings are to bird as fins are to . . .   (swim, fish, water, fly)
2. 49 is to 7 as 16 is to . . .

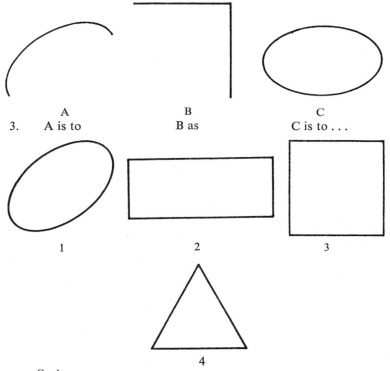

3.   A is to   B as   C is to . . .

Series

1. What comes next in the series?
   penny, threepence, sixpence, shilling, . . .
                    (one and sixpence, florin, half-crown, pound)
2. 1, 4, 8, 11, 22, . . .

If A is first, which is last?

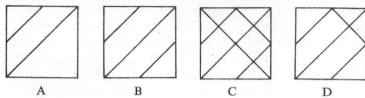

A   B   C   D

Classifications:
Which does not belong?
1. sheep, lily, cart, thrush, trout
2. 5, 7, 12, 13, 17
3.

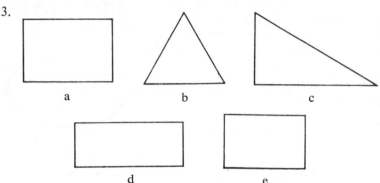

a   b   c

d   e

Vocabulary
1. What is an 'athlete'?
   What does 'diligent' mean?
2. 'Sinister' means: single, evil, careless, slight, powerful.
   Comprehension
1. What should you do if you are in a strange town and someone asks you the way?
2. John is younger than James, and William is older than John.
   Who is the youngest?

The number of kinds of questions, such as analogies, which
appear in intelligence tests is fairly limited, about a dozen in all.
One kind of item which cannot be demonstrated here is that
requiring the use of concrete materials such as coloured wooden
blocks, which appear in individual performance tests.

Kinds of Intelligence Tests

Some of the items we have quoted above are very like those
which would be used in school work. Others require the same
pattern of thinking, though the content may be diagrams rather

than words or numbers. Though there are tests of intelligence which do not use school knowledge of language and number, these tests, called non-verbal group tests or individual performance tests, are not as satisfactory tests of intelligence as group and individual tests involving the kind of school knowledge a pupil would normally acquire. For one thing, they do not allow the intelligent pupil, who requires words and numbers to think with, an opportunity to show how intelligent he is. Nor is the claim that they are 'culture free' justified, because the more we remove educational and cultural elements from an intelligence test, the less does it test intelligence. For the pupil whose educational opportunities have been inadequate or exceptional, such tests as these have their uses, but for the pupil who has gone through the normal schooling the group verbal test is probably the most satisfactory assessment of his intelligence. A more thorough assessment can be made by using a mixed verbal and non-verbal individual test like the Stanford–Binet Intelligence Scale, the Wechsler Intelligence Scale for Children, or the new British Intelligence Test. These tests, however, take time to give, and require a degree of psychological skill beyond what is expected of a class teacher.

Intelligence tests can therefore be classified into four main types. Group tests, which can be given to a group of children at the same time and can be administered and marked by a class teacher, are of two types, verbal and non-verbal. Individual tests, which require a trained psychologist to administer and mark them, are also of two types, mixed verbal and non-verbal, and performance, which is wholly non-verbal. For general, non-specialist use, the group verbal test is the most satisfactory.

Requirements of a Satisfactory Intelligence Test

As an intelligence test is intended to give in the short time of an hour or so the same assessment as an observant teacher may take some weeks to reach, the test must be constructed with great care. The general principles governing mental measurement discussed in Chapter 6 apply here. For content validity, the items in the test should agree with the generally accepted idea of what intelligence is, and should, of course, be suited to the ages of the pupils for whom the test is intended. The kinds of test item have changed but slightly over the past fifty years; this is illustrated by the difficulty of constructing a new or original kind of intelligence test. The criticism would be that it is not a proper test of intelligence. But there have been gradual changes in test content reflecting changes in school practice and psychological thinking. The appearance of new scientific and mathematical ideas, like sets, in the elementary-school syllabus is now being reflected in recent intelligence tests, as is the influence of Piaget's work on children's thinking.

The predictive validity of a test cannot be judged by inspection of the contents of a test. How effectively test scores enable a forecast to be made of a pupil's future educational progress, or his suitability for different levels of academic education, is a matter of factual information. The predictive validity must be known, and the general rule is that a test whose properties have been established is preferable to one which has not been thoroughly tried out in practice.

Reliability in the technical sense is achieved by making the test of adequate length. A short, snap-shot assessment of intelligence is unreliable in all senses of the word. In fact, a well-established group test is one of the most reliable educational measures we have. Individual tests are a little less reliable, but still compare favourably with the conventional school examination.

Group tests of intelligence reach a high level of objectivity in the scoring, and individual tests usually provide a list of typical answers, so that different testers are guided towards a uniform standard of scoring.

How an Intelligence Quotient is obtained from a Test

The pupil's performance in an intelligence test is first expressed in 'raw score': that is, total number of correct answers according to the scoring system used. A pupil may obtain a high raw score on a test because he is intelligent, or because he is older than the others taking the test, or because the test is an easy one to do. The first reason is the one we want, so differences in age and level of difficulty of the test need to be eliminated. This is done by converting the raw score into an Intelligence Quotient, or IQ. Regardless of the easiness or difficulty of the test, the average raw score for all pupils of the same age is calculated, and this becomes an IQ of 100. By definition, therefore, a pupil with IQ 100 is of average intelligence for his age. Age groups can be in intervals of one month, three months, or four months, but seldom more. For each age group the average pupil obtains an IQ of 100, though the average raw score for each age group will not be the same.

It is also necessary to establish the spread of IQ. This is done by deciding on a figure for the standard deviation of IQ; the common practice is to select 15 as the figure. For each age group, the raw scores are converted to a 'normal' distribution with the prescribed standard deviation.

The result of this is that each pupil's performance on the test is expressed in terms of a 'normally' distributed scale of IQ. The 'normal' distribution was chosen because its mathematical properties were well known (Chapter 6) and because it did not offend the common observation that children of average intelligence were more numerous than children of either very high or very low intelligence. But it cannot be concluded from a study of children's IQs that intelligence is 'normally' distributed in the population; the distribution of intelligence quotients is normal because it has been made so. Nor can it be said that two pupils of IQ 100 are equally intelligent. This is true only if the pupils are of the same age. A ten-year-old of IQ 100 does in fact behave more intelligently than an eight-year-old of the same IQ because he is older.

Finally, the use of the term 'quotient' in IQ is now largely of historical interest. In the earlier intelligence scales a pupil's mental age was obtained, this being the average age of the pupils who obtained the same score on the test as he did. The pupil's mental age was divided by his chronological age, and the quotient so obtained was multiplied by 100 (to eliminate decimal points). This was his intelligence quotient. Though the idea of mental age still has some value, quotients are no longer obtained in this way, the mental age now being treated as a form of raw score.

HOW DO WE THINK ABOUT INTELLIGENCE?

Whether a teacher gets his knowledge about differences in intelligence from observation in the classroom or the more precise assessment of an IQ, it is the educational implications of that information that count. We can discuss these under three main headings.

A. The interpretation of differences of intelligence, or how we think about intelligence.

B. The social and personal characteristics accompanying differences of intelligence, or the broader implications of differences in intelligence.

C. Differences in intelligence in the classroom, or how the knowing of a pupil's IQ helps the teacher.

We shall discuss them in that order.

Schemes of Thought or Cognitive Structures

We have already discussed the acquiring of cognitive structures by learning and the development of cognitive structures or, as we shall refer to them here, schemes of thought, by maturation. We have likewise noted earlier in this chapter that some school learning, such as ordering the development of an English composition, is considered as more indicative of intelligent behaviour than others, such as learning to spell correctly. The distinction very broadly is between what is learned in terms of cognitive structures and what is learned in terms of S-R behaviour. Both kinds of learning are a necessary basis for intelligent behaviour, but differences in intelligence are judged much more on the cognitive structure than on efficiency of S-R learning.

The examples of intelligence test items we have given above embody schemes of thought. Analogies are a scheme of thought, as are series, classification, and the other types of item. In tests of intelligence, pupils are being compared with others of the same age. For the younger pupils, the acceptable responses are distinguished from the wrong responses in the context of the pupils' level of intellectual maturity. Thus to the question, "What is an envelope?" the answer defining by use, "For a letter", is acceptable from a younger pupil. For the older pupil more formal definition is required. "Mosaic", for example, is defined as "A picture made out of little blocks". This is a formal definition and is acceptable. A definition at a less mature level is not accepted. Intelligence tests therefore attempt to assess pupils' schemes of thought as appropriate to their age, and there is no single intelligence test which is equally applicable to pupils of all ages. Where a test is devised to cover a wide age range, such as the Binet and WISC individual tests, it will be found that in fact pupils of different ages are doing different sections of the test. Both these tests include a section on vocabulary, the same list of some fifty or more words being used for ages from six to sixteen. But the six-year-olds soon find the words too difficult; the sixteen-year-olds easily get through the easier words, and begin to show differences in the later items in the list.

The difficulty, which we have discussed earlier, of distinguishing between maturity and efficiency of schemes of thought appears in the assessment of intelligence. To use vocabulary again, two definitions of "ochre" are ,"It's a kind of yellow, but isn't quite yellow—a medium-brown and yellow colour", and "You use it in oil paints". The first pupil is struggling towards a definition by classification, the second gives a firm and clear definition by use, a less mature scheme of thought. The point of interest is that the first pupil could probably have given an equally efficient definition by use, but is less efficient because he has not mastered his more advanced scheme of thought. Which is the more intelligent?

The assessment of differences of intelligence from observed behaviour is essentially an assessment of the extent and complexity of the schemes of thought a pupil has acquired. Included in the term 'schemes of thought' is the recognition of their relevance to any given stimulus situation. We noted in the discussion of heuristic systems of thinking that the machine which had certain ready-made schemes of thought fed into it operated more efficiently than a machine which had to develop its own schemes of thought from, as it were, first principles. The same condition applies to assessments of intelligence, whether by classroom observation or by formal test. The pupil who has available the scheme of thought to reach a correct and rapid solution to the problems presented to him is judged more intelligent than the pupil who, with a more limited range of schemes of thought, has to work out the solution from first principles.

Finally, we cannot separate intelligence from knowledge. To solve correctly the simple problem *cat: kitten — cow: (calf)* a pupil must not only be able to operate the scheme of analogy, but to know what a cat, a kitten, a cow, and a calf are. If he does not know what a kitten is, he cannot solve the problem. To a very great extent, differences in intelligence are based on acquired systems of thought; but it is also a matter of common observation that all pupils are not equally able to acquire such schemes of thought. Wherein lies the source of the differences in behaviour? It becomes necessary to try to clarify our thinking on this point.

Intelligence A, B, and C

If a man returns from a social occasion, is asked by his wife what some of the women were wearing, and he replies, "Clothes", the answer, though correct, would be regarded as singularly unhelpful. But that is the position for intelligence. We have only one word to use for a number of our different schemes of thought, all of which must be called intelligence, because there are not enough words to distinguish them from each other. It has become increasingly evident that the one term, intelligence, is being used with different meanings, and this is one of the main sources of confusion in our thinking about intelligence.

One attempt to clear up some of this confusion was made by the Canadian, D. O. Hebb, who distinguished between two meanings, which he called Intelligence A and Intelligence B. The British psychologist, P. E. Vernon, added a third meaning, Intelligence C. These three terms are not different views about the nature of intelligence; they are different but not conflicting ways in which the word is used. Hebb defines Intelligence A as, "an innate potential for the development of intellectual functions", and Intelligence B as, "the average level of that development at some later date". In this discussion we have adopted the idea of schemes of thought as being the form that "intellectual functions" take. Thus Intelligence A would be a pupil's innate capacity for acquiring schemes of thought, and Intelligence B the store or repertoire of schemes of thought he had acquired. We cannot observe all the schemes of thought a pupil has acquired, we can only observe a sample of them. This sample or selection of the pupil's schemes of thought, which is assessed in a classroom or an intelligence test, is Intelligence C.

A pupil's IQ, therefore, gives us a direct assessment of Intelligence C. From it we can infer Intelligence B, in the same way that we infer that a pupil who gets twenty-eight division sums correct out of a possible thirty (Arithmetic C) is good at division (Arithmetic B). From Intelligence B, which can be measured by sampling, we in turn infer Intelligence A, which cannot be measured. We need the meaning, Intelligence A, because it is observed that pupils given equal opportunities of acquiring schemes of thought do not all acquire them equally well. It is this limitation on a pupil's ability to acquire schemes of thought that Intelligence A refers to.

These differences in meaning are obviously relevant to certain questions of educational importance, such as the effects of heredity and environment on a pupil's ability, and the constancy of a pupil's IQ. These we shall return to later.

Is there One Kind of Intelligence or Several Kinds?

Intelligence A, B, and C are different meanings that we have for one word, intelligence. But it is also a matter of common observation that children, whether of high intelligence or not, are not equally good at all school subjects. Some excel at languages, but are relatively poor at arithmetic. The question is, therefore, are there different patterns of intelligence, or can a pupil of high intelligence be equally good at any subject, provided he is interested and applies himself?

Observations of different levels of attainment in the conventional school subjects are not, however, very helpful. There is no reason to believe that the pattern of children's intellectual abilities coincides with the pattern of school subjects found in schools in the latter half of the twentieth century. Also, if a class is listed on a timetable as doing English, a visitor entering the classroom cannot predict what kind of activity the class will be engaged in. They might be listening to poetry, or learning to spell, or writing an imaginative composition, or doing exercises in correct usage, or acting a drama, or reading silently for rapid comprehension.

What we are asking is whether there are different ways or modes of thinking among pupils, such that one pupil readily acquires schemes of thought in terms of language, another in terms of number, and a third pupil in terms of spatial relations. Take, for example, the number 169. One who had acquired a considerable repertoire of numerical schemes of thought would readily recognize it as the square of 13, and as the sum of 12^2 and 5^2. It would also be obvious that apart from 1 and 169, the only factor could be 13, as 13 is a prime. Similarly, what is the meaning of 4096? These 'meanings' would be as evident to anyone who thought easily in terms of number as the different meanings of the word "fair" would be to one whose pattern of thought was linguistic. Consider also a cube of white wood, painted black on the outside. If the cube were cut in a plane parallel to two opposite sides, the white surface revealed would be a square. How would it be cut to show a parallelogram, an equilateral triangle, a regular hexagon? These three examples, 169, "fair", the cube, demonstrate respectively, numerical, verbal, and spatial schemes of thought.

But how many are there? Verbal, spatial, numerical, musical, mechanical, memory, perceptual speed, verbal fluency, inductive reasoning, auditory perception, artistic, and so on? There is no agreement on what different modes of thought there are; and there are about as many lists as there are persons making them. And how do we identify them? Tests of spatial relationship may indicate how good a pupil is at that particular kind of problem, but they do not tell us how the pupil solved it, or whether those who can do it well are using different modes of thought from those who do it badly.

There appears to be no clear way of reaching a firm conclusion about the relationship between such special abilities or modes of thinking and intelligence. A rather complicated mathematical process called factorial analysis can be used to classify scores from a battery of different kinds of tests into what are called factors; the difficulty is that different classifications can be made, and in any case, the factors, which are mathematical, have to be identified psychologically. Differences of interpretation are therefore possible.

Two typical interpretations are those of Spearman and Thurstone. Spearman interpreted intelligence in terms of two factors, called 'g' and 's'. The first was a single factor common to all intellectual activities, and may be considered as general intelligence. The 's' factor was the specific knowledge necessary to do each intellectual task. In the terms we are using, he held that there were only two schemes of thought, the eduction of relations and the eduction of correlates. Thus, if we are given the terms 'tall' and 'short' we educe the relation of opposite. In passing, we may note that other relations are possible, such as similarity, as both are measures of height. If we are given 'tall' and the relation 'opposite' we can educe the correlate 'short'. Broadly speaking, the operation of these processes of eduction represents the 'g' factor. If we are given the terms 'stammel' and 'synalk' we can educe no relation, as the words are unknown. This specific knowledge of the content of the relationships is the 's' factor, which is different for each item; the eduction of relations or correlates is common to all items.

Thurstone's interpretation is that what we call intelligence is an average of a number of different modes of thought. His is a multi-factor theory implying that there is no single function called intelligence, but there are a number of different kinds of intelligence. The main primary factors are: V (verbal comprehension), W (word fluency), N (number), S (space), M (memory), P (perceptual speed), and R (reasoning). There are other factors, as well as specifics. To Thurstone, intelligence should be used in the plural, not the singular.

A 'hierarchical' interpretation of intelligence by Vernon represents a commonly accepted compromise. He considers 'g' or general intelligence as a major factor in intelligence, but also recognizes different kinds of ability, the principal ones being v:ed (verbal–educational) and k:m (practical–mechanical). There are also the specifics (s) which with 'g' he regards as the main sources of differences in intelligence.

Our discussion of Intelligence A, B, and C was concerned with the different meanings of the word intelligence. The discussion here is concerned with whether our use of the one word 'intelligence' obscures the fact that there may be different kinds of schemes of thought. The two discussions are not in conflict. It is possible, for instance, that there may be different patterns of Intelligence A, such that one person may have the capacity to acquire schemes of thought in numerical or verbal terms more readily than another person. Similarly with Intelligence B and C. Whether this is so or not is a matter of interpretation. The general opinion is that there are such differences; there is disagreement about what they are and how important they are.

Intelligence and Creativity, or Convergent and Divergent Thinking

A more recent distinction has been that between 'intelligence' and 'creativity'. The words used are rather unfortunate, as creativity has associations with artistic talent and self-expression, and intelligence does not necessarily exclude certain forms of creative thinking. A better distinction is that between convergent and divergent thinking. When discussing Spearman's idea of eduction as a thought process, we noted in passing that various relations could be educed between two terms, such as 'tall' and 'short'. The number and variety of possible relations represent divergent thinking, the reaching of the one 'correct' solution represents convergent thinking. Here is an item from a draft of an intelligence test:

(*a*) The hermit lives at the ____ of the hill.
(*b*) The lion had a thorn in its ____ .
What is the word which can be used in both sentences?

The intended answer was "foot" but pupils gave various answers' such as "side", "bottom", "foot", "top".

To make the item a test of convergent thinking, the second sentence would need to be changed, for example:

(*b*) I slept like a ____ .

The one acceptable word is "top". To make the item a test of divergent thinking the original sentences (*a*) and (*b*) would remain but the question asked would become, "How many different words can be used in both sentences?" Besides illustrating the difference between convergent thinking, which is the "drawing of fully determined conclusions from given information", and divergent thinking, which means that "a variety of responses is produced from the given information", the example also demonstrates why the conventional intelligence test is strongly biased towards convergent thinking. The reason is that tests of convergent thinking, where there is only one correct answer, can be marked so much more accurately and objectively.

The idea of creativity as distinct from intelligence was put forward by J. P. Guilford in 1950, the distinction being later developed into that between convergent and divergent thought. The pioneer experiment in the field of school education was reported by J. W. Getzels and P. W. Jackson in 1962. The examples of intelligence-test items, mainly convergent, given on page 171 should be compared with the items used by Getzels and Jackson to assess creativity or divergent thinking. Examples of the kinds of items used are:

1. *Word Associations*—e.g., How many meanings are there of words like "fair", "duck", "cap"?

2. *Uses—e.g.*, How many uses are there of a brick, a paper-clip, a tennis-ball?

3. *Hidden shapes—e.g.*, Is a simple shape hidden in more complex shapes?

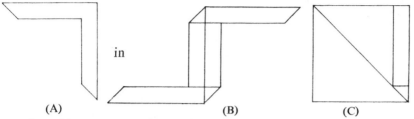

(A)   (B)   (C)

4. *Fables—e.g.*, The fable of the ant and the grasshopper is left unfinished; give a moral, and a sad and a humorous ending.

5. *"Make Up" Problems—e.g.*, A passage containing much information is given; make up as many problems as possible from the contents of the passage.

In such tests pupils are marked on the number, the variety, the originality, and the relevance of their responses. There is clearly much room for differences of opinion, and tests of creativity cannot be marked as precisely as the traditional convergent types of group intelligence test. Nevertheless, a broad measure of difference in divergent thinking can be obtained, and scores on creativity tests compared with these on intelligence tests. As the contents of the two kinds of tests are not absolutely different, a positive correlation between them is to be expected. This has, in fact, been found; though Getzels and Jackson reported very little correspondence between intelligence and creativity, this can be adequately explained by the fact that their initial inquiry was upon a highly selected group of pupils, with an average IQ of 132.

What are the Meanings of Intelligence?

If someone ignorant of Italian went to Italy and crossed busy roads where it said (in Italian) "Don't cross", or entered areas marked "Danger" and so on, the Italians would, correctly, judge him stupid. He returns, after learning Italian, and the Italians remark, again correctly, on how much more intelligently he now behaves. Has he become more intelligent, or was he equally intelligent on both occasions? It is this kind of confusion that the distinction between Intelligence A and B is intended to clarify. If we are talking about Intelligence A, the visitor was equally intelligent whether he knew Italian or not, but in terms of Intelligence B, he was more intelligent on the second occasion, because he behaved less stupidly. A similar situation occurs where a pupil has had his education seriously interrupted, or where his home conditions are very adverse, or where he suffers from some physical, sensory, or emotional handicap. The teacher of a hard-of-hearing pupil who says, "I think he is really quite intelligent, but he is handicapped by his hearing difficulty", is meaning Intelligence A; the teacher who says, "I am afraid he is not very bright, but that is because he has hearing difficulties", refers to Intelligence B.

The other question discussed was, in effect, what is the psychological recipe for intelligence? In an intelligent pupil, can the teacher distinguish the proportion of divergent and convergent thinking in the pupil's behaviour? What are the different ingredients, such as general ability, more special abilities like spatial and verbal, and different items of specific knowledge, which make up the performance of pupils who may be judged equally intelligent? When assessing intelligence the teacher should be looking not only at differences in degree of intelligence, but also differences in kind of intelligence. It is not enough for a teacher to know the intellectual level of his pupils, it is equally his duty to be able to think clearly about what he knows.

THE BROADER EDUCATIONAL IMPLICATIONS OF DIFFERENCES OF INTELLIGENCE

Heredity and Environment

If differences in intelligence are determined mainly by heredity, the best that education can do is to identify the bright and the dull pupils, and give them a chance to make the most of what abilities they have. This is the concept of the 'pool of ability', which implies that there are fairly definite proportions of pupils of different levels of ability, and that these proportions are fixed by means out of the educator's control. If, on the other hand, differences are largely determined by environmental opportunities, chiefly educational, then the proportion of very intelligent pupils can be increased by social and educational improvement. Besides being of great theoretical interest, the relation of heredity and environment is also of considerable educational importance.

Unfortunately, we know very little about the ways in which intelligence is inherited by one generation from another, and not enough about what aspects of environment are most influential in developing intelligence, and in what degree they are significant. The differences in IQ among children can be attributed to three sources: heredity, environment, and interaction. Heredity, the genetic component, is virtually the same as Intelligence A, which cannot be measured directly. Environment, which is the opportunities for acquiring Intelligence B, appears to be mainly a matter of educational opportunity, though we are far from understanding the effects of environment in the earliest years of a child's life. Interaction operates in various ways; children of intelligent parents not only inherit intelligence, but are also living in an intellectually stimulating home; also, a child of high intelligence can gain more from his environment than would a child of lesser intellectual capacity in the same environment.

We have only bits and pieces of evidence on which to build a scheme of relationship between these three components. We have not enough adequate information about the relationship between the intelligence of parents and children in a representative population; we suspect it is of the order of $r = +0.5$. Apart from some severe cases of mental defect, we are not certain how intelligence is inherited. We do know that in our kind of society there is differential fertility for intelligence, such that the average IQ of children in small families is higher than that of those in large families. (See Table 8.) There is some doubt about whether this relationship applies at the two extreme ends of the IQ scale; it does not apply to very low IQs, and may not apply to the very high IQ range. It is also uncertain to what extent, in the middle range of IQ, the feature of differential fertility is a biological or a social feature. Probably it is both. We also know that the correlation between IQs of children in the same family is of the order of $r = +0.5$. This is a finding of some interest, as it means that it is not at all impossible to find one pupil of IQ 75 and another of IQ 100 coming from the same family. A recent Scottish inquiry tested all the younger brothers and sisters of a representative sample of children, tested at eleven years old. These younger brothers and sisters were in nearly all cases brought up in the same home,

7

usually attended the same school, were tested at the same age on the same test, often by the same tester as the originally tested member of the family. Taking the children in families of four children or more, where all children had been tested, it was found that the median difference between the highest and lowest IQ recorded for the same family was, for all these families, 26 points of IQ. This is a substantial difference, especially when it is remembered that for half the families this difference was greater than 26 points. Differences of 50 or more points of IQ within a family were not unusual. As children brought up in the same family are within fairly uniform environmental conditions, it is difficult to see how differences in IQ can be attributed in any substantial degree to environmental conditions. There are, of course, differences between families, the average IQ for some families being much higher than for others; the difficulty in interpretation is that we cannot disentangle the effects of better environment from the effects of inheritance, which tend to reinforce each other.

The most effective approach to the problem is one which we have already mentioned, the comparison of identical twins. The evidence is limited, as few identical twins are reared in substantially different environments, but the classical investigation of Newman, Freeman, and Holzinger showed that of nineteen such pairs, the fourteen individuals who by independent assessment were in the more favourable environment had higher IQs than the other member of the twin pair. The five exceptions showed only small differences in IQ. Length of education was the most significant environmental influence.

This scheme of heredity, environment, and interaction is the skeleton of our thinking, but as yet it is thinly clothed with knowledge. There is no absolute answer about the influence of heredity and environment on intelligence; any answer must be relative. If there is little difference between the environmental opportunities of children, then the major source of differences of IQ is heredity. We have used the term 'environmental opportunities', not 'environment', as the two terms do not mean the same. Equality of opportunity means environmental conditions related to the child's ability to benefit from them. Educationally, the same curriculum and the same teaching is not an equality. The same environmental and educational opportunities exist only when these are adapted to the intellectual level of the pupil. An illiterate and a literate child in the same library are not in this sense in the same environment.

We suspect there may be an analogy between education and nutrition. If a child's diet is short of vitamins, health suffers; if the diet contains vitamins adequate for his needs, the child can flourish; if the vitamin intake is further increased, health may again suffer from the overloading of the child's excretory system in getting rid of excess vitamins. But the vitamin needs of all children are not the same, and it may well be that in the development of intelligence there is a different level of environmental stimulation adequate for each child, and an 'over-rich' educational environment may hinder rather than help intellectual development. Probably for each child there is a 'threshold' of cultural environment above which additional opportunities have no effect. Increased educational opportunity is not a universal remedy for low intelligence; the effective education of intellectually dull pupils is based on the principle of simple and slow rather than of maximum enrichment.

One word of warning. It is very easy to attribute the low IQ of a pupil from an unfavourable cultural and social environment to his lack of opportunity. He is the conventional 'under-privileged' pupil. But he might have a brother further up the school with an IQ above average. And evidence is accumulating to indicate that, as far as we can assess, many such 'under-privileged' pupils are of limited intellectual ability in any case, and the environment is not such a handicap as might be imagined. The pupil of high ability is most likely to be affected by an unfavourable environment, and the truly 'under-privileged' child is the one who presents himself with an average IQ, but whose intellectual development is damped down by an impoverished environment.

The Constancy of Intelligence Quotient

It is administratively convenient to consider children's IQs as relatively stable. How far is it also true? Certain inquiries, now almost legendary, are frequently quoted to show how much IQs may change. H. Gordon's investigation in 1923 into English canal-boat children is one such. The children below school age had an average IQ of 90, but the average IQ of those who were over twelve years old was 60. The difference is reasonably attributed to the lack of schooling affecting adversely the IQ of the older children, whose relative intellectual rank had fallen. Another type of instance is that quoted by F. Lloyd, where a pupil, with IQ 73 at seven and a half years old, reached an IQ of nearly 90 three years later, after receiving special schooling. It is, however, the exceptional cases that reach the text books, and the more spectacular the changes in IQ, the more likely are they to be quoted. Large changes do occur, but the circumstances are nearly always exceptional, as in the canal-boat children. It is well established that for the great majority of children in normal circumstances, the IQ level does remain fairly stable, and if a pupil's IQ is found to be 85, it is very probable that later assessments will be somewhere between 80 and 90. Table 2, Chapter 3, gives some data about the constancy of IQ.

Selection by Intelligence Test

The practice of selecting children for different kinds or levels of education on the basis of intelligence has attracted more than its fair share of support or abuse, according to how fashions change among educational theorists. Intelligence tests have been used for educational guidance and selection for over fifty years, and a very considerable body of knowledge about them has been built up. Educational selection by IQ is not infallible, but no measure is. The IQ is probably the most efficient single instrument for educational selection that has, as yet, been devised, and it is the results of its efficiency that tend to attract criticism.

The difficulty is that children cannot be selected by intelligence alone. Selection by IQ necessarily involves selection by social class, family size, physique, and emotional stability. Table 7, taken from the 1947 Scottish Survey data, is typical of the relationship found between intelligence and social class as defined by

TABLE 7   *Percentages of Eleven-year-old Children of High and Low IQ by Father's Occupation*

Father's Occupation	% High IQ	% Low IQ
(1) Professional	71	0
(2) Salaried Employee (Non-professional)	37	9
(3) Skilled Manual	23	15
(4) Semi-skilled Manual	15	22
(5) Unskilled Manual	12	21
All Occupations	23	17

father's occupation. 'High IQ' means the pupils in the top 23 per cent of the school population, 'Low IQ' means the lowest 17 per cent of the same population, all eleven years old.

If therefore we select the most intelligent 23 per cent of the children, we find that this group contains 71 per cent of all the children whose fathers are professionally qualified, 25 per cent of all the children of skilled manual workers, and only 12 per cent of the children of unskilled manual workers. In the lowest 17 per cent of the school population, no children of professional men appear, but 21 per cent of the children of unskilled manual workers are there.

Table 8, from the same Scottish Survey, demonstrates the tendency for the average intelligence of children in smaller families to be higher than that of children in larger families. The figures are test raw scores, not IQs.

TABLE 8 *Average Test Score of Eleven-year-old Children by Family Size*

Father's Occupation	Family Size				
	1	2	3	4	5
(1) Salaried Employees	49	48	49	43	43
(2) Skilled Manual	42	41	39	36	33
(3) Unskilled Manual	35	36	33	33	30
All Occupations	42	42	39	35	32

From Table 8 it is clear that selection by high intelligence would tend to include more of the children from the smaller families. Though it is not shown in the table itself, the high IQ group, which is the top 23 per cent of the eleven-year-olds referred to in Table 7, contains 36 per cent of the children from one-child families, but only 3 per cent of the children from families of twelve or more. The low IQ group contains only 10 per cent of the one-child families, but 43 per cent of the families of twelve and over. Family size and overcrowding are, of course, related, but the relationship between intelligence and family size is not a direct result of overcrowding, nor indeed of social class.

There is no evidence to support the picture of the undersized, delicate, bespectacled, brainy bookworm. The children who are above average in intelligence tend, more often than not, to be above average in height and weight and in general to be healthier.

The Scottish high IQ group were over two inches taller, and six pounds heavier, than the low IQ group, at age eleven.

In the U.S.A., L. M. Terman followed up the future progress of a group of gifted children born in 1921, all with IQ 135 or over. Besides confirming the general findings stated above, Terman found that his 'gifted' group were significantly below the national average in mental illness, crime, alcoholism, and suicide. Delinquent and maladjusted pupils appear at all levels of intelligence, but more frequently at the lower levels of IQ than the higher.

Finally, selection by intelligence implies selection by sex. Provision has to be made in schools for the mentally handicapped for at least two places for boys for each place for a girl. Correspondingly, there are more boys than girls with very high IQs; the sex difference is not in average intelligence, but in the greater scatter of intelligence among boys.

The findings of the last fifty years of fairly intensive research into differences of intellectual ability affords no comfort to those who hold egalitarian views. There is no evidence of uniformity in the distribution of intelligence, and no evidence of compensation, in the sense that those who are not good with their heads are good with their hands. Educationally, selection by intelligence is effective, but it depends on the swing of the pendulum of educational philosophy whether the social and other consequences of such selection is or is not too high a price to pay. It also seems at present that educational selection by intelligence is more readily accepted for low IQ than for high IQ.

HOW DOES KNOWING A PUPIL'S IQ
HELP THE TEACHER?

Here are the answers given by three pupils, each aged ten years nine months, to the same two questions from an individual intelligence test.[1] AA is above average intelligence, with IQ 141, A is of average intelligence, with IQ 108, and BA is below average, with IQ 78.

(1) "In what ways are paper and coal alike?"
    AA "Well, they're both made from trees. Paper is made right from trees today. Back in the time of the dinosaurs trees were pressed down, and the Ice Age came, and all

[1] R. Strang, *Helping Your Gifted Child* (New York, E. P. Dutton, 1960).

the pressure and time turned the trees into coal deposits."
A "They both can burn."
BA "I don't know—(brightly) you can make marks on paper with coal."

(2) "What is a diamond?"
AA "It is the hardest known and next to the most valuable substance. It is pure carbon. Volcanoes erupt and the smoky carbon is trapped. After hundreds of years of pressure—
(examiner's hand gave out)
A "It's pretty and shiny and costs lots of money. It comes from mines. People wear it in jewellery."
BA "A diamond ring."

These answers are typical of the different quality of the schemes of thought acquired by pupils of different IQs. At the age of ten the difference is very marked, and as the pupils grow older the difference will increase. AA is an indication of what a teacher can expect of a pupil of IQ 140, and BA indicates what is to be expected of a pupil of IQ 80. The level of attainment and, more important still, the educational needs of these three pupils are obviously different. The presence of such pupils in a class virtually forces the teacher to teach at different levels. For the above-average pupils, the traditional answers to the teaching problem are either enrichment or acceleration, or a mixture. Both methods lead to difficulties.

The Pupil of High IQ

Enrichment means that in the basic curriculum the pupil proceeds at the same rate as the class, but he does supplementary work as each teaching topic is covered. The curriculum is extended sideways. Besides raising difficulties of class organization, the weakness of this approach is that the bright pupil is prevented from progressing in the main stream of his studies at his own rate, and that it is usually in the academic studies that the intelligent pupil is most able and interested. In any case, a highly intelligent pupil who is interested in, say, mathematics, cannot in fact be prevented from following his interest outside the classroom. If the teacher can give help, it would seem reasonable that he should do so.

If such help were given in the classroom, the policy would be that of acceleration. This implies allowing the able pupil to proceed through the curriculum at his own rate with as much call on the teacher's assistance as any other pupil. It may well be that programmed learning will find a place here. This course of action also raises obvious difficulties of organization. Within a class, the accelerated pupil is liable to complete the requirements of his elementary-school education a year or two before he is supposed to. If he continues, there are difficulties in fitting into the scheme of secondary education, and from secondary education into higher education, where there is almost invariably a lower age limit for acceptance. The other consideration, frequently put forward, that younger but highly intelligent pupils are not personally or socially mature enough to be advanced up the school, is based on prejudice. At present there is no satisfactory measure of personal or social maturity available; there is a lack of information because the practice of accelerating pupils is not carried out to its conclusion, and what evidence there is from occasional experiments in the U.S.A., like that of admitting fourteen-year-olds to a Chicago university, shows that the practice seems to have little, if any, adverse consequences for the pupil where acceleration is part of a planned educational policy. We cannot, in fact, know the effects of acceleration till it has been tried much more extensively.

The Pupil of Low IQ

What has been said about the very intelligent pupil can be said in reverse about the very dull pupil. Satisfactory progress through school depends on letting him proceed at his own rate, which is often very slow. A pupil of IQ 70 may not be ready to begin reading till he is eight years old, and his progress will be correspondingly slow. Unlike the highly intelligent pupils, the pupils of low intelligence have had special educational provision made for them. Pupils unable to cope with ordinary school work, the borderline being usually between 65 and 75 IQ, can be educated in special schools, where the expected rate of progress is adapted to the slow learning rate of such pupils. In the long run, they frequently reach a higher level of school attainment than pupils of higher IQ who have remained in the main stream of school education.

Differences between IQ and School Attainment

A class teacher can make a reasonably good estimate of a pupil's intelligence, and can make a good estimate of a pupil's attainment. But it is difficult for the teacher to compare his two estimates, as they are not independent but are based on the same set of observations. It is here that an intelligence quotient, obtained from a standardized intelligence test, is of value to the teacher; so too is an assessment obtained from a standardized test of school attainment.

A discrepancy between level of IQ and level of school work proves nothing in itself; it is, however, an indication to the teacher that investigation is desirable. There are several sources of discrepancy, and if one is established, it does not follow that others are not also operating.

Since there is not a perfect correspondence between IQ and school attainment, some discrepancy is the rule rather than the exception. As a result of regression to the mean it would be expected that the pupils with the highest IQs would not always be the pupils with the highest attainment levels, and the pupils with highest attainment not always those with the highest IQs. The same principle operates for pupils at the other end of the scales of IQ and attainment, the lowest IQs not necessarily being those of lowest attainment. The effects of regression are often difficult to assess, and it is probably wiser for the teacher to consider only those pupils who show a gross or unexpected difference between IQ and school work.

Another source of discrepancy, often overlooked, is age. An IQ is relative to a pupil's age, and a pupil of IQ 120 at the age of ten is of approximately the same level of ability as a pupil of IQ 100 at the age of twelve. The younger pupil cannot be expected to do better than the older pupil, and the higher IQ may easily mislead the teacher. The ability of older pupils with lower IQs may similarly be under-estimated.

The 'Under-Achievers' and the 'Over-Achievers'

Those whose IQ is higher than their school work would suggest are commonly called the 'under-achievers'. Various possible explanations are offered. Lack of application is one. The intelligent pupil may find school work too easy and lose interest, or he may, if he is older, be living in social circumstances where neither his family nor his friends give him any encouragement to apply himself to school work. Laziness is not unknown among pupils, but before a pupil is labelled as lazy the fact of laziness should be clearly established. Among the less intelligent pupils repeated failure may lead to discouragement, and the lack of application lead to even poorer work than the pupil is capable of. An awareness of success, even in simple school tasks, can often remedy this.

The effects of personality disturbance or emotional stress may take various forms, but a very common effect is a lowering of standard of school work, often due to inability to concentrate. The IQ is affected too, but to a lesser extent. The remedy is a matter for the school psychological and medical services. So too are physical conditions, arising from lack of sleep, malnutrition, or chronic minor disease, the first indication of which may be the growing discrepancy between the pupil's IQ and his school work.

The list of possible causes given here is not complete; each pupil has to be considered as an individual, but it is desirable for the teacher to inquire into the commoner sources before inquiring into the less usual ones.

There is also a substantial number of 'over-achievers' whose progress equally needs to be watched by the teacher. These are the pupils whose level of school work is higher than their IQs would suggest. Over-application by pupils does occur, usually as a result of family pressure. If the pupil shows no signs of stress, it is not in itself wholly undesirable; but the teacher should bear in mind that for a pupil of mediocre intelligence the strain of keeping up a high level of school work will become increasingly great, and that, for the pupil's future education, evidence shows that IQ is a better basis of prediction than school attainment.

Emotional disturbance can occasionally reveal itself as over-achievement. A pupil emotionally rejected in his home may compensate by trying to gain recognition and approval in school. Further, over-application and over-achievement in arithmetic particularly may indicate a personality disturbance of a com-pulsive-obsessional type.

Also among the over-achievers are those pupils whose quality of intelligence is not adequately assessed by the conventional intelligence test. Whatever his level of 'general' intelligence, a pupil may be well above average in such special abilities as 'verbal' or 'number', with the result that his school work in English or in arithmetic may be above the level expected from his IQ. If more detailed observation by the teacher confirms that this is so, then the assessment of the pupil's intelligence requires to be revised. He then ceases to be an over-achiever.

In the same way a pupil with a higher level of divergent thinking (or creativity) than convergent thinking (or intelligence) may also appear as an over-achiever. School work can involve divergent thinking to a greater degree than intelligence tests do; and, once again, if the teacher, keeping in mind the characteristics of divergent thinking, finds that the pupil's school work shows a considerable element of this kind of thought, then the level of the pupil's intellectual ability will require to be reassessed. In making such observations, however, the teacher should be aware that certain characteristics of divergent thinkers are not such as endear them to the teacher. The divergent thinkers are said to be more introverted—that is, more concerned with meeting the needs of their own inner experience than in conforming to the requirements of the external world, and therefore less ambitious and in need of conventional success. They show greater flexibility of attitude, and are more willing to question and to change their opinions. They have greater intellectual self-confidence and are independent to the point of being self-willed. Finally, if an activity engages their interest, they pursue it with energy, often to the apparent neglect of other studies. Not all divergent thinkers, of course, show all these characteristics, but there is some evidence, not yet conclusive, to indicate that the distinction between divergent and convergent is not only between kinds of thinking, but also between kinds of persons.

CONCLUSION

If a teacher is to perform his duty of reconciling the needs of the children to the needs of the society in which they are being educated to live, he cannot afford to throw away any information about his pupils. IQ is very relevant information. No intelligence test ever placed a pupil in a particular class, or school, or ever decided what kind of education he needed; only people can do that. Hence comes the need not only for accurate information, but also for clear thinking about what the information means.

8

Personality

"What manner of man is this?" That is the question which any student of personality is trying to answer. The psychologist sets out to answer it by using his well-tried psychological techniques of definition of sectors of behaviour, observation, and measurement of differences. He constructs a theoretical interpretation on the basis of his observations, and then tests his theory against further evidence. Personality is such an extensive and complex sector of psychological study that it cannot be defined, nor differences assessed, in a few simple terms. It is as if we were looking at a very large building whose whole structure cannot be observed from one point of view only. We can observe the frontage, the wings, the sides, the back, but not all at the same time. And like such a building, there are different doors through which we can enter to study what goes on inside. We can select our aspect or sector, we can select our entrance, but we cannot see it all at once.

Not that there have been no attempts to formulate a comprehensive definition of personality. Possibly the best single definition is that of G. W. Allport: "Personality is the dynamic organization within the individual of those psycho-physical systems which determine his unique adjustment to his environment." A number of concepts about personality are packed into this definition. The words 'dynamic organization' imply that the individual is continuously developing, and actively seeking the most satisfying way of living; the emphasis is not wholly on the earlier stages of life. The word 'psycho-physical' indicates that physical constitution is an element in determining personality pattern. Besides the differences in physiological functioning that may underlie differences in temperament, such as lethargy or emotional instability, there is also the fact that differences in physical strength may lead to differences in behaviour and values, or that being short and fat is a condition which the individual has to adapt himself to. The use of the word 'unique' reflects Allport's view that each individual has to achieve his own special pattern of personality, arising out of differences of physical constitution, level of ability, and social experience. The uniqueness of personality is not so much that each of us is born different from all the others, but that each of us reaches his own particular solution to the problem of finding a way of living with ourselves and our environment.

Allport's definition, though broadly based, does imply that he has taken up a definite position in respect of how he views personality. He regards the building from a particular aspect, and enters by a particular entrance. He places emphasis on the unique nature of personality, rather than on those elements of personality which are common to all. He stresses continuing adjustment rather than taking the view that the unalterable foundations of personality are laid down in the first few years of life. There are other ways of looking at personality, and other avenues of approach to the psychological study of personality.

APPROACHES TO THE STUDY OF PERSONALITY

(1) We can begin by studying personality either as manifest in 'normal' behaviour, or in its 'abnormal' manifestations. The abnormal personality is not essentially a different kind of personality; it is one in which normal behaviour has become unbalanced, so that certain functions of the normal person are either exaggerated or underdeveloped. The difference is one of degree and proportion and the dividing line between normal and abnormal depends on the limits of tolerance of the society in which the individual is living. Some psychologists regard the disorders of personality as revealing most clearly the mechanisms of personality, and from the understanding of the way personality functions in the extreme cases, proceed to the study of the normal personality, where the same processes are manifest, but to a less obvious degree. We are all, for example, prone to attribute the blame for our shortcomings, to some extent at least, to other persons. The extreme cases of such a process are paranoid, suffering from delusions of systematic persecution by other

persons or organizations. Other psychologists prefer to begin by studying the characteristics of the normal person, to establish the 'norms' of observed behaviour, and to regard deviations from these norms as exceptional aberrations of behaviour. In practice, they argue, we act on the assumption that people, including pupils, are normal, and we must first find out about normal personality before proceeding to the exceptions. Both approaches ultimately reach common ground; but the different observations they begin with tend to colour their interpretation of personality.

(2) We can begin the study of personality by observing the differences in the ways individual persons respond to their own particular circumstances. This we shall call the clinical approach. Clinical interpretation depends on careful observation of individual cases, and a more general interpretation is built upon extensive experience of such cases. Usually, the clinical approach is linked to the study of the abnormal, but this is not necessarily so. A teacher in a classroom is in a good position to adopt a clinical approach. By contrast, what we shall call the scientific approach adopts the method of objective assessment of different sectors of behaviour, finding the dispersion of differences and establishing how the different sectors are related to each other. We discuss the scientific approach of Eysenck and Cattell in more detail later.

(3) We can begin from the assumption, as Allport does, that each of us is a unique personality, and concentrate on establishing the origin and kind of differences between persons. Alternatively, we can adopt the view that we are only marginally unique, that the resemblances among us are more significant for the study of personality than the differences. Then we concentrate on establishing the common components in personality, and from these common characteristics proceed to examine how observed differences in behaviour may be attributed to a common source.

(4) We may also begin our investigations by an analysis of the manifestations of personality into different sectors or traits, investigate these traits individually, and examine how they are combined into different personality patterns. The approach is similar to that of Thurstone in his investigation of intelligence; there was, he held, no single function of intelligence, but a number of distinct functions which combined to form the intellectual level

and pattern of the individual. A trait is a habitual mode of response, such as depression or suggestibility, or even characteristics like intelligence or bodily build. Using traits as the ingredients we can, as it were, find the recipe for each individual's personality. The alternative is the holistic view, that personality is a unity and functions not in parts but as a whole. The study here is of the organization of the total personality, how the individual adapts himself to his environment as a total person. The study of traits is more limited in scope, but is precise; the holistic view is more comprehensive, but lacks precision.

(5) Another difference between psychologists is whether they interpret personality in terms of its development or in terms of its present functioning. Some are interested in the origins of personality: how the present characteristics developed, and what is the history of the individual's personal development. Such psychologists attach great importance to the early years of life when the foundations of present personality structure were laid down; they consider that present personality characteristics can best be interpreted in terms of their growth and development. Others prefer to concentrate their studies on the on-going personality, how the individual as he is copes with each new development in his life, and what his aims and purposes are. Two of the psychologists whose theories of personality we shall examine more closely represent these two approaches, Freud attaching great importance to early life, and Rogers being more concerned with how the individual responds to his current problems and situations.

(6) Finally, the study of personality can be approached from different theoretical points of view. For example, there are psychologists who find it most useful to interpret observed behaviour in terms of unconscious drives, who regard our own awareness of our motives and experience as only a part of the functioning of our total personality. Others find it more profitable to begin the study with the individual's concern with his problems and motives as they appear to him. The person's own idea of self is the central point of study. Another distinction is between those psychologists who interpret behaviour as purposive, stressing drives and goals, and those who interpret behaviour as reactive, a series of responses to changing circumstances and new environments. These theoretical differences lead not only to differences in interpretation, but to differences in methods of study, and to

different emphasis on such processes as learning in the development of personality.

It is beyond the scope of this book to examine in any detail the consequences of adopting all these different approaches to the study and interpretation of personality. What we shall do is to examine more fully three rather different theories and methods of investigating personality. S. Freud represents those psychologists who approach the study through abnormal psychology, who stress the importance of the early years of life, and who regard the unconscious elements of personality as of first importance in determining our behaviour. H. J. Eysenck is taken as an exponent of the scientific approach, concerned with establishing and assessing a system of traits, interpreted in terms of a theory of personality involving three dimensions: introversion–extroversion, neuroticism, and psychoticism. C. Rogers concentrates on the study of the personality of the individual as he is at the time, and interprets personality mainly in terms of the conscious self—that is, the individual person as he knows himself. His approach is therefore clinical rather than scientific and holistic rather than analytical.

There are certain fundamental questions about personality which all explanations are required to answer, and no single theory of personality answers them equally well. The questions are:

(1) What is the structure of our personality? In what terms is it best described?

(2) How does our personality function? How do we acquire and establish new motives and new patterns of behaviour?

(3) What are the sources of energy? What are the motive forces determining how we behave?

(4) How much does our personality change? Are the foundations of our personality inherited, or are they laid down by our earliest experiences, or are the features of our personality liable to develop and change as we go through life?

With these questions in mind, we examine how far three different approaches attempt to answer them.

FREUD'S INTERPRETATION
OF PERSONALITY

Sigmund Freud was born into a middle-class Jewish family in Vienna in the latter half of the last century. He was a physician who had an interest in neurotic illness, and developed his ideas on personality from his attempts to understand the fundamental nature of mental illness. He regarded his views as having almost universal application, but it has also been argued that they reflect strongly the conditions of his own upbringing as a middle-class Jew in the latter half of the nineteenth century. Be that as it may, there is no doubt that his interpretation of personality, which met at first with violent opposition, has become part and parcel of our psychological thinking.

According to Freud, the energy sources of our behaviour are the instincts, which are of two kinds, Life instincts and Death instincts, or *eros* and *thanatos*. The life instincts are those directed to satisfying the bodily needs, hunger, thirst, and sex. Freud uses the word sex with a much wider meaning than in common language. For him sex means any kind of sensuous pleasure, warmth, caressing, and the like, and the gratification of this instinct may be obtained through various channels of behaviour. In the infant, there is oral gratification, centred in the act of sucking. When the infant is weaned, and the hunger need is satisfied by eating rather than sucking, direct oral gratification is prohibited, but may continue in substitute forms of behaviour like thumb-sucking and blanket-chewing. In adults, substitute satisfaction may continue in the forms of gum-chewing, smoking, or kissing. It is noteworthy that it is not uncommon for smoking or gum-chewing to be described as filthy habits, and in other societies kissing is regarded in the same way.

The second phase of sexual gratification in the infant is anal gratification, which is centred in the act of excreting bodily waste. Here again social disapproval intervenes in the form of 'toilet training' and again the word filthy is used. Once again substitute satisfaction may continue in such forms as finger painting, pottery, and, according to Freud, the hoarding of money and other objects. The third phase, that of genital gratification, is reached, according to Freud, about the age of five years. The child seeks gratification from sexual activity. But here again social prohibitions enter very powerfully. Sexual activity is not permitted at the age of five years, or indeed till much later. All the social devices to prevent gratification and learning are brought into action. The forces of repression are so powerful that what Freud calls a latency period follows till about the age of twelve or thirteen, when visible signs of sexual maturity are evident; adult society recognizes the instinct for sexual satisfaction, but endeavours still to restrict its gratification till the acceptable age for the social institution of marriage is reached. The channels of gratification are socially limited; sexual relations are tolerated, but there is a not uncommon attitude that celibacy is a virtue, coupled with a long list of words like lust, lewdness, and so on, indicating disapproval of sexual activities in general, and extra-marital and homosexual activities in particular. Games of physical contact are one of several substitute activities for homosexual relations, and dancing for heterosexual.

Freud has less to say about the death instincts. There is a destructive, aggressive component in behaviour attributed to the life instincts which may paradoxically involve hate and destruction of the loved object itself. The expression of the life instincts is inherently selfish, and involves a complex love–hate relationship with other persons, and indeed with oneself. The death instincts are invoked to explain those components of our behaviour in which we seek to withdraw from the continuous struggle for self-gratification; we desire peace, uniformity, and nothingness. We withdraw from reality, renouncing the values of this world or escaping into schizophrenic illness. We seek the ultimate refuge of death, where we overcome the insistent demands both of the life instincts and of external reality. This insistence on the conflict between life and death instincts is one of Freud's doctrines which has been attributed to his being a Jew in a German society in the first part of this century.

The Id and the Ego

In order to find a way of living with these conflicting desires, and with the prohibitions of their free expression in behaviour, the individual develops a system of structures which embody different forces shaping the personality, and a system of mechanisms by which relations between these conflicting structures are regulated. Freud calls the structures the Id, the Ego, and the Super-ego. The id is the original and unstructured personality from which the later structures emerge. The instincts of the id are the sources of the energy which directs our behaviour. The nature of these desires and impulses is unknown to us, so the id is wholly unconscious. The activities of the id system are governed by what Freud calls the Pleasure Principle, which means that the instincts of the id drive us to seek direct gratification of themselves in behaviour. If we are hungry we eat what we can lay our hands on, if we seek sexual satisfaction in any of its Freudian forms we take it as we take food, if we are thwarted we attack and destroy.

At an early age conflict arises not only between the conflicting instincts of the id, but also beween the desires of the id and the external world of persons and things through which the desires of the id can be satisfied. This external world is governed by the Reality Principle. The infant seeking food and sex satisfaction from the mother is sometimes gratified, sometimes thwarted. The frustrated infant cannot attack his mother; the reality is that she is stronger, and in any case the infant cannot destroy his source of gratification. Some scheme of behaviour has to be developed to resolve the conflict. The system of such compromises between the id and reality is the origin of the ego structure. In the same way a young man may find a young woman sexually attractive. He cannot directly gratify his sex desires, as such behaviour would, among other things, destroy the favourable impression he wants to create. If the young woman remains unresponsive there are several ways in which he may resolve his conflict. He may find satisfaction in fantasy and daydreaming. He may attack her, and himself, by committing suicide. Or he can come to believe that she is not a desirable person, worthy of his desires. Or he can repress any manifestation of sexual behaviour as too distressing, and protect himself by adopting an attitude of puritanical disapproval of sex, obtaining substitute satisfaction, unknown to himself, by spotting sexual implications in words and situations where other persons may not notice them.

It is the development of such forms of behaviour that constitute the ego structure, and later the super-ego. The ego is partly conscious, partly unconscious, which means that we are not always aware of the real motives for our behaviour. The ego consists of a system of behaviour patterns which enables the individual to find a way of living with the conflicting demands of the reality principle and the pleasure principle. Frustration of desires, or conflict between desires, produces emotional distress, anxiety, and guilt; the function of the ego system is to reduce this tension by developing forms of behaviour which satisfy the desires indirectly without direct conflict between the pleasure principle and the reality principle. Such forms of behaviour Freud calls ego-defence mechanisms.

Defence Mechanisms

We have already indicated some of these mechanisms. One is repression. The difference between the terms repression and inhibition is that inhibition is a conscious process. We are aware of an impulse, but the conscious ego so organizes its behaviour that the impulse is not expressed in action. A teacher experiences a desire to slap an impertinent pupil, but inhibits the desire. Repression on the other hand is a process involving the whole ego system, and we are not conscious of the process occurring, as the repressed desire is one which is not accepted into the ego system. The ego system provides no acceptable form of behaviour by which the desire can be gratified, and both the desire and the experiences associated with it are repressed; the desire is not extinguished, it is denied expression in conscious experience. No-one, therefore, can know their repressed impulses, only a skilled observer can infer them. The obvious sign is amnesia or forgetting of an incident, or complete unawareness of a desire. Freud believes that a very large amount of repression is needed in early childhood to establish an acceptable and civilized form of behaviour later in life; this is another reason why we have scarcely any memory of our very early years. Hate of the mother who denies the infant the gratification of his desires is often completely repressed, and the older person would strongly deny ever experiencing such an emotion. Another example could be the parents of a handicapped child, who repress their feelings of guilt associated with the situation, and cannot entertain the idea that the child is permanently handicapped. Either he will grow out of it, or all the diagnoses are wrong.

Repression may be complete, but frequently it is accompanied by other defence mechanisms which allow indirect satisfaction of the repressed desire. Reaction formation is one, in which the repressed desire is replaced in the conscious ego structure by its opposite. A teacher may entertain, unconsciously, aggressive feelings towards children, especially if the offending behaviour of the child is in the area of sex or destructiveness. This hate, Freud suggests, is the result of the teacher's own childhood conflicts, and reflects the child the teacher desired to be, but repressed. The hate is also unacceptable to the teacher, and is in turn repressed, and to protect himself against the conflict and distress arising from this unacceptable hate, the teacher tends to the opposite attitude of tolerance and permissiveness. The reaction formation may, for example, take the form of strong emotional opposition to corporal punishment. The teacher's childhood sexual and destructive impulses have been repressed, the hate towards these forms of behaviour has in turn been repressed, and the function of the reaction formation is to keep them repressed.

Rationalization is another form of defence mechanism, which consists of developing a rational system of thought to justify the satisfaction of a desire which is not in itself acceptable. A teacher may satisfy aggressive impulses in administering corporal punishment, but render his behaviour acceptable to himself by arguing that pupils need it and that he is acting on sound educational and psychological principles. Likewise, a person disturbed by his desire for alcohol may convince himself of its medicinal value. There are, according to the French proverb, more old drunks than old doctors.

Fantasy is another defence mechanism. Desires which cannot be gratified in reality can be satisfied in fantasy. The process of compensating for failure in reality by dreaming of triumphs is common enough. Other common mechanisms are:

Compensation, in which a failure in one sector of behaviour is compensated for by over-gratification in another. The underling at work may be the domestic tyrant, the poor learner may become the school bully.

Projection, in which we blame our failures on other people, and attribute to them desires and motives which we are afraid of recognizing in ourselves. The dishonest man is most likely to assume dishonesty in others, and the man who cannot accept his own sexual desires is most ready to suspect sexual irregularities in others.

Sublimation, in which an unacceptable form of gratification is obtained by acceptable substitute behaviour. Boxing can be sublimated aggression, pottery sublimated anal satisfaction, and dancing sublimated sex gratification.

It must be emphasized that these mechanisms are in no way abnormal or undesirable. They are necessary for us to be able to live with our own instincts and with the external world. Our personality development is such that we are all driven to acquire such mechanisms, the particular form or balance of mechanisms in any given individual being largely a matter of learning. It is only when the defence mechanisms fail to function, or become developed to an exaggerated degree, that a person becomes emotionally disordered. The paranoid who suffers from delusions of persecution by others is ordering his life by the mechanism of projection, the schizophrenic who withdraws from reality into fantasy is again over-dependent on one mechanism. Successful functioning of the defence mechanisms leads to enjoyment of life, failure to distress and guilt.

The Super-ego

The super-ego structure, which is in part conscious, arises mainly as a result of the mechanisms of introjection and reaction formation. The infant finds pleasure in activities which society, as represented by his parents, regard as nasty and bad habits. His parents react emotionally, and to keep their approval, because he is dependent on them for his other gratifications, the infant adopts these attitudes into his own personality (which is introjection); he becomes a 'good' boy by identifying himself with his parents' attitudes and by rejecting as 'nasty' the unacceptable forms of behaviour both in himself and in other children. This adopting of the condemning attitude of the parents into his own personality is the origin of the super-ego. The super-ego is the embodiment of disapproving authority, from parents to teachers, to law, and ultimately to God. The super-ego functions as our conscience, and we are aware of it in the form of feelings of guilt. The forces motivating the super-ego are the life instincts and the death instincts; the super-ego structure permits satisfaction from being righteous, and satisfaction from hate of transgressions. Conscience is emotional rather than rational; it is noteworthy that it functions most effectively about the five-year level of behaviour. It is easier to modify a claim for expenses than to steal a shilling, and a direct lie is more difficult than a sophisticated evasion of truth, though both are intended to achieve the same result. The ego defence mechanisms protect the ego from the super-ego as well as from the reality and pleasure principle conflicts.

Characteristics of Freud's Personality Theory

For Freud, the personality is the relations between the three systems of the id, the ego, and the super-ego. The structure is rather crudely expressed in the diagram below, where the horizontal line represents the fact that the functioning of the ego and super-ego is in part conscious and in part unconscious. What Freud is

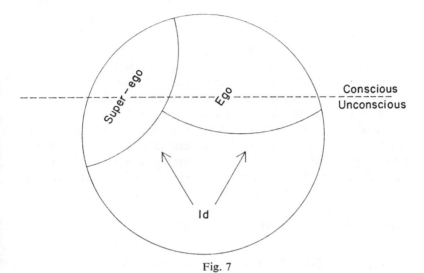

Conscious
Unconscious

Fig. 7

trying to do is to find a scheme in terms of which our total behaviour can most easily and convincingly be explained. His explanation stresses the irrational and emotional elements in our behaviour, and our imperfect awareness of the motives which direct our behaviour. The pattern of these motives and the forms of behaviour which they originate are developed in their main forms in the first few years of life, and change little thereafter. Personality develops through certain phases, and fixation at any one of these phases can lead to a failure to develop a fully balanced personality. Though the early years are the important years, education has little relevance, as the processes of the evolving personality structures are reflected but little in day-to-day behaviour. These underlying processes can only be reached through the method of psycho-analysis which, besides being lengthy, also requires a high degree of skill and is but seldom used with younger children.

The Freudian explanation is of direct relevance to the teacher in only a limited number of aspects. It stresses the ineffectiveness of rational argument on matters where emotion is involved, too much so according to some psychologists. Where it does apply is in the insistence that the teacher's attitudes and behaviour are as much determined by unconscious emotional needs as the child's are, and that teachers' behaviour is basically determined by their own childhood experience. Also, as the teacher has learned his defence mechanisms, so the child is learning his. The defence mechanisms are as necessary as air and food; the child has to develop his fantasies, his rationalizations, his sublimations to make life tolerable, and it would indeed be an unwise teacher who attempted to prevent him or direct him. It is also to Freud's credit that he has put forward the most satisfactory psychological explanation of conscience to date. It is necessary for the child to develop a conscience to avoid intolerable conflict in his early years. The duties and prohibitions, largely unconscious, of the parents' and teachers' super-egos determine their behaviour, and it is to behaviour and attitude rather than teaching that the child must adapt himself. It is in this way that moral imperatives are passed on from one generation to another.

THE SCIENTIFIC APPROACH
TO PERSONALITY

In this approach, the established methods of objective assessment and statistical analysis which were developed in intelligence testing are applied to the study of personality. The two psychologists most closely associated with this method of study are R. B. Cattell and H. J. Eysenck. Both employ the technique of factorial analysis, a mathematical technique rather too complicated to discuss here. But a crude analogy may illustrate the nature of the process. Solid objects, such as boxes, can all be defined in terms of three dimensions—length, breadth, and height. Two dimensions are sufficient to define plane surfaces, like sheets of paper. As persons differ in many characteristics, so we can have boxes of all shapes and sizes. Factorial analysis is a method of ascertaining how many independent dimensions are necessary to define all boxes. The same method applied to assessments of different sectors of behaviour aims at giving us the number of dimensions or factors necessary to define the various behaviour patterns reflecting personality differences. With the boxes, the answer is known; in personality studies, the aim is to find the smallest number of factors which account for the widest range of behaviour; thus interpretations of the assessment in terms of factors may differ. Cattell finds sixteen personality factors best to define personality characteristics. Eysenck, on the other hand, finds three dimensions adequate. These are: introversion–extroversion, neuroticism–non neuroticism, and psychoticism–non psychoticism. As a box can be described as tall, long, and narrow, so an individual's personality can be defined as introverted, non-neurotic, and tending to be psychotic. The standard of measurement is the average of the population measured, so introverted persons can be described as introverted to greater or lesser degrees relative to the population in general.

For Eysenck, any sector of behaviour that can be objectively measured is a sector of personality, so his measures include such diverse sectors as IQ, vocabulary, night vision, manual dexterity, bodily build, level of aspiration, political attitudes, aesthetic preferences, speed of reaction, age, number of symptoms of illness, employment history. Whether or not these are relevant to the pattern of the individual's personality can only be determined by investigation. At this stage, a description of personality would be a catalogue of test scores; but by factor analysis certain clusters of these specific behaviour sectors can be identified. These clusters are called traits, and can be described in such terms as suggestibility, liability to depression, type of bodily build, level of intellectual ability, rigidity of habits, speed of working, and so on. A further factor analysis can in the same way establish clusters of traits. As traits can be arranged in various numbers and kinds of groups, Eysenck turned to psychological theories of personality, and adopting the basic structure of personality from Freud and more particularly Freud's associate, Jung, set up the three dimensions we have mentioned. These three dimensions were found to form a framework which corresponded well with a grouping of traits established by factor analysis, and became the foundation of Eysenck's interpretation of personality. These dimensions enable us to recognize certain distinct personality types, which appear at the extreme ends of the three dimensions. The completely average man, who is the exception, would show characteristics between the extremes of each dimension. On the other hand the extreme introvert would tend to possess such traits as persistence, rigidity of habits, shyness, tends to be tall and thin, and has a slow but accurate style of work. In the introvert, the super-ego is dominant; in the extrovert, who has the opposite characteristics to the introvert, the id dominates the personality structure. The extreme neurotic tends to exhibit behaviour traits which can be classified as anxiety, depression, low energy level, below-average intelligence (unless also introverted), high suggestibility, good dark adaptation, and low persistence. The non-psychotic would score high in tests of mirror drawing, reversible perspective, memory, and dexterity; he would exhibit such traits as emotional stability, clear social attitudes, and good concentration. Not all traits appear at the extremes of the dimensions and therefore do not clearly distinguish personality types. But within this framework of three dimensions it is possible to identify such consistent personality types as the neurotic extrovert, or the introverted psychotic.

The feature of Eysenck's method is that all traits and personality types are identified by performance on a specific set of tests of measures. These include personality inventories, asking such questions as "Do you prefer action to planning for action?" or "Do you frequently feel depressed?" or "Do you feel unhappy without social activities?" Other tests used are tests of suggestibility, tests of persistence in holding the breath or keeping the leg in a given position, speed of dark adaptation, history of illnesses, and the like. In the more extreme personality types such as extrovert-psychotic, the findings on the various tests reinforce each other, so the identification of such types is on the basis of performance on a number of tests, each corroborating the other. The intermediate personality types nearer the average do not necessarily show the same consistency of test scores.

The validity of Eysenck's identification of personality types stands or falls by the agreement between the clusters of test scores and other objective measures on the one hand, and independent observations of behaviour on the other. We have mentioned in the discussion on assessment both concurrent and construct validity, and it is these kinds of validity that can be investigated for Eysenck's tests and classification. Concurrent validity is established by administering a battery of Eysenck's

measures to a group of persons known to be neurotic and under-
going treatment for neuroses. Those tests on which there was a
marked difference of scores between the neurotic patients and a
normal group were confirmed as those which defined the dimension of neuroticism. The construct validity of the introversion-
extroversion dimension is derived from the personality theory
of Jung, who postulated two main types of personality function.
The introvert is one whose dominant response is to the needs
of his own experience and emotions, the extrovert's main response
is to the external world of people and events. The development of
this theoretical distinction would lead to the prediction that certain
observed patterns of behaviour would be different in the two
personality types. These predicted differences were measured by
a series of Eysenck's objective tests and observations, and again
there was substantial agreement between the actual clustering of
the tests and the predicted clustering from theoretical considerations. The validity of the dimension of psychoticism was established
in the same way as for neuroticism.

Eysenck's methods and theory are of more interest to the psychologist than to the teacher. He has attempted consistently to apply
scientific psychological methods used in other aspects of psychology
to the study of personality, and has achieved a certain measure of
success. His conclusions are firmly based on objective observation,
not on theoretical principles, which are only used as a structure
to classify the test findings. His description of personality types is
precise and detailed and directly related to specific items of
behaviour. One weakness of his approach is that the tests used,
at least the psychological ones, are not particularly reliable.
Also the classification from tests to traits and from traits to types
is not as clear-cut as this rather condensed discussion might
suggest. There is some difficulty in that the dimensions are not of
the same order. A scale from extreme introversion to extreme
extroversion, with the average person in the middle, is not difficult
to understand, but the normal–psychotic scale is not such that the
average person is half-way between normality and psychotic
illness. Eysenck's answer would properly be that his scheme is
what the facts compelled, and theoretical balance takes second
place to observation. Nevertheless, though the more extreme
personality types are clearly enough defined, the 'mixed' or
'average' personalities, who are the majority, are not clearly

defined or explained. Finally, Eysenck shows little interest in the processes whereby personality types and traits develop. Some information has been obtained about children; for example, the neurotic or disturbed child who is at the extroverted end of the scale manifests his difficulties as conduct problems, such as swearing, fighting, truanting, stealing, and lying. The introverted neurotic exhibits what are better called personality problems. He tends to be sensitive, ineffective, depressed, anxious, and daydreaming. But there is nothing to approach Freud's emphasis on the phases of development through early childhood. Freud, however, was concerned with fundamental processes of development far removed from the observation or control of the teacher. Eysenck is dealing with a very specific set of observations, many of them within the scope of the class teacher's activities, but he offers little guidance to the teacher as to how such observations can be related to the developing personality of the pupil. Eysenck's interpretation is essentially adult and static.

CARL ROGERS'S NON-DIRECTIVE THERAPY

The use of the word 'therapy', or treatment aimed at the cure of a disorder, indicates the essentially clinical approach of Rogers. Like Eysenck, he has developed his scheme from observation, but his evidence is derived from psychological guidance rather than from scientific objective measurement. Like Freud, his main purpose is to help an individual to a better understanding of himself and his relations with reality. Unlike Freud, however, Rogers accepts what a person says about himself as evidence, and he is more concerned with the person as he is and as he sees himself than in the origins of his personality and the unconscious motives of his behaviour. Rogers aims at change in the person's idea of self, rather than explanation in terms of a doctrine like Freud's. His method of 'non-directive' or 'client-centred' therapy is to encourage the individual to develop and clarify his ideas about the kind of person he is and would like to become; Rogers refrains from advice or deep analysis of motives.

Rogers has extended his inquiries by techniques other than clinical observation. He uses, for example, the technique of Q sorts, which was developed by W. Stephenson. A Q sort uses a set of about one hundred cards, on which appear such statements as, "I am an impulsive person" or "I am well liked by others". These cards are sorted by the individual into prescribed proportions. He may be required to find the ten statements which best describe him, the twenty next most applicable, and so on to the ten statements least applicable to himself. Having sorted the cards according to what he thinks he is, he can be asked to repeat the sort in terms of what he would like to be, or what he believes other persons think he is. The method has its weaknesses, the statements are often too general and vague, and 'defence sorts' may be used by the sorter to present himself in a favourable light and to defend himself against being forced to acknowledge his defects. Rogers's method of non-directive therapy is the application of a theory of personality developed from his clinical records and the evidence from Q sorts.

Rogers's Theory of Personality

The basis of Rogers's theory is the organism, which is the total individual. The organism behaves as a whole in response to the 'phenomenal field' in order to satisfy its needs. The phenomenal field is the environment as it is perceived by the organism, not necessarily consciously. The phenomenal field of a hungry organism is the experience of hunger, together with the perceiving of food, and the organism acts accordingly, by eating. If there is food physically present, but it is not perceived, the organism acts differently, because food is not part of the phenomenal field. The basic motive of the organism's behaviour is to maintain and develop itself.

The self, which is the centre of the theory, arises out of the organism's reaction to the phenomenal field. The organism has the ability to 'symbolize' experience, which then becomes conscious, or to deny experience, which then becomes unconscious. A teacher taking a new class symbolizes by identifying the pupils by names and faces. Symbolizing is the ordering and labelling of the phenomenal field, mainly through language. The same teacher, travelling home by bus, may be perceiving but not symbolizing the names and appearances of the streets he passes through, and the experience is not explicitly conscious.

The self, therefore, is that part of the phenomenal field which is symbolized as 'me'. This self strives for consistency—that is, we try to be a particular kind of person—and in Rogers's view this need for consistency is reinforced by our emotions. Emotions he regards as motives towards the realization of our idea of self, rather than as a disruptive element needing to be inhibited. The idea of self has four different aspects to it. First there is the way the person perceives himself—that is, the knowledge he has about himself. We are unaware, for example, of our unconscious motives, or on a more trivial level of some of our habits that may irritate others. We can only perceive ourselves from inside, as it were. Second, there is the way the person thinks of himself. This is the symbolizing of our perceptions of ourself. We can have different systems of thought about the kind of person we perceive ourselves as. We may think of ourselves in terms of motives; we may mean well, and that is what we think matters. Or we may think of ourselves in terms of our behaviour, and use our actions as the basis on which we judge ourselves. We may think of ourselves mainly in terms of our abilities, intellectual or other. Or we may think of ourselves as unique individuals, or think of ourselves as part of a larger humanity. We may think of ourselves specifically as women, or teachers, or Christians, or fathers. We must classify and label our idea of self to symbolize it. Third, there is the way we value ourselves. We have different systems of values against which we can compare our idea of what we think we are. What is it important to us to be? What does not matter so much? Are we good teachers, good Christians, or good fathers? And does it matter to us whether we are or not? Fourth, there is the way we defend our selves against threats, and enhance or develop our selves and the values we accept in the self. A person who regards himself as sympathetic and humanitarian, and who values these qualities, will direct his anger against what he perceives as cruelty or injustice. His emotions reinforce his idea of himself, not only as an opponent of injustice, but as a supporter of the oppressed. On the other hand, a person who regards himself as a person of common sense and realism will direct his anger against reformers and 'agitators'.

Experiences which conflict with the idea of self are perceived as threats. We speak of temptations and pressures which have to be resisted. The resistance takes the form of ego defence mechanisms as described by Freud. In their clinical experience both Rogers and Freud made much the same observations, and found it necessary to explain them in much the same way. Rogers, for example, uses the ideas of introjection, which is the basis of Freud's super-ego, of projection, and of repression, which he calls denial of experience. Rogers also explains the experience commonly expressed as, "I could not stop myself from doing it" or "I don't know what made me do it", by pointing out that here the organism is responding to the phenomenal field in a way which is not compatible with the idea of self. Further, any such experience not acceptable by the self, and therefore experienced as a threat, tends to make the person's concept of self still more rigid as a defence. This rigid defensive attitude prevents the development or expansion of the self, and this in turn frustrates the main motive of our living, to actualize, to maintain, and to enhance the organism.

Non-directive Therapy

It is to the prevention of this limiting and inhibiting effect of threats upon the personality that Rogers's system of non-directive therapy is devoted. The individual has a need to develop the self; he has a need for self-regard, for the esteem of other people, and a system of values by which he can accept or reject experience as being of worth and concern to him. Though these needs are common to all, there is no ideal pattern; each person develops and organizes his experience in his own way, creating an idea of self not necessarily the same as that of others, and trying to become the kind of person he thinks it is worth being. In Rogers's scheme, the counsellor or therapist does not attempt to 'cure' the individual or to establish any kind of approved pattern of behaviour. What he does is to help the person to clarify his ideas of self, to formulate what kind of person he thinks he is, wants to be, and can be. The obstacles in the way are those events in the phenomenal field which are perceived as threats. The counsellor acts by letting the individual freely discuss these threats and talk about himself; above all, the counsellor accepts seriously all that the individual has to say about himself. This attitude of acceptance and encouragement reduces the threats; what the person says he would like to do, but is afraid of doing, is not condemned by the counsellor, the threat loses some of its menace, and the rigid defence structure of the self becomes less necessary.

This is not so easy as it sounds. Skill is needed to assess changes or movement in the person's conceptions of himself, to refrain from interpreting too much, and to know when some direction or discussion is needed and when to leave the individual to work it out for himself. Much counselling and therapy, Rogers believes, is ineffective because the counsellor is too ready to advise solutions acceptable to the counsellor but not necessarily to the person being counselled, and too ready to offer interpretations on the same basis. The essence of non-directive therapy is to support and encourage the individual's efforts to organize himself into clearer awareness of the kind of person he is and would like to be.

There are fairly obvious resemblances between Freud's psychoanalysis and Rogers's non-directive or client-centred therapy. But the differences are equally significant. Freud does not accept what the client says as valid statements about himself—he seeks the unconscious motives underlying the awareness of the conscious ego and super-ego. Rogers accepts that the person himself is the one who knows most about himself. Freud seeks to help the client by interpreting to him 'really' why he behaves in a particular way; Rogers accepts and encourages, but does not direct or interpret. Freud seeks the origin of conflicts in early childhood, Rogers in the client's present situation.

CONCLUSION

From the considerable number of model schemes and explanations of personality offered by psychologists we have selected three which are clearly different from each other. Each of the three represents a cluster of theories of the same general type and approach. The Freudian interpretation, for example, has been developed by psychologists like Jung, Adler, Fromm, Erikson, and others, who accept the same principles of interpretation and are generally called the psycho-analytic school. Eysenck and Cattell represent a group who apply the principles of measurement and statistical analysis to personality, and Rogers represents another group of psychologists who attempt an interpretation of personality in broad psychological terms without committing themselves to a deep or doctrinaire point of view. But despite their differences, there is a greater common element in their interpretations than is at first sight apparent. Rogers's explanation can be reworded in terms of Freud's conscious ego and super-ego, and it is found they are both talking about much the same processes. Rogers does not deny unconscious processes, but finds them unnecessary for his immediate purpose of counselling. Eysenck accepts introversion–extroversion as one of his dimensions; this is derived from the psycho-analytic theory of Jung. Rogers is concerned with the observable behaviour and characteristics of the individual; so is Eysenck, who prefers, however, to attempt to assess them on a scale of measurement. The dimensions of neuroticism and psychoticism are dealing with the same areas of conflict as those from which Freud derives his system of defence mechanisms. The observed behaviour of Eysenck's neurotic and psychotic types can be readily explained as the manifestation in behaviour of the defence mechanisms at work. Rogers too uses the explanation of defence mechanisms, as ways of responding to threats. The difference between the theories we have discussed is to some degree one of emphasis and the language used.

Personality Theory in Context

Nor are personality theories unrelated to topics already discussed. The investigation of personality employs the same psychological procedures and principles as are used in the investigation of learning, development, thinking, or intelligence. The treatment of personality as a separate topic is but another instance of the psychologist's practice of analysing, defining, observing, theorizing, and verifying. But in so far as a person tends to function as a single individual, the various psychological processes we have so far described do not operate independently of each other. In the development of a personality structure, learning is again fundamental. Personality has been concisely defined as a system of motives and memories. The learning and retaining of S-R units of behaviour includes a wide social and personal sector, where the stimulus is the behaviour of other persons. A set of established responses to such stimuli, by the processes of stimulus discrimination and generalization, can readily be observed in the form of a personality trait such as timidity or aggressiveness. The pupil whose immediate and unconsidered response to an accidental push is to retaliate is not uncommon. Learning in terms of cognitive structure is equally relevant. The structure of social and personal relations is of great importance to the growing child, and what Rogers calls the phenomenal field is essentially a system of cognitive structures. The area of problem solving, for example,

8

is not confined to science and mathematics; there are equally difficult social and personal problems in which the pupil's formal education gives him little clear guidance. He is given a few principles, either moral or practical; if struck by a bigger pupil it is prudent to learn not to retaliate, but if struck by a smaller pupil it is wrong to retaliate. Much of the pupil's thinking is concerned with personal behaviour and attitudes; so far this aspect has not been fully investigated, but there is no reason to suppose that the processes of thought are essentially different when related to predicting a card from when they are concerned with the prediction of another person's behaviour.

Both Piaget and Freud lay considerable stress on sequences of development. The ages of transition from one major phase to the next are approximately the same for both schemes; whether there is a connection is not known. But Piaget has explored certain areas of children's thinking about social and personal matters. He finds, for instance, that younger children are unable to interpret events from anyone's point of view other than their own. If I hit him, that is one thing, but if he hits me that is quite a different kind of event. Also, such children tend to regard punishment for an act as part of the act itself; they do not distinguish between the act itself and the punishment, or praise, which may or may not follow, nor do they appear to distinguish between intentional offences and accidents. Similarly, moral rules appear to be regarded by such children as absolute—an untruth is wrong, whatever the circumstances. The way in which children reinterpret these attitudes as their modes of thought develop and change is likely to have considerable influence on the development of their personality; the rigid puritan and the plausible politician must have begun some time. Unfortunately, perhaps, Piaget did not pursue these earlier inquiries systematically, but turned his attention rather to the more strictly logical aspects of children's thinking, with the results we have outlined earlier.

There is one caution to be noted. We must not assume that the plausibility and consistency of a theory is necessarily an index of its validity. The final test of a theory of personality is the extent to which it agrees with the evidence. Freud and Rogers do not stand up to this test as well as Eysenck. On the one hand, Eysenck's interpretation is less coherent and intelligible, but is more firmly based. On the other hand, Freud's is a more co-ordinated and fundamental interpretation, but the hard, objective confirmation is lacking.

Personality Theory and Education

How is the discussion of these theories relevant to education? Children have only appeared incidentally in our discussion. The relevance is this. When we talk of the social and personal development of children we use terms like society, adults, teachers, parents. These are in fact abstractions; each child has to respond to particular adult individuals, whose personalities, attitudes, and expectations are different. When we come in the next chapter to examine the way children develop in the social context, we shall be taking the view that the shape of the child's personality is determined as much by the expectations of adults as to how a child should behave as by the nature of the child's developmental pattern. The structure of the social and personal context of the child's development is that of adult personalities, with the differences in types, defence mechanisms, and patterns of behaviour that we have outlined. The adult society in which the child is reared does not consist of neutral, objective, or indeed wise people educating the child, and guiding his development; rather it consists of a number of individuals, motivated more or less irrationally by their own childhood experience, operating within the framework of their various defence mechanisms and uncertain both of themselves and their relationship with growing children. The interaction between the child's developing personality and this social context is the next topic we discuss. The evidence available is not extensive, but what there is of it has to be translated from abstract terms into individual personalities manifesting the kinds of behaviour we have indicated here.

9

Personality Development in the Social Context

In the discussion on the relationship of learning and maturation to the process of education, we considered three sets of requirements, or structures, that had to be amalgamated. These were the requirements of the school subjects to be learned, the requirements of the developing child's cognitive structures and levels of maturity, and the requirements of the learning process. There is a parallel set of requirements in personality development. There is the system of expectations represented by adult society, to which the child is continuously under pressure to conform. There is the structure of the child's personality both in respect of differences in types of personality and in level of development. And there is the process of learning, by which the child finds ways of reconciling the requirements of his own psychological nature to the expectations of the society in which he lives. If it is difficult to distinguish between changes of behaviour attributed to learning and to cognitive maturation, it is still more difficult to make a distinction between those features of personality which can be regarded as constitutional and those which have been learned. We shall take the view that the main influence determining the personality development of children is the child's adaptability. The stages of development and the kind of person a child becomes are more a reflection of the attitudes and expectations of society than of the psychological characteristics of children. In other words, a study of personality development tells us more about the adults' ideas of what children are and should be than about the children themselves. The limits of differences in personality are largely the limits of tolerance of the society in which the child develops. Failures to conform to the pattern of expectations of society are principally due either to failure to learn the appropriate behaviour, or to a constitutional personality pattern which does not easily fit the patterns required by society. But failures, it must be remembered, are the exceptions.

CONSTITUTIONAL PERSONALITY TYPES

It is to the Greek philosopher and scientist, Aristotle, that we owe the idea of entelechy. This is the principle according to which the tadpole develops into the frog, and the oak tree is the end of the acorn's growth. The acorn is such that it can develop only into an oak tree. Among human beings we accept without too much difficulty that some people are born to be tall, some are constitutionally lean, others fat, and that some are born with a greater liability to certain diseases than others. It is not difficult to accept the same view with personality differences, such that one person may respond to success or failure in a different way from another person; the accumulating development of such different types of response may build up different patterns of personality, though the situations to which these responses are being made seem very much the same to the outside observer. In practice, however, it is very much more difficult to identify constitutional differences in personality than it is in stature, for example.

Physical Types

There have been numerous attempts to identify and classify different constitutional personality types. One line of approach is to try to establish a relationship between physical characteristics and personality types. This has a long history from the choleric, sanguine, phlegmatic, and melancholic types of the Classical writers through Lombroso's 'criminal types' with low hair lines, particular head and ear shapes, and so on, to more recent and sophisticated studies where abnormality of the sex chromosomes has been shown to be associated with criminal psychopaths. One of the most fully developed of recent schemes is Sheldon's. He identifies three main types of bodily physique. The endomorph is physically rather soft and round in appearance, with a tendency to fat. He, or she, is sociable, fond of food and comfort, and is tolerant and easy-going. The digestive system is well developed. The mesomorph has a hard muscular body. He or she is physically strong, tough, and enduring. The mesomorph is physically active, adventurous, aggressive, and callous. Bone and muscle are well developed. The ectomorph is more slightly built, and in appearance is thin and flat, relatively lacking in physical strength and endurance. In personal characteristics, he or she is inhibited, retiring, self-conscious, and prone to anxiety. The brain and nervous system are well developed.

Sheldon has produced evidence to show that these differences in physique are constitutional and not acquired, and that physical and psychological characteristics are linked. But that is about as far as it goes. It cannot be conclusively shown that the psychological characteristics are themselves constitutional, and not the product of the physical constitution, in the sense that the mesomorph, with physical strength above average, will tend to respond to certain situations by using his physical superiority, thus acquiring habits of aggression. Also, most people are of mixed types physically, and though the mixture may be constitutional, their characteristics are not easy to identify.

Despite its theoretical and practical limitations, Sheldon's scheme is of some value to the teacher. In most classes there are pupils who are clearly recognizable as endomorphs, mesomorphs, or ectomorphs, and most have personality characteristics as described by Sheldon. The teacher would be ill advised to try to change them. To send little Edward Endomorph on cross-country runs or mountaineering expeditions would not only cause him genuine distress, but also would more probably reinforce his characteristics than change them. On the other hand, Michael Mesomorph would enjoy such expeditions and benefit from them. His tendency to be a bully may require to be checked, but no amount of teaching or preaching is likely to give him the easy-going sociability of Edward Endomorph.

Jung's Psychological Types

Another well-known system of personality types has been developed by Carl Jung, a Swiss psychologist whose thinking was closely associated with that of Freud. He proposed two main types of personality, the extrovert and the introvert. Whether this difference is constitutional or not is uncertain, but Jung considers that the adoption of one of these two modes of mental attitude is fundamental to the development of personality. The main concern of the introvert is adapting to his own needs, to the inner world of his ideas, fantasies, and feelings. To the extrovert, the external world of things and events is the more significant, and his energies are directed to adjusting his behaviour to them. As Jung put it, in extroversion the id instincts are outwardly directed, in introversion inwardly directed. Extroversion and introversion are not in themselves different kinds of personalities; they are rather differences in attitudes from which different kinds of personalities develop. This is how Eysenck was able to infer the characteristics of the introvert–extrovert dimension, and verify the inference by observation of behaviour.

Because of the value he attaches to events and other persons, the typical extrovert tends to be socially involved, seeking power and prestige, with easily aroused but not very profound emotions, carefree, insensitive, and materialistic. The typical introvert is socially withdrawn, often caring little for convention, guided more by his own convictions and ideals, emotionally sensitive, and more deeply involved personally in events. When in difficulties, the introvert tends to respond by anxiety and depression, developing obsessions and withdrawing into a world of fantasy. The typical extrovert response is hysteria, the escape into illness; extroverts tend either to develop an objective disability, or to make the most of such disabilities as they have. They themselves are not depressed or anxious about their symptoms; their illness is a barrier to protect themselves from the pressures of the outside world.

To the extrovert–introvert distinction, Jung has added further distinctions concerning the mode of mental activity to which the person is inclined: namely, thinking, feeling, sense perception, and intuition. Where thinking is the predominant mode, the person is concerned with consistent logical relations between events; his approach is basically rational. Where feeling predominates, it is the person's likes and dislikes, his emotional attitudes, that determine behaviour. With sense perception the attention is mainly to details; with intuition it is the broad pattern that is of interest. These four different modes of functioning have not stood up too well to stricter investigation, and have not proved easy to identify. The major distinction between introvert and extrovert is both better established and more useful. In education, the position of Jung's types is very similar to that of Sheldon's types. Those who are markedly extrovert or introvert are recognizable kinds of person; most are somewhere in between with a bias to one or the other end of the scale. There is no educational reason for attempting to develop extroverted behaviour in an introvert; what is most likely to happen is that a 'normal' introvert becomes a neurotic introvert.

CHILDREN'S NEEDS

These and other theories of personality structure tend to assume that we are born with a particular physical and psychological disposition, which determines the basic pattern of our personality development. There is some little evidence at present to prove that such dispositions are inborn, and there is none to disprove; so we accept the assumption as a basis for discussion. Though an ectomorph may aim to excel as an athlete or adventurer, and an introvert as a carefree social man of affairs, they learn to play these roles only with difficulty; often the price is conflict and personal unhappiness. Many who fancy themselves as adventurous Secret Service agents would in reality be laid low with stomach ulcers in a few weeks.

Why then should a fat, good-tempered, easy-going boy yearn to be the dominant athletic team captain, or a thoughtful, sensitive, and retiring girl dream of being the gay, popular social star? Part of the answer can be obtained by looking again at the personal characteristics of Sheldon's and Jung's types. Which is most likely to be esteemed by his or her school-fellows? Or be regarded by adults as the kind of boy or girl they like to see? In general, it is the active, athletic, dominant, and adventurous mesomorph. So too the forthcoming, managing, and socially interested extrovert tends to gain more approval than the more self-centred, anxious, and withdrawn introvert.

The developing pattern of a child's personality is determined not only by his psychological constitution but also by the standards and values of the society in which he lives. The conforming to the expectations of society is basically a process of learning. He learns how he is expected to behave, and learns to adapt his behaviour to the different kinds of personalities he encounters as he grows up. The mesomorphs and the extroverts are those whose behaviour and attitudes are likely to make the most direct impact on the children they meet; the child learns either to adopt their ways or, with more difficulty, learns to protect himself against them. Society has been likened to a maze which children learn to run, as rats do in learning experiments. Society is of course a much more complicated maze; the expectations of adults are not all the same, the demands change as the child grows older, the expectations are different for boys and girls and for different social classes, and the child has not only to learn what society expects of him, but also the ways to meet, or safely evade, its expectations.

Primary Needs

To continue the comparison, the rat learning a maze needs a goal—food, freedom, or the avoidance of punishment. What are the goals of the children learning their way through the social maze? These goals are best defined in terms of children's needs, which they seek to satisfy. Any discussion of children's needs must be approached with caution. As we have already pointed out, the needs of children are to a considerable extent a function of adult society's expectations and opinions about children. The ideas about children's needs change from generation to generation; probably each generation's opinions reflect their own childhood experiences. These ideas also vary from one type of society to another, so all we can properly discuss here is the needs of children as accepted by our society in our time. With this in mind, we can consider one possible classification of these needs. Children's needs may be considered as primary and secondary. The primary needs can be accepted as a statement about children; they are food and drink, bodily comfort, and sleep. In earliest life these cover almost all of the child's needs, and he is wholly and directly dependent on adults for their satisfaction. These needs, of course, remain with us through life, but from an early age there appear secondary needs, which arise out of living in an organized society. The need for food is related not only to hunger, but also to social requirements. "Please, can I have something to eat?" "No, you will have to wait until tea-time", or later, "But I'm not hungry." "Now eat your tea like a good boy." Such conversational exchanges are but one example of how secondary needs arise. To be a 'good boy' means gaining the approval of the adults around the child. Not only does the 'good boy' avoid the risk of not getting his food, but also the risk of temporary loss of the affection and approval of his parents, which is an important need in itself.

Secondary Needs

Secondary needs have been classified in various ways, but there is general agreement that they can broadly be described as feelings of worth and feelings of security. They are not unrelated. Feelings of worth mean that approval and acceptance by others is important; the child feels he is of concern to others. These feelings are worth seeking; this involves learning and achievement in activities which are approved of by other people, the family, the school, the peer group, and so on. Very young children are demanding and self-centred to a degree that would not be tolerated in older children, so the growing child is continuously learning how to gain acceptance by others as somebody worth knowing, as it were. There is a small number of persons, usually known as psychopaths, who develop intellectually like others, but whose ways of satisfying the need for the esteem of others remains at the 'toddler' level. Their need for feelings of worth is satisfied by gaining immediate praise from others, but the integration of this need into the developing personality is incomplete. Some well-known criminals are of this type; their characteristics are a calculating callousness towards others, a childish vanity and desire for admiration, indicating a marked immaturity of personal development. The normal development of personality has been, by some means, arrested; the need for feelings of worth normally finds satisfaction in different behaviour as the child's personality develops and matures.

Feelings of security also depend on the acceptance, approval, and affection of others; and awareness of security seems necessary for individual personality characteristics to develop. All people are not conforming to society's demands all the time. Children who feel secure will from time to time 'test the limits' by aggression, stubbornness, and other sins of commission and omission. This is as necessary to personality development as conforming, but a secure base is needed for adventuring forth. The insecure child on the other hand cannot extend his range of behaviour and experience in the same way; he tends either to be anxiously conforming, or to seek his own security by a defensive aggression and rebellion, depending probably on his constitutional personality type.

One form of security sought by older children particularly is acceptance as a member of a group. This, in turn, means the accepting by the child of the behaviour of the group. How strong this need is may be illustrated by two similar experiments by Asch and

Bernera. The experiment by Asch required the subject to judge whether two lines, up to 1·75 inches different in length, were of equal length or not. In each case the subject was one of a group of eight who were shown the two lines. Unknown to the subject, the other seven had been previously instructed to state that the two unequal lines were equal. In these circumstances, it was found that one-third of the subjects were willing to agree with the group that the clearly unequal lines were equal. Further, they stated that they indeed saw the lines as equal. The remaining two-thirds of the subjects, who disagreed with the group, on no occasion stated that the rest of the group were wrong; they only reported difference of opinion. A very similar experiment was conducted by Bernera on younger children, in the ten to eleven age group, and he obtained similar results. The additional findings reported by Bernera was the distress of most of the children who disagreed with the group. They wanted to agree but could not contradict their own perception of the lines. We quote these experiments as illustrations of the strength of the individual's motivation for the security of belonging to a group.

These secondary needs for worth and security represent one classification of the needs which motivate children to social learning and hence to develop their personality structure. Other classifications are possible, such as Maslow's, for example, which we discussed in Chapter 3. But we repeat the warning; in so far as children's motives and needs are inferred from their behaviour, it must be remembered that this behaviour is in turn a reflection of adult expectations.

THE SOCIAL CONTEXT

To analyse the structure of the maze, society, we turn to the study of sociology, which is concerned with the structure and working of society, as distinct from the individual persons or groups of persons in it. We can speak of social institutions like the family, the school, the peer group, which can continue to exist as institutions, though the individual persons occupying places in them may come and go. We can examine the relationships between persons occupying places in these institutions, such as that between a head teacher and the staff of the school, or a mother and daughter in a family. We can try to define the status or position of each person in this structure of social relationships. The position of a head teacher is not the same as that of an assistant teacher; and even within the staff room, where assistant teachers may in one sense be of equal status, the status of the older and more experienced teacher is not the same as that of the recent newcomer. The phrase 'pecking order' is derived from studies of poultry, but there is among school staff a structure involving pegs for hanging coats, seats near the fire, and places for parking cars.

Role

Closely related to status is role, which is the form of behaviour appropriate to a person's status or position in the network of social relationships. Though persons may have different personality patterns, those occupying the same status are expected to act in the same appropriate manner. This concept of role is central to an explanation of how children's personalities develop, as the expectations of society are expressed in terms of the roles that children are expected to adopt. A formal definition of role is given by Banton: role is "the set of norms and expectations applied to the incumbent of a particular position". The importance of role is further shown by its being possible to define an institution as "a cluster of roles". A school, therefore, would be an institution in which the head teacher behaves according to the standards expected of a head teacher, assistant teachers behave as assistant teachers, the caretaker as a caretaker, and infants as infants. In so far as each individual conforms to the norms and expectations of others regarding his behaviour in his position, the school exists and functions as a social institution. The term 'society' can also be defined as a system of roles. When we say "in our society" we imply that in other societies persons behave differently. For example, in our society the proper role of the child is a school pupil from the age of five; in other societies helping to cultivate the family plot is the proper role. In our present-day schools young pupils are expected to be active and inquiring, in Victorian schools they were expected to be respectful and diligent. The idea of self has also been defined as the total pattern of the roles that a person plays in society; in other words, I know what I am by knowing what I do. The essence of Rogers's non-directive therapy is to help a person to formulate the roles he wants to play, and to encourage him to play them more effectively.

It is impossible to trace all the complexities of social requirements to which a growing child learns to conform, and by which
his developing personality is shaped. One way in which adults'
ideas about children are expressed is in the status of children in
society. It is made clear to children that they are not old enough
or considered responsible enough to drive cars, purchase tobacco
or alcohol, take employment, marry, or vote. On the other hand,
the child is required to attend school, and is not expected to support himself. If he is under the age of criminal responsibility he
cannot be punished in the same way as an older child or an adult,
though he may commit the same offence and be able to distinguish
right from wrong acts. These formal definitions of status do not
greatly affect younger children; they can influence the personality
development of adolescents who may easily rebel against continuing in the status, and therefore the role, of a child. They are
often judged by adults not on the merits of their behaviour, but
on how far the behaviour offends this adult system of status.

Age Role

There is also an informal system of status, more widespread
and more continuously influential, which is expressed principally
in the expected roles, sex roles, and social-class roles of children.
When a child is told, "You should be able to tie your own shoe-
laces by now" or, "You are not old enough yet to go out on
your bicycle alone", the age role is being impressed on the child.
School organization in classes is a system of age roles, the behaviour required of infants being different from that of eleven-year-
olds, and that in turn different from fifteen-year-olds. It is interesting to note how age roles appear to have changed over the centuries
in accordance with changes in adult ideas of what children are.
Painters of the sixteenth and seventeenth centuries portrayed
children not only in the same clothes as adults, but also with the
same bodily proportions. To them, children were miniature adults.
The corresponding psychological view was expressed by, for
example, John Locke, who considered the child's mind as a blank
tablet, on which were inscribed the child's sense impressions, these
being organized into a system of knowledge by the powers of the
mind, which included such faculties as memory and reasoning.
Personality was regarded in much the same light, the child's personal characteristics being created by formal training reinforced by

rewards and punishments. Children with constitutional personality characteristics that did not fit easily into the approved pattern were disciplined into it, and failure to conform was attributed to sin or bad upbringing. Discipline could be severe, though Locke himself was more humane than most. Children were regarded not only as miniature adults, but also as incomplete adults.

The present system of thinking about children is almost the direct opposite. Children are regarded as persons in their own right, having modes of thought consistent in themselves, but different from those of adults, which are ultimately reached by a process of maturation through various stages. We are back to entelechy. Young children are considered as having clear personality characteristics, integrated in different fashions according to the child's age, but never incomplete. We do not try to repress or discipline these characteristics, but try to guide and develop them into forms of behaviour which are acceptable. It is easy to see the defects of the earlier view of children; it is not so easy to see the assumptions that underlie our own. The seventeenth-century teacher probably saw the active, impulsive, and somewhat aggressive extrovert as in need of discipline. Are we doing the same kind of thing when with our modern methods of activity and discovery we are in effect saying to the rather shy, sensitive introvert, "Be active, and discover something"? And are we quite sure that when we encourage younger children to experiment and think for themselves that we are not establishing personality characteristics which we shall later want to discourage in adolescents?

Sex Role

What has been said about age role can equally be said about sex role. The two roles are not independent, as the distinctive sex roles tend to develop with age. Little boys may play with dolls, older boys may not. Little girls may adopt unladylike postures in the playground, older girls may not. The school system again reflects the attitudes of society to sex roles; there is no solid evidence that single-sex schools have any advantages or disadvantages over co-educational schools, or indeed classes. Arguments are about our ideas of sex role, not about children. Girls dressed as we think boys should dress, or boys with flowing locks, affront our ideas of sex role; forgetful of rumbustious, long-haired Renaissance gallants, our super-egos may override our reason. Physically, fourteen-year-old girls are bigger, stronger, and more robust than boys of the same age; socially, they are not supposed to be. So they must learn to behave according to social requirements, and the active, adventurous, mesomorphic girl may find it difficult to conform.

Social-class Role

The expected age role and sex role varies according to social class. The term 'social class', though it reflects differences in way of living of which everyone is aware, is difficult both to define and measure. The convention is that social class refers to families rather than to persons, and that it is best identified by the occupation of the father. The difference in social-class attitudes may be illustrated by the anecdote of the two ladies who attended plays by Shakespeare. The first, middle-class, saw *Antony and Cleopatra*, and her comment was, "How unlike the home life of our own dear Queen!" The other, working-class, saw *Hamlet*, and her comment was, "I felt real sorry for them Hamlets—they had a rare lot of trouble in the family!" Though there is some evidence, not always easy to interpret, about the relation of social class to intelligence and educational attainment, there is little firm evidence of the effects of different social-class roles on the development of personality. People in different social classes learn to behave differently, but there is no evidence that the conforming personality in upper and in lower social classes may be other than the same personality type learning to conform to different ways.

The social-class differences are expressed in the parents' expectations of children's behaviour. Middle-class mothers, for example, seem to have less confidence in the effects of their attitudes and discipline than working-class mothers, who appear to be more ready to interpret behaviour in terms of black and white rather than shades of grey. In working-class homes, good behaviour often means obedience, and discipline tends to be simple and direct. Middle-class parents are often more influenced by their interpretations of current psychological opinions on the upbringing of children, and tend to stress internalization—that is, to enforce discipline by creating feelings of guilt by the withdrawal of affection and approval. Their approach is by reasoning with the child, and by placing greater responsibility on the child to work through his own social and personal difficulties. It has been said that with the decrease in brutality and physical ill-treatment of children, the centre of cruelty to children has shifted from the working class to the middle class. For the working-class child the social requirements are probably easier. His father may be driving a bus, or building houses, jobs which make sense to the child, and the code of discipline is simple, though possibly inconsistent at times. Compare him with the child whose father is a Civil Servant, or 'something in the City', and who is never quite certain whether misbehaviour is going to be treated as trivial or lead to serious disapproval and disappointment of his parents. Whether such differences as these tend to create different kinds of personality is uncertain; it is more certain that different types of personality may have a more difficult passage in some social classes than others. Middle-class exploitation of guilt feelings, for example, may tend to reinforce super-ego dominance in the personality, and cause more distress to introverts than extroverts.

Another way in which the social-class role affects the child is in school. Schools are essentially middle-class institutions, staffed by teachers who tend to maintain middle-class ideas of the pupil's role. The 'good pupil' is one who is interested, conscientious, and honest. What the teacher may describe as indiscipline, carelessness, and lack of interest is often the sign of conflict between the teacher's social-class-role expectations and the working-class-home's expectations that the pupil should be able to 'stand up for himself' and expect punishment only if he breaks known rules and is caught. It is probably the lack of internalization that troubles the teacher most.

There is little doubt that such differences in role expectations related to social class must have effects on personality development, but even the few examples we have given are suspect. There is much opinion, some prejudice, and very little reliable evidence. With social-class roles, as with age and sex roles, educators are very far from knowing how these different demands on the growing child influence his personal development, how undesirable personality characteristics can be avoided and desirable ones established. Indeed, we are far from clear what desirable characteristics are, and our aims and limits of tolerance are themselves the various products of the same age, sex, and social-class roles as we see affecting the pupils. We know very much more about how to teach French or arithmetic than we do about how to guide personality development.

Similarly, the process by which the behaviour appropriate to the various roles is acquired is not clearly known. Basically it is a process of learning, not significantly different from other forms of behaviour as far as learning is concerned. The motives which direct the learning process are the satisfaction of the needs of the child, one classification of which we have outlined earlier. We have no solid evidence on how this learning process is related to the maturation of the child's personality structure, and no information on whether learning reinforces or inhibits development of the behaviour characteristic of personality types. Does the introvert learn to become more consistently introverted, or does his social learning tend to make him less so?

We can induce personality disturbances in animals. For example, Pavlov carried out an experiment in which dogs were conditioned to give different responses to two stimuli, such as a bright light and a dull light. When the two lights were gradually brought to the same intensity, so that they became indistinguishable, the dogs began to behave in a way that would in humans be called an anxiety state. In a different set of experiments, this time on operant conditioning, cats learned to press a lever for food. A puff of air was then introduced when the cats pressed the lever; there was conflict between the response of seeking food and the response of withdrawing from the puff of air. The cats became withdrawn and listless—in short, neurotic. But when the conflicting stimuli were removed, both sets of animals returned to 'normal' behaviour. We do not know how. We arrange for maladjusted children, those with personality disturbances, to receive education in special schools. Some such schools establish a simple and regular routine, in the hope that the consistent and clear demands made on the child will lead to his learning more stable behaviour. Other schools give these children more than average freedom, hoping that the child will act out his conflicts and return to a more stable behaviour. Both methods succeed with some children, partly succeed with others, and fail with others. But we do not know why there is success with some and failure with others, nor what kinds of children benefit more from one school than another. Any educator who aims at developing desirable personal qualities in children can only place the children in what he thinks is a 'good' environment, and then hope for the best. We are far too ignorant to be able to control or guide personality development. We do not know why we sometimes succeed, or why we sometimes fail.

SOCIAL GROUPS

There is still another complication in the social maze the child has to learn. He has to learn to distinguish between the roles he is expected to play as a member of different social groups. He is first a member of a family, later he becomes a member of a school and class group and a member of a peer group which may or may not include his classmates. A group may be defined as a number of persons in a state of interdependence. A group has the properties of:

(1) Interaction, which means that the persons in the group have some means of communicating with each other.

(2) Cohesiveness, which means that the members are aware of belonging to one group and not to another.

(3) Structure, which means that the group has some system of status and roles.

(4) Common objective, which means that the group has some reason for its existence, whether it be to play together, to escape from adults, to listen to music, or to make mischief. The common objective of a family group is not easy to define, but the objectives of care and affection are implicit.

(5) Norms, which means that the group has certain standards of behaviour to which members are expected to conform.

Each of these requirements implies certain common personality characteristics, and the child who does not develop personality characteristics compatible with group requirements is unable to satisfy certain of his basic needs. The extremely withdrawn and introverted child has difficulty in becoming a member of a group; the extremely impulsive and aggressive child has difficulty in remaining a member of a group. With these group properties in mind, we examine more closely the main groups to which a school pupil usually belongs.

The Family

The basic group is the nuclear family, the group of father, mother, and children who make up the normal household in our society. In other societies, the unit is the extended family, the wider network of relatives by marriage, by kinship, or by social adoption. In our society, the extended family is disappearing, probably because the welfare services are taking over part of its function, and partly because houses are built for nuclear and not extended families. The characteristics of the nuclear family therefore become increasingly vital in the child's personality development. Feelings of worth, which imply affection, and feelings of security appear to be necessary for a child to develop a stable personality. Bowlby has shown that lack of a mother's personal care and love in early life can have adverse effects on personality development, but such deprivation has to be long and severe before permanent damage is done. Children, like Pavlov's dogs, appear to be able to reconstitute their personality structure by means we do not understand. Other studies show that children rejected by their parents tend to be unstable, resentful, and quarrelsome, and a vicious circle can easily develop, by which the child's personal characteristics, established through unsatisfactory relations within the family, tend by their presence to make relationships still more difficult. An aggressive parent tends to provoke the child to aggression, to which the parent responds with still more aggression, and so the personality pattern becomes established.

If the norms of child behaviour within the family are within the child's ability to attain, he tends to identify himself with the parents' behaviour and attitudes (not their precepts) in order to gain security and acceptance in the family group; the child internalizes these norms and his personality pattern tends to conform with those of his parents. If the norms are too exacting, for example for a child who is too young, or intellectually dull, or whose constitutional personality is not in accord with the family system of roles and norms, then anxiety, withdrawal, or aggression result, the particular form of response probably depending on the constitutional dispositions of the child's personality. Where there is warmth and affection, according to Sears, withdrawal of parental acceptance leads to the development of a strong conscience, or super-ego, in the child; on the other hand, according to McClelland, where the parents' role is authoritarian, discipline is effective in securing conformity by the child, but leads to a personality pattern in which conscience plays a lesser part.

Though there have been many studies of child and family relationships, especially in the U.S.A., clear conclusions regarding the effect of these relationships on personality are not numerous. But certain broad conclusions can be drawn. The relationships within the nuclear family are probably the most important single factor influencing the child's personality development. Also, it is becoming clearer that the emphasis placed on family relationships in the earlier years of life is not wholly justified. Deprivation in early life can be compensated for by later care and affection, and the results of early care and affection can be undone by later conflict. It is difficult to say that, throughout the child's life from infancy to adolescence, there is any one period in which family relationships are more important than another. It also appears that the 'efficient' or well-organized family may lead to better achievement in school and employment; in the matter of stable personality it is the affectionate and accepting family that is most effective.

School and Peer Groups

The peer group is one in which all members are of the same status, though within the group itself there may be some difference of status. The peer group does not seem to have much effect on personality development until the pupil has been at school for three or four years; the important peer groups are those of the older primary-school children, and the adolescent clique or gang. In the peer groups of the children, the leaders are usually of the mesomorphic and extrovert type of personality, but other personalities can find an appropriate role. Whether the group membership remains stable or not seems to depend mainly on how easily the members can manage to meet. Pupils attending the same school or living in the same neighbourhood tend to form groups easily. Those of high status within the group prefer security and order, and tend to create a formal organization of leaders, committees, secretaries, and so on, while those of lower status prefer flexibility and mobility within the group so that each member has an opportunity of occupying positions of higher status. The resulting conflict of personalities can easily be observed by anyone who has tried to let a group of twelve-year-old boys organize a game of football or cricket. More time is spent on arguments about rules, positions, and procedure than on the game itself.

It seems to be necessary for the pupils to sort out their appropriate roles, to test the strength of their personalities against others and to find a pattern of personal behaviour which satisfies themselves and is acceptable to the group.

Even those pupils whose personalities do not fit easily into the main stream of the group's activities can establish themselves as acceptable members by finding special roles. The clown, the scapegoat, the tomboy, the daredevil, or the mischief-maker are such roles. There is some risk that the features of the special role may become integrated into the pupil's personality, such that the child who readily bursts into tears may play himself into being a daredevil, or the insecure child play himself into a clown. Whether this is desirable or not must remain a matter of opinion; what is undesirable is to expose the daredevil's timidity or the clown's insecurity without another acceptable role being available. Another way of overcoming conflict between personality and peer-group role is found by those children who attach themselves to groups of younger or older children. Again the role may become a feature of personality, as in the younger boy who becomes the 'hanger-on' of older boys' groups, or the girl who becomes the 'mother' of younger children.

Another group to which all pupils belong is the school and the class. Sociological analysis of the school as an institution is still in its infancy, and despite numberless statements about the influence of school on the pupils' characters and personalities, there is virtually no psychological evidence on the relationship between the aims and functioning of the school and the development of the personalities of pupils in it. What can be said is that the school class is not a group of the same kind as the family or peer group. A school class is a formal group involving only a limited number of roles, essentially the adult role of teacher and the children's role as pupils. The social and personal relationships within a class tend to operate in smaller groupings. To most younger pupils, for example, the school class consists of a teacher, a small and not always permanent group of friends and enemies, and an undifferentiated background of other pupils.

The informal structure within a class can be revealed by a sociogram. This is a way of setting out the results of a process called sociometric analysis. In it, the pupils are asked to state which other pupils are their friends, whom they do not want as friends, whom they would most like to sit beside, to play with, or to have in a work group. A series of such sociograms can be constructed for a class, and the structure of informal relationships revealed. The resulting sociogram for a class of thirty or more pupils can be rather complicated, but a simpler one is illustrated in Fig. 8. The heavy-line arrows between pupils mean

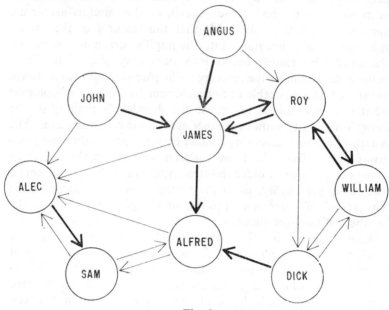

Fig. 8

that the pupil would like to associate with the one at whom the arrow points. The thinner-line arrow indicates the opposite. Those pupils whose company is sought are called 'stars', those who tend to be rejected by the others are called 'isolates'. The sociogram does not represent conclusions about class relationships; it is only a way of laying out the information about personal relationships within the class or group. Nor does it follow that the isolates are socially unacceptable or non-conforming; they may be so within the class, but could equally well have central roles in another peer group.

Another difference between the school class and the peer group arises out of the importance to pupil, teacher, and parent of achievement in school work. Whether we approve or not, children get satisfaction from doing well in school work, and those who do not, tend to seek alternative forms of satisfaction for their needs of esteem and security. The pupils who do well are approved by the teacher, they are recognized by their classmates as being 'good at English', and often success at school is accompanied by greater acceptance within the family. On the other hand, the pupil whose school attainment is noticeably below average is aware of his lack of success. The extrovert may respond by becoming a professional dunce, or a bully, or find compensation in social or athletic excellence. Other types of personality may develop patterns of anxiety or withdrawal. Success at school may also have its disadvantages. To quote Musgrove, "There seem to be few rewards in our educational system (and perhaps in our society generally) for 'normality' or even for humanity. The driving, demanding home, with exacting standards and expectations, and remorseless pressure on children appears to be the 'good home'. The kindly, reasonable, understanding, tolerant and helpful home pays less handsome dividends."[1] If this view is correct, some of the children who achieve satisfaction from the role of 'good pupil' may pay the penalty in other aspects of their personality development. It is also true that many pupils enjoy school work.

ADOLESCENCE

To examine in more detail the social interaction between the developing individual and the social context of adult expectations, we consider the last stage of the personal development of children, adolescence. The child of about eight to eleven years old has a relatively easy set of roles to learn, and he moves easily within his system of roles, in a fairly clearly defined status. His emotional life is also relatively simple, and though he may withdraw into fantasy to solve some of his difficulties, there is little questioning of his assumptions, and few doubts about the underlying nature of humanity, freedom, justice, and so on. The period of adolescence is broadly that between eleven and eighteen years old in girls, and twelve and twenty in boys. The pupil enters adolescence as a child, and emerges as an adult. During this period various changes are

[1] F. Musgrove, *The Family, Education, and Society* (London, Routledge and Kegan Paul, 1966, p. 79).

taking place. Physically, the adolescent is maturing sexually, and gaining a physique much more powerful in both physical and sexual strength. To this the adolescent must learn to adjust. Emotionally there are new difficulties, sexual success and frustration, transferring from school to employment, and deeper and wider questioning of the order of things and people. With the appearance of formal relations as a mode of thought, the simpler and more concrete philosophy of childhood is no longer sufficient. Socially, the adolescent must learn a new set of roles, which lack the stability of those of the child and the adult, and which often drive the adolescent to seek the security of exaggerated aggressive and defensive behaviour as a radical, a bohemian, or a delinquent.

The adult society is not prepared to accept the adolescent easily. This resistance does not rise wholly from the behaviour of the adolescent himself, but also from the psychological attitudes, often unconscious, of the adult. The adolescent is seen as invading the adult society, but not yet conforming to its roles and norms. The stereotype of the adolescent, as seen by the adult, is twofold and contradictory. On the one hand, the adolescent is perceived as the attacker and the non-conformer, a stereotype symbolized by the leather jacket, gang violence, sex, and obtrusively different forms of behaviour.

On the other hand, the adolescent is also seen as the inexperienced victim of society, exploited by commercial interests and in need of protection and discipline 'for his own good'. These fears are present to some extent in most parents and teachers of adolescents, and there is the expectation that the adolescent will behave as they fear he might. Such expectations become apparent to the adolescent, who tends to adopt these roles, thus convincing the adults that they were right.

We have to ask whether the more distinctive personality characteristics of adolescents are a necessary feature of adolescent development as such, whether they are the adolescent's response to the uncertainty of his role in society, and whether the difficulties that adults meet in relation to adolescents arise from psychological factors operating in the adult rather than in the adolescent. To the first question, the answer appears to be no. It would seem that most adolescents are reasonably responsible and stable persons engaged in growing up in somewhat difficult circumstances. The association of adolescence with delinquency and with strain and

stress is an adult attitude of long standing which does not seem
to be supported by the evidence available.

To the other two questions, the answer seems to be yes. An
interesting suggestion is that the adolescent is showing many of
the characteristics of a minority group in a society, such as
American Negroes, or French-Canadians. Parents and teachers
do not adopt the same attitude to younger children, who are not
perceived as a threat to the adult personality. The adolescent
threat is that of a lost parent-child relationship, and that of a
competing adult. Adults respond in various ways, for instance
by turning a blind eye to the developing sex interests of the
adolescent and attempting to prolong childhood roles. The mother
resists the adolescent's change of dress, choice of friends, and use
of make-up. The father is scornful of his daughter's 'dates',
and the teacher tends to be continuously concerned about hair
and skirts that are either too long or too short. The adult may
respond by cutting the adolescent down to size. Apprenticeship,
examinations, and various legal prohibitions are institutionalized
examples of this. Youth clubs and the like are instituted to keep
the adolescent within his status, and to prevent him or her becoming too adult. Another form of adult response is to identify with
the adolescent, so that the adult attempts to meet the challenge
by maintaining his youth. The mother who looks as young as her
daughter, the father who shares his son's activities till stopped by
a coronary attack, or the teacher who shares his pupils' interest
in 'pop' music, are not unfamiliar figures.

These adult responses are ultimately based on fear and envy.
A quotation from a classic on adolescence illustrates this fear:
"Sex asserts its mastery in field after field, and works its havoc
in the form of secret vice, debauch, disease and enfeebled heredity,
cadences the soul to both its normal and abnormal rhythms, and
sends many thousand youth a year to quacks, because neither
parents, teachers, preachers or physicians know how to deal with
its problems. Never has youth been exposed to such dangers of
both perversion and arrest as in our own land and day. Increasingly urban life with its temptations, prematurities, sedentary
occupations and passive stimuli just when an active life is needed,
early emancipation and a lessening sense for both duty and
discipline, the haste to know and do all befitting man's estate
before its time, the mad rush for sudden wealth and the reckless

fashions set by its gilded youth—all these lack some of the regulatives they still have in older lands with more conservative traditions."[1] This was written in 1904, but the language could easily be translated into contemporary terms, and most of the statements would have a familiar contemporary ring. But is he really talking about boys and girls?

The maze of social status, role expectations, and behaviour norms which the adolescent must learn is both more complex and more emotionally involving than that of the child. If the adolescent's personality development is more fundamentally affected, it is not because he or she is adolescent, but because the demands of society are both more exacting and more conflicting. To meet this threat, using the term as Rogers does, adolescents seek security in various directions. They may find it in an accepting and affectionate family, where conflicts can be amicably resolved, or in adolescent peer groups. These groups are characterized by their exclusiveness; they form a society within which the roles and norms are those of the adolescent, not the adult, and within which the roles and norms are known and accepted by its members. They show all the properties of a group, interaction by means of a common language within the group, cohesiveness in that there is a social exclusiveness if not snobbery between groups, structure in that certain leaders tend to set the pattern to which others conform, common objective in that the group resists adult participation and interference, and norms which are expressed in dress, language, activities, and 'crazes'. Such adolescent groups lend themselves to commercial exploitation; but whatever view is taken of this, the commercial interests do offer the adolescent a security arising from conformity to an accepted set of roles, in music, in dress, or in recreation. The effects of adolescent groups on personality are uncertain; probably they are beneficial in the long run by offering protection to the adolescent against the emotional threat of adults at a rather vulnerable phase. The evidence on adolescent personality development is conflicting and is confused by adult attitudes. The late-developing adolescent does appear to suffer some disadvantages; his more mature contemporaries tend to retain their confidence and stability; the late developer tends to retain a certain anxiety and sense of inferiority into adult life. The personality changes in adolescence

[1] G. S. Hall, *Adolescence* (London, S. Appleton, 1904).

can be quite marked in some children; we are led to doubt whether the earlier stages of personality development are as important as is sometimes claimed.

CONCLUSION

This discussion about personality development in the social context has of necessity to be in rather general terms. One reason is that we lack valid and precise methods of assessing personality differences and personality changes. Certain rather extreme personality types are identifiable, as are certain forms of personality disturbance. But the great majority of children and adolescents are not extreme in either sense. Information from clinical observation is valuable, but it tends to be confined to individual cases, most of whom are in some way or another disturbed or exceptional. We have spoken about the mature, stable personality, but we have no precise way of assessing or indeed defining its characteristics. Until such instruments are available, discussion must be general.

Much of what we call personality has to be learned, and the processes of learning are those which we discussed earlier. The difficult question, for the pupil as well as for the psychologist, is what is being learned. School studies, like French or mathematics, constitute a fairly stable and clearly defined structure of knowledge and skills. Sectors of these can be presented to the pupil and assessments can be made as to the pupil's rate of progress and his level of attainment. The teacher has a handle, as it were, to control and direct the pupil's learning. In the learning associated with personality development what the pupil has to learn are other people's attitudes and expectations, often conflicting and not clearly presented in orderly stages. And much of what he has learned, as in age role, has to be discarded or modified as it is being learned. What has to be learned is as psychologically variable as the learners themselves, who have to learn how best to satisfy their own changing needs in a society of adults, many of whom are themselves learning to cope with developing children. What the mechanisms of interaction between the children and the adults are is not at all clearly known. We can identify a few, but cannot predict with any confidence. Until our range of knowledge is established in more precise form, we can only try to observe ourselves as closely as we try to do the children in our care. Some children fail to learn the social maze adequately; is it because they are poor learners or because we have made it too difficult?

10

Handicapped Children

Who are handicapped?

Our educational system is mainly concerned with the education of the 'normal' pupil, with certain additional and special arrangements for those who cannot fit easily into the main stream of education. For various reasons, these children have difficulty in meeting the requirements of the system of roles and expectations discussed in the previous chapter. This difficulty may be the result of poor vision, poor hearing, poor muscular control, low intelligence, specific intellectual disability, or inadequate and unacceptable behaviour patterns like delinquency, epilepsy, or emotional maladjustment. From the point of view of the teacher and the educational administrator, the pupil who is hard of hearing obviously requires different educational provision from the pupil who is seriously short-sighted; from the point of view of the psychologist interested in personality development, these children all face the same difficulty, that of adapting to the requirements of society and developing those feelings of worth and security which follow from acceptance by other people. The view of some educators that doing one's best is more important than doing well does not appear to be one which is acceptable to many children. To pupils, especially to the younger ones, achievement in school is as important as satisfaction and esteem in his occupation is to an adult; any disability that prevents a pupil from attaining such satisfaction can be a barrier to the development of a stable and effective personality. The nature of the disability is of secondary importance.

Who are normal?

There is no precise definition which enables us to distinguish between handicapped and other children. A distinction is made in practice, as is shown by the existence of special schools and classes;

the distinction, however, is largely a matter of degree and practical convenience. The word 'normal' refers to norms, which are used in two senses. There is an ideal norm, the model of what is desired, perfect health, full functioning of the sensory organs, satisfying and effective personality, and so on. There is a statistical norm, which is what people are; occasional illness is more normal than perfect health, some conflict more normal than wholly satisfactory adjustment. No child, therefore, is wholly normal in the ideal sense, and no child is wholly abnormal. Colour-blind and left-handed children suffer from a disability, but not to a degree which prevents them from following a normal, in the statistical use, life and education; it is just a little more difficult. Some children with more severe disabilities, such as inadequate vision or marked speech defect, can adjust both to their handicap and to the expectations of society, and develop 'normal' personalities. Others, with possibly less severe disabilities, find the frustration of their handicap or their interpretation of the requirements of society more than they can learn to cope with, and become emotionally maladjusted as well. Educationally, the normal pupil is one who can attend school with other such pupils, without too much interference with the education of other pupils, and without too much difficulty to himself. How much 'too much' is, is a matter of judgement; it is impossible to assess or define precisely. Handicapped children can therefore be considered as belonging educationally to three broad groups; there are those who are able to attend ordinary schools, there are those who require different educational provision in special schools or classes, and there are those whose handicap is so severe that they are not educable in the school sense of the term. We are concerned here mainly with the first group.

CHILDREN WHO ARE VULNERABLE AND CHILDREN AT RISK

We have taken the view that the nature or degree of disability is not the important question; it is the pupil's mode of adjustment to his handicap and his society that matters. A useful distinction can be made between pupils who are vulnerable and pupils who are at risk. A vulnerable child is one who suffers from some disability that is likely to give him more than average difficulty in adjusting his behaviour to the pattern expected by society. A short-sighted child, for example, who cannot see a cricket- or tennis-ball till it is within two or three feet of him will find these games difficult and rather terrifying. The short-sightedness, unless very severe, is not such a handicap in reading. But he can have difficulty in finding acceptance by a peer group, who may attach more value to being good at games than at school work. An emotionally unstable child, easily provoked to tears or anger, is also vulnerable, as he can have difficulty in fitting into his age role; behaviour acceptable in a four-year-old is not acceptable in an eight-year-old.

A child at risk is one who is exposed to more than average demands by society, regardless of any disability the child may or may not have. A child whose parents are in a conflict leading to divorce is at risk; the loss of feelings of security and the emotional stress involved may readily lead to the development of defence mechanisms which, in turn, may lead to the development of a personality structure which does not easily find acceptance by adult society or the peer group. Another child at risk is the one of average ability whose parents expect a particularly high standard of academic and moral behaviour. Such a child may adapt himself very easily to a less exacting social environment, but as long as the parental pressure is being applied, usually in the form of withholding esteem, security, and affection, the child may respond with anxiety symptoms, withdrawal, or rebellion. Such a child is in no sense vulnerable; he is being subjected to greater emotional and social demands than he can reasonably be expected to meet.

It is, of course, not only children to whom the concepts of vulnerability and risk apply. The occupational illness of teachers is neurosis, the adult form of emotional maladjustment in children. A teacher whose personality is characterized by a tendency to anxiety and conscientiousness can find the continual striving for perfection with a class of indifferent, hostile, and active young adolescents too much to continue to endure. He, or she, finds the professional role increasingly difficult to maintain, worry drains energy, and social relationships within and without the school suffer; feelings of failure and frustration replace feelings of worth and security; defence mechanisms come to establish the pattern of the personality, and neurosis follows. Teachers with such personal dispositions, like those whose personality functioning is introversion and withdrawal, are vulnerable in a substantial sector of their professional duties. Teachers can also be at risk. There are some kinds of schools and classes which make much greater demands on the teacher's skill and personality than others. A young man, of middle-class upbringing and of academic interests, as yet inexperienced as a teacher, may find himself faced with a class of fifteen-year-old girls, of working-class standards of behaviour and attitudes to education, not academically interested and becoming aware of their sexual powers. The 'reality shock' can be severe and emotionally disturbing to such a teacher, who in less exacting circumstances might have come to adapt himself more easily to both the frustrations and satisfactions of his professional role. A less obvious form of risk awaits the efficient 'born teacher'. The satisfaction obtained from success in the teacher role can be such that this role comes to be the dominant behaviour pattern in the personality, and one who began life as a human being may end as a school-teacher.

An example of the vulnerable parent is the widowed mother, often in poor health and circumstances, who is unable to establish satisfactory relations with an adolescent son or daughter. Parents at risk are those who find themselves with a handicapped child with whom they do not know how to cope. In this sense, all parents are to some extent at risk. The ideas of risk and vulnerability can be applied to peer groups. In a peer group a younger or more immature member is vulnerable to bullying by the older and more developed members, as is a child with unacceptable personality characteristics. A child from a 'good home' may be at risk in a peer group dominated by a few children with delinquent tendencies. The plea that he was "a good boy led astray by other children" can often be true.

It is clear that risk and vulnerability are not independent. One of the aims of special education is to place the handicapped child in a situation where the risks are reduced, and where the educational and social demands are such that the child has a chance of meeting them. The pupil of limited intelligence, or with hearing or sight disability, or with physical handicap in a special school does not present a serious educational problem. There has been much research on the education of such pupils, methods of teaching have become established, and such pupils can, and usually do, develop personality patterns that enable them to find satisfaction in their special educational situation. The critical areas of difficulty for handicapped children lie elsewhere. One is at the point of leaving school. Another is the position of the moderately handicapped child in the ordinary school; such a pupil is vulnerable to a lesser degree, but he is not protected as he would be in a special school. A third area of difficulty is the personal relationships between a handicapped child and his family.

THE HANDICAPPED CHILD IN THE FAMILY

A handicapped child is usually under a double handicap. He has his disability, but he also has to learn a system of adult expectations which are less clear and less stable than those presenting themselves to the normal child. A feeling of guilt is seldom absent from the attitudes of parents to a handicapped son or daughter. Often, too, there is some resentment that this misfortune should have happened to them. Such feelings of guilt not only influence the emotional relations between parent and child, but also lead the parents to feel a need to defend themselves against real or imagined criticism by the society in which they live. The response of the parents may take various forms, determined as much by the personality of the parents as by the condition of the child.

The parents may reject the child, and try to have the responsibility transferred to an institution or a residential school; parents have been known to try to emigrate and leave a handicapped child behind. The rejection may be rational, the interests of other members of the family being weighed against those of the handicapped child; it may also be irrational, based on guilt and resentfulness. Another form of parental rejection is for the child to remain with the family, but to be treated differently, without the affection and esteem given to the other children.

Another form of response is for the parents to refuse to accept that the child is handicapped and to attempt to treat the child as 'normal', perhaps a little different from other children, but not seriously so. Mentally-handicapped children are regarded as 'slow learners' or 'late developers'. Autistic children—that is, children of so withdrawn a personality that they have difficulty in responding to the behaviour of other persons—may be described by their parents as shy or dreamy. The parents never give up the hope that their child may one day suddenly develop and begin behaving like other children. Any sign of 'normal' behaviour is noted and encouraged by the parents; the child is ever under the anxious observation and pressure of the parents, and may in the end become

9

aware of their frustration and possible rejection when the expected development does not occur. A similar form of refusal to accept the child's disability is seen in the parents who take the attitude that the child is basically normal, but is suffering from some other condition which has not been properly diagnosed. The child is taken from one specialist to another, and his disability becomes the central concern of his family and other social relationships. The child may easily acquire a feeling of failure when the expected cure fails to be found.

Even those parents who accept the child and his disability often tend to develop defensive attitudes involving the child. One is to be over-protective; the parents may overlook the fact that the disability may only affect some sectors of the child's behaviour. No child in school is wholly vulnerable, but such parents tend to over-emphasize the degree of handicap, often to reassure themselves that, by handicapped-children standards, their child is above average in ability, considering his handicap. In the belief that they are doing all that is possible for their child's welfare they may be denying their child the opportunity to develop normal personality traits in those sectors where it is possible for the child to do so. This is a risk that children whose parents do accept the disability are exposed to; the risk is that the parents' expectations are based on the attitude that the child has a general disability rather than one based on a particular area of behaviour only.

THE HANDICAPPED CHILD IN SCHOOL

These different parental attitudes have been revealed by various investigations; what is not known is the relative frequency of the various attitudes. What is known is that children who are vulnerable on account of a handicap are also at risk on account of the parents' expectations. It is for this reason that there is a greater incidence of emotional maladjustment among handicapped than among normal children. The risk is least for children with 'clean' or 'respectable' disabilities, such as physical or sensory defect. It is greatest for children whose handicap involves difficulties with bowel or bladder control, and for children who are emotionally maladjusted; the latter have no visible signs of handicap, their disability is often shown as socially unacceptable and unreasonable behaviour, and they frequently have parents who are personally disordered themselves.

In considering the handicapped pupil in school we shall confine the discussion to those attending ordinary schools or classes; the special education of handicapped pupils is a large and specialized topic in itself. The teacher is not so emotionally involved as the parents, and the feeling of guilt is not a significant element in the teacher's attitudes and expectations, so that the pupil is less at risk in the school than in the home. Also, the attitudes of the pupil's classmates and peer groups are less complex than those of the parents; indeed, apart from some forms of emotional maladjustment, school pupils can be very tolerant of handicap, and more readily accept the handicapped pupil as he is.

A teacher may have in a class a small number of children known to suffer from a moderate disability, and possibly a few others in whom the presence of a disability has not yet been recognized. The extent to which the teacher can help such pupils depends on the amount of information about the pupil that the teacher has. It is not expected that the teacher should have the specialized knowledge and experience to diagnose the nature and degree of a pupil's disability. There is a danger of being either too ready to accept the pupil's behaviour at its face value, or to attribute complex causes to a relatively simple condition. There is a short strip cartoon showing two children discussing a third, who is crying bitterly. The captions read (1) "He must be under-privileged" (2) "Or maladjusted" (3) "Or perhaps he's frustrated" (4) "Let's ask him" (5) "He says his shoes are too tight". There is another showing two psychiatrists meeting each other. First psychiatrist, "Good morning." Second psychiatrist (thinks) ,"Now what made him say that?" In the same way a teacher may be tempted to overlook a child's difficulty by stressing too much the irrelevant factors; it may be equally easy for a teacher to attribute an immediate and simple explanation to a situation which may in fact be very complex. For example, one of the common experiences in educational clinics is for children to be referred for reading difficulties. In many cases these difficulties are only the presenting symptoms of a serious personality disorder. Reading difficulty is a relatively respectable condition, for which parents can blame the teachers, and is therefore more readily acceptable to parents than emotional maladjustment would be. On the other hand, it is not unknown for children from homes where there is some poverty, conflict, and neglect to show signs of lassitude and lack of concentration; some such children are found to be suffering from a chronic infective condition, of the nose or tonsils for example, and simple medical treatment transforms the child's whole behaviour.

The obvious explanation of a child's disability is not necessarily the correct one. The behaviour of a mentally-handicapped child in class is very difficult to distinguish from that of a pupil with moderate hearing defect. A survey testing the hearing of primary-school pupils in an education authority area showed that about one-half of the pupils with a definite hearing disability (30-plus decibel loss) had not been previously detected. The degree of disability was such as to affect their educational progress; most were, however, described by their teachers as intellectually slow or dull. Moreover, a number of pupils were both slightly deaf and of low IQ; their hearing disability led to their intellectual ability being somewhat underestimated.

Maladjusted Pupils in School

Apart from the moderately mentally handicapped, say from IQ 65 upwards, the most frequent form of disability found in most classrooms is emotional maladjustment. Such pupils may range from those who suffer from some personality disorder which makes adjustment to the ordinary requirements of society difficult for them, to those of normal personality structure who are in a state of emotional disturbance arising from exceptional stress or conflict in their social environment, usually the family. Not all forms of maladjustment are observed in school behaviour. In 1928, an inquiry by Wickham showed that teachers were most observant of aggressive behaviour, stealing, truancy, and impudence, but tended to overlook withdrawing behaviour, such as shyness, suspicion, and anxiety. Child psychiatrists, on the other hand, regarded withdrawing behaviour as the more serious condition. Later inquiries in the U.S.A. show much the same pattern, but an increasing awareness by the teacher that the withdrawing pupil may be seriously disturbed emotionally. An English inquiry by Rutter and Graham in the Isle of Wight showed that from ten- and eleven-year-olds in school, who were known to be having emotional or social difficulties, the parents and teachers did not each select the same set of children as being maladjusted. Agreement was greatest where the condition was severe, or where the maladjusted behaviour was very specific. But there were children having emotional and personality conflict in the home situation who were not noticed by their teacher, and children whose school behaviour was causing difficulty but whose parents noticed nothing wrong.

What is Maladjustment?

It is evident that teachers, parents, and psychologists do not all share the same view of maladjustment. Educationally, maladjustment is considered as a form of handicap, requiring special educational provision either in special schools or in ordinary schools, with or without expert guidance. It is doubtful whether the term 'handicap' is appropriate, as this implies a certain permanency of the condition, which the pupil and society have to learn to live with, and implies also a certain deficiency in the child's equipment for living. Neither of these implications apply to all maladjusted children. The prospects of a return to 'normal' living are probably greater for maladjusted children than for those with other handicaps, and frequently the emotional disability can be remedied by changes in the home and parents rather than in the child himself. There are also some maladjusted children who appear to have a constitutional personality defect, and to those the term handicap may more properly be applied.

In the discussions of learning and of intelligence we noted that the use of a single term for different psychological processes causes some confusion. The same applies to maladjustment. Any definition of the term would have to take into account at least three main components.

First, there is the nature of the pupil's behaviour; in some way it departs from the pattern of social norms, whether it be a reaction of an essentially normal child to intolerable social and emotional conflicts in his family, or whether it reflects personality characteristics incompatible with the norms of society. This behaviour cannot be clearly defined; limits of tolerance vary.

Second, there is the origin of the behaviour. Children who are vulnerable need a different approach from those who are reacting to difficult conditions. Unacceptable behaviour is no criterion here; one expression of maladjustment may be an anxiety to conform, and a pupil whose behaviour gives no cause for social complaint may be an anxious, insecure child seeking refuge in meticulous conformity to the roles expected of him.

Third, there is the age role. Forms of behaviour which are acceptable in a younger child may indicate maladjustment in an older child. The stages of development which the child passes through are often referred to as milestones. In this context the maladjusted child is one who has failed to keep up with his age roles, who finds the increasing demands too difficult and who meets these difficulties by retaining or reverting to a familiar but immature form of behaviour.

Quite apart from individual differences among children, it appears that the term 'maladjusted' is applied to different kinds of children. The maladjusted child's behaviour, also, is liable to overlap with other forms of behaviour, not necessarily indicating maladjustment. There may be confusion between maladjustment and delinquency; petty theft, for example, is not an uncommon sign of emotional disturbance in children. The distinction is that delinquency is a form of behaviour socially and legally unacceptable, while maladjustment is a psychological condition which may or may not find expression in anti-social behaviour. Some delinquent acts are signs of emotional and personality disorder, whereas others are deliberately committed by children or young persons for personal gain or satisfaction. Most lie between these extremes, and in any individual child the assessment of these two components may be difficult. Also, unhappiness is not necessarily an indication of maladjustment. Some children have reason to be unhappy and emotionally distressed; some maladjusted children are irrational optimists, living partly in an unreal world in which the next venture is to be the solution of all their problems; such children are often the least worried or unhappy persons in their social situation.

Maladjusted Behaviour

Rather than attempt a definition of maladjusted behaviour, we give below one list of behaviour typical of most emotionally maladjusted children. This list, the teachers' scale compiled by Rutter for the inquiry mentioned earlier, is intended for pupils around the age of ten or eleven years. Such a scale would require modification for seven-year-olds or fourteen-year-olds, and a different scale is used to obtain information from parents.

CHILD SCALE B[1]

(To be completed by Teachers)

Statement

1. Very restless. Often running about or jumping up and down. Hardly ever still.
2. Truants from school.
3. Squirmy, fidgety child.
4. Often destroys own or others' belongings.
5. Frequently fights with other children.
6. Not much liked by other children.
7. Often worried, worries about many things.
8. Tends to do things on his own—rather solitary.
9. Irritable. Is quick to 'fly off the handle'.
10. Often appears miserable, unhappy, tearful, or distressed.
11. Has twitches, mannerisms, or tics of the face or body.
12. Frequently sucks thumb or finger.
13. Frequently bites nails or fingers.
14. Tends to be absent from school for trivial reasons.
15. Is often disobedient.
16. Has poor concentration or short attention span.
17. Tends to be fearful or afraid of new things or new situations.
18. Fussy or over-particular child.
19. Often tells lies.
20. Has stolen things on one or more occasions.
21. Has wet or soiled self at school this year.
22. Often complains of pains or aches.
23. Has had tears on arrival at school or has refused to come into the building this year.
24. Has a stutter or stammer.
25. Has other speech difficulty.
26. Bullies other children.

The items can be scored by giving a score of zero if the behaviour stated is not observed in the pupil, a score of one if the description applies to some extent, and a score of two if the description clearly applies to the pupil. A score of ten or more is taken as indicating a significant degree of maladjustment; this level of score agrees substantially with teachers' subjective judgements.

[1] Rutter, M. L., *Journal of Child Psychology and Psychiatry*, vol. 8, pp. 1–11.

There are certain points to be noted about the scale. The behaviour items are specific to the age of the pupils for whom it is intended. If used for younger children, many items would not be inappropriate for their age role, and therefore not indicate maladjustment. Nor does the scale include behaviour items indicating severe personality disturbance. It refers to the moderately disturbed pupil who may be found in a classroom; the psychotic child who may exhibit extremely withdrawn or bizarre behaviour is not included, and most psychologists would make a sharper distinction between school refusal, which is a serious sign, and truancy which is not necessarily so. A working distinction is that the school refusal is usually to be found at home, the truant elsewhere. It remains, however, a precise and comprehensive list of the behaviour signs of maladjustment the teacher is likely to encounter; a teacher using the scale should expect to find clusters of items which described the different behaviour patterns of the emotionally maladjusted pupil. The next question is how these different patterns develop.

Origins of Maladjustment

The origins of maladjustment are one aspect of the development of personality, and can be considered in terms of different personality theories. Eysenck, for example, would tend to classify the different behaviour patterns of maladjustment in terms of extrovert–neurotic, introvert–neurotic, and so on. Rogers would regard maladjustment as a failure to develop a self which is satisfactorily able to meet the threats of the phenomenal field. Freud would interpret in terms of ego and super-ego relationship to the pleasure and reality principles. A simpler, though less adequately developed system theoretically, is to consider the signs of maladjustment as arising out of the pupil's relations with other people, and the defence mechanisms he develops to operate these relations. Pupils can be thought of as those whose behaviour is towards other persons, and those whose behaviour is away from other persons.

In the first group are the aggressive children, who look on others as enemies; they distrust other people and are concerned with defending themselves against a hostile society by attacking. They provoke other persons, and are ready to blame those others for real or imagined slights and setbacks. They are the mischief-makers, the bullies, and the experts in righteous indignation. But the root of it all is usually fear and insecurity, against which they protect themselves by such defence mechanisms as projection and reaction formation. These mechanisms become established, and so the pattern of personality crystallizes. The aggression may take various forms. One boy, a dapper, intelligent twelve-year-old, had been adopted by a middle-class couple, who brought him up, not too strictly, to be a credit to the family, but who showed little warmth of affection and little tolerance of childhood lapses of behaviour. His response to the lack of security based on affectionate acceptance was to behave like a little gentleman whenever there were other people in the house, but to show every form of disobedience and mischief when alone with his two adoptive parents. At school he appeared as timid and anxious, but was not a difficult pupil. Psychological treatment helped his immediate difficulties, but he still retains a basic suspicion and fear of other persons, and the prospects of a satisfactory personality development are not very good.

Also in the first group, the children whose behaviour is towards other persons, are the over-dependent children, those who are too anxious to please and conform. They seek feelings of worth in the approval of others, seeking attention and reassurance continually. They prefer to play a minor role to avoid conflict, and frequently display immature forms of behaviour, being unwilling to give up the protection and acceptance gained in the younger age roles they have already learned. Some such pupils learn to conform to the extent of causing little trouble in school, but others can be difficult in a classroom. One such, a girl, was brought up in a family in which the mother was an ailing, nagging person, and the father a domineering, tempestuous man, genuinely fond of his children but very unpredictable, and engaged in frequent quarrels with his wife. The girl, dependent on her father's unpredictable behaviour for affection, sought to establish a special relationship with her teacher, playing the role of the perfect pupil and attempting to monopolize the teacher's attention. She became such a nuisance in class that she was finally transferred to a residential unit for maladjusted children where a sympathetic but firm approach, together with an explanation of her difficulties, enabled her to return to both school and family more able to learn to live with the situation. There was a considerable element of fantasy in her defence mechanisms, as well as the obvious one of using the teacher as a substitute mother. A younger brother rebelled against the same home situation by delinquency, drawing pointed nails along the paint-work of parked cars. Both can be considered as children at risk, both have overcome their emotional difficulties, and the future prospects are good.

The second group is the withdrawing children. They are the daydreamers, to whom the world of fantasy may be as real as the external world of people and events. In their fantasy, the pupils can play satisfying roles and attain feelings of worth and security which they do not find in their relations with real people. Such pupils withdraw from social and personal relations with others; they are afraid of committing themselves and being rejected, and are often difficult to communicate with. The shy, retiring, dreamy child is not maladjusted, so long as he responds to other people in a reasonable manner appropriate to his age. The withdrawn child, who erects a barrier against others, who fears and distrusts their intentions, and who projects his fears into misinterpretation of the attitudes of other people, is maladjusted. The child who internalizes his difficulties, such that his inadequate defences against his conflicting emotional relationship with others becomes built into his personality structure, who ceases to seek a resolution of his conflict in action, but who has protected himself by becoming no longer aware of conflict or dissatisfaction, and to whom the imaginative roles he can create for himself in fantasy are sufficiently satisfying for the external world to become largely irrelevant and unnoticed—such a child is seriously maladjusted.

A childless couple, the husband a free-lance writer and the wife an artist who designed furniture fabrics to supplement the household income, which was adequate if not large, adopted a baby boy. Why they so decided is not clear. Their way of living was gay, Bohemian, and disorganized, and the boy was brought up in an almost complete absence of recognizable routine. When he went to school he appeared to welcome the class routine as a refuge, but took little part in class activities and showed a tendency to daydreaming. As he grew older he became more remote in his behaviour, and more difficult to arouse from his daydreams. Unlike the shy pupil, he had no special friend, nor did he show any desire to join in play; he showed no interest and just stood around at playtime, alone. This, combined with increasing neglect of routine activities like eating, washing, and the like, together with occasional episodes of bizarre behaviour, possibly quite a logical outcome of his fantasies, led to the boy being referred to the school psychologist and thence to a child psychiatrist. The finding was that he was quite severely mentally ill, and the outlook not very promising. It is likely that this boy was vulnerable, having a personality disposition prone to disorder, but he was also at risk in the nature of his upbringing, and his defence mechanism of retreat into fantasy came to set the pattern for his whole personality development.

The various kinds of defence mechanisms used by maladjusted children to protect themselves against threats and conflicts are the same as those used by the normal child. The differences lie in the fact that those adopted by maladjusted children are less effective in relation to the external world, though not necessarily so for the child himself. Also, the maladjusted child tends to cling to his particular system of defence mechanisms, apparently lacking the feeling of personal security which would enable him to change to other mechanisms. And finally the dependence on a limited and often ineffective system of defence mechanisms tends to lead to the establishment of a rather rigid and limited personality structure. How far this process is due to constitutional disability in personality development, and how much to the insecure child becoming habit bound, is unknown. Studies with identical twins would suggest that a constitutional disability is by no means impossible.

Milestones in Personality Development

This approach to personality development implies that a series of progressive adjustments have to be made by the child, both to his own needs and the expectations of society, if he is to be able to establish satisfying relationships with other people. This progression can be expressed as the learning of successive age roles, and failure to progress at any stage is manifested as maladjustment at a later age. Various systems of milestones have been suggested; we take that of Erik Erikson as a typical scheme of development. He describes progress as a series of developmental tasks, in each of which certain disabilities have to be overcome. His system of developmental tasks is based on Freud's personality theories, with some modifications. Erikson stresses the importance of the ego to a greater extent than Freud; he is less concerned with the deeper unconscious processes. Freud tended to centre the development of personal relationships in the nuclear family; Erikson is concerned with the child's adjustment to the wider society. And finally, Erikson considers that successful accomplishment of the developmental tasks is necessary for satisfactory growth of personality; development is a continuous process throughout all ages, and each crisis or task surmounted means a further progression in development.

Erikson recognizes eight milestones or developmental tasks, the first five belonging to childhood, the remainder to adult life. Each he expresses as a contrast between what has to be acquired and what has to be overcome. The eight tasks are as follows, those numbered 3 to 5 being those involving children of school age:

1. (Infancy) Acquiring a sense of trust, against basic mistrust. The infant is mainly concerned with bodily needs, and this developmental task is dependent mainly on how the infant is cared for and handled.

2. (Up to about four years) Acquiring a sense of autonomy, against doubt and shame. The child learns in this stage that his behaviour is his own, and that he can control it. He is, however, still dependent and finds this dependency difficult to escape from. The child is now able to move about more freely and explore; he is also aware of his emotions, anger, fear and the like, which he finds difficult to control. His dependency, the disapproval of his parents at his emotional behaviour, and the incomplete security resulting from partial dependency and partial responsibility lead to uncertainty and feelings of shame. He overcomes these by fantasy and playing with toys which he can direct and control, and with which he can express his conflicts and doubts. At this stage adults and other children become significant elements in the child's world.

3. (About four to seven years) Acquiring a sense of initiative, against overcoming guilt. As the child's sense of autonomy and responsibility extends in the family, and beyond the family into the school and neighbourhood, his activities are no longer dependent on his parents and under their direct observations. This freedom is accompanied by a feeling of guilt, and conscience is taking the place of parental rules in controlling his behaviour. Internalization is taking place, or in Freud's terms, the super-ego is emerging. The child is learning various social roles, but there is uncertainty, with the feeling of guilt, that he may exceed the acceptable limits,

and lose security and approval. At this stage the appropriate sex role is being learned, which again has certain overtones of guilt.

4. (About seven to ten years) Acquiring a sense of industry, against a sense of inferiority. At this age the child is inquisitive and active, seeking new experience. He is still not able to play adult roles, and recognizes his inferiority to adults in strength and skills. He sets out to master the skills and behaviour appropriate to age and sex. He takes school work seriously, as a means of establishing his status, and attaches importance to physical skills also. The child needs the peer group at this stage, as a standard against which he can test the behaviour he is learning to acquire.

5. (About ten to fifteen years) Acquiring a sense of identity, against identity diffusion. Identity here means confidence in facing the adult world as an equal. It is the stage of commitment to roles, occupational for example. The questions to be answered are "What am I?" and "What am I going to be?" This is a period of seeking and examination, especially of adult values with which the child realizes he will soon have to identify himself. At this age the peer group is the dominant influence, providing security and standards with which the child can identify himself while testing out adult values.

6. (Adolescence and early adulthood) Acquiring a sense of intimacy and solidarity, against isolation. One of the fears of the older adolescent is that of not belonging, of not being accepted into the adult society. He or she seeks and obtains this sense of belonging mainly through love and work.

7. (Adult) Acquiring a sense of generativity, against self-absorption. This refers to the establishment of a satisfactory family life.

8. (Adult) Acquiring a sense of integrity, against despair. This refers to later adult life, where the adult seeks the sense of having lived a worthwhile life.

This is a very condensed summary of Erikson's scheme of developmental tasks, and does not do justice to the implications of each step. But the general line of approach is fairly clear, and though Erikson did study psycho-analysis in Vienna for a period, it must be remembered that he is referring to the process of socialization in a North American culture, which has probably influenced both the selection of the tasks and the social context in which he sees them operating. Our purpose, however, is to give an example of the way of thinking which sees the psychological development of personality in terms of milestones. Maladjustment is the outcome of failure to accomplish these tasks, and hence of failure to develop the ability successfully to meet the challenge of the succeeding tasks. This failure to meet the requirements of developmental progress leads to fixation at an earlier stage, with immature behaviour as the result, and to the development of defence mechanisms as a protection against failure in the later tasks. According to this approach, maladjustment is basically arrested personality development, and unacceptable behaviour is the sign of it.

THE HANDICAPPED PUPIL AND THE TEACHER

We have discussed three lines of approach to the problem of emotional maladjustment. To the psychologist, interested in defining and analysing the processes of personality development, each has its contribution to make. To the teacher, who may often be the first to suspect the presence of a handicap, and who may have the task of educating the handicapped pupil according to his abilities, the first approach, the observation of the pupil's behaviour, is the most useful. Of the three children whose case histories we have briefly described, the first pupil, though emotionally maladjusted, was not a difficult pupil. The second, the girl who was least seriously disturbed, presented the greatest problem to the teacher. The third, the boy who was seriously disordered, gave the teacher no disciplinary or personal difficulty, but his behaviour was markedly abnormal. A teacher may be excused for overlooking the first pupil, though perhaps reference to what psychological services were available would have been a wise precaution, but the second and third both presented personality and behaviour problems beyond the teacher's function to deal with. It is not expected of the class teacher to diagnose either the nature, the severity, or the treatment of handicapped pupils; but the discovery of handicap often depends on a teacher's observation. The detection of the development of multiple handicap in pupils is also dependent on the teacher's observation. Pupils of low intelligence, for example, are at risk for emotional maladjustment, as are pupils with sensory or physical handicap. And it does not follow that all pupils with handicap have difficulty with school work. Excellence at routine arithmetic may on occasion be a sign of personality disturbance, and children of high intelligence with, for example, some hearing disability may be able to maintain at least an average level of school work.

Not all handicapped pupils require special classes; some may be more effectively provided for in the ordinary school situation. What then is the function of the teacher with handicapped children, particularly emotionally disturbed children, in the class? First, there is the need to assess the educational capabilities of the pupil, and adjust the school work to these. This means assessing what sectors, if any, of school work are not affected by the disability, and requiring the same norms of behaviour as from other pupils. It is not unknown for handicapped pupils to seek punishment to establish their standing in the peer group and to support their own feelings of worth. If the disability is more general, it becomes a matter of finding, not manufacturing, something that the pupil can do adequately, that he knows he can do adequately, and building as much of the pupil's educational progress as possible on that foundation.

Second, there is the need for the teacher to assess, as objectively as possible, his own limits of tolerance, and having done so to adhere consistently to them. Some pupils can be expected to be difficult; there is the pupil with a heart condition who must not be punished or excited—and knows it. There is also the hyperactive pupil who cannot stay still, and there is the emotionally maladjusted pupil who demands attention. The teacher has to consider the interests of the rest of the class, and may have to be fairly ruthless in suppressing attempts by handicapped pupils to demand too much of the teacher's time. Where the line is to be drawn is a matter for the teacher's discretion, but consistent application of the limits is better than variability. The teacher has to try objectively to assess his own personal characteristics; there is no advantage in a teacher setting wider limits of tolerance than he knows he is likely to be able to maintain. The permissive teacher is probably better able to cope with these difficult pupils than the more authoritarian teacher, but again, the latter may be more effective in the teaching of other pupils in the class.

Finally, there is a need for the teacher to assess the total situation the handicapped pupil is living in. It is often stated as self-evident that a teacher should know the home and family background of his pupils. This is not the obvious truth that it may appear to be. For most pupils a sense of autonomy and identity is achieved by acquiring an independent and separate status in the home, the school, and the peer group. The younger pupil is eager to relate at home what happened in school, the older pupil's reply to the question, "What happened at school today?" is frequently, "Nothing much." An English inquiry into pupils' attitudes to different methods of punishment revealed that what older pupils disliked most was having their school offences reported to the home. Too close collaboration of parents and teachers may act as a barrier to the pupil's search for personal independence and responsibility. The exception is the handicapped pupil, where it is necessary for the teacher to know what the parents' attitude is, and what pressures they are exerting on the pupil. His status in the school may be vital for the rejected pupil; school may provide a means of achieving greater independence for the over-protected pupil.

General rules are no substitute for careful observation and clear thinking about individual pupils. With emotionally maladjusted pupils, who are the most common problem to teachers, it is best to consider the pupil's behaviour as a defence against people and events with which he feels unable to cope. The pupil is either vulnerable, or at risk, or both. As far as he is vulnerable, he has to protect himself against his disability; if at risk he has to protect himself against society. A boy whose behaviour was characterized by boastfulness, attention seeking, and aggressive insistence on his rights and property formed an ambivalent relationship with his class teacher. On the one hand, he was anxious to gain the teacher's approval and to establish a close and special personal relationship with him. On the other hand, he felt a pressing need to be sure of being accepted by the teacher, and by disobedience and provocation was seeking a kind of absolute certainty of acceptance and security. He was testing the teacher's acceptance to the limits, and on one occasion overstepped the limits of the teacher's tolerance. The teacher, perhaps naturally but unwisely, demolished the boy's aggressive defence, and in effect rejected him. The boy rushed out of school in an emotionally disturbed state, with mixed feelings of worthlessness and resentment that anyone should have the power and authority to spurn him so, and a desire to show that he was not as worthless as he felt. He rode furiously down the road on his bicycle, did a spectacular and daredevil turn into a main road, and narrowly escaped being killed by an oncoming car. It took some months of psychological help to restore enough stability for him to return to school, and he remained vulnerable to disappointment or frustration, responding as before with self-assertion and aggression. This boy lived to tell his story; another may not. And with this cautionary tale we close.

Further Reading

This list of suggestions for further reading has two purposes. One is to supply the references to most of the books discussed in the text. These are of varying levels of difficulty, and are marked with an asterisk. The other purpose is to give a list of books, not too advanced or technical, on the main topics discussed. The selection has been mainly from more recent publications, and nearly all these contain bibliographies from which a further selection of reading can be made.

GENERAL PSYCHOLOGY

BRUNER, J. S.: *The Process of Education* (Harvard University Press, 1960).

COMBS, A. W., and D. SNYGG: *Individual Behaviour* (New York and London, Harper and Row, 1959).

FERNALD, L. D., and P. S. FERNALD: *Overview of General Psychology* (Boston, Houghton Mifflin, 1966: London, Harrap, 1966).

GARRETT, H. E.: *Great Experiments in Psychology* (New York, Appleton-Century-Crofts, 1951).

HYMAN, R.: *The Nature of Psychological Inquiry* (New Jersey and London, Prentice-Hall, 1964).

MILLER, G. A.: *Psychology: the Science of Mental Life* (London, Penguin, 1966).

SKURNIK, L. S., and F. GEORGE: *Psychology for Everyman* (London, Penguin, 1964).

YOUNG, M.: *Innovation and Research in Education* (London, Routledge and Kegan Paul, 1965).

READINGS

FOSS, B. M. (ed.): *New Horizons in Psychology* (London, Penguin, 1966).

FULLAGAR, W. A., H. G. LEWIS and C. F. CUMBEE (eds.): *Readings for Educational Psychology* (New York, Cromwell, 1964).

MORSE, W. C., and G. M. WINGO (eds.): *Readings in Educational Psychology* (Chicago, Scott Foresman, 1962).

PAGE, E. B. (ed.): *Readings for Educational Psychology* (New York, Harcourt, Brace, and World, 1964).

ROSENBLITH, J. F. and W. ALLINSMITH (eds.): *The Causes of Behaviour* (Boston, Allyn and Bacon, 1962).

LEARNING: GENERAL

BORGER, R. and A. E. M. SEABORNE: *The Psychology of Learning* (London, Penguin, 1966).

*BUGELSKI, B. R.: *The Psychology of Learning* (New York, Holt, 1956; London, Methuen, 1957).

CRAIG, R. C.: *The Psychology of Learning in the Classroom* (New York, Macmillan, 1966; London, Collier-Macmillan, 1966).

CUNY, H. (trs. P. Evans): *Ivan Pavlov* (London, Souvenir Press, 1964).

ELLIS, H.: *The Transfer of Learning* (New York, Macmillan, 1965; London, Collier-Macmillan, 1965).

*GAGNÉ, R. M.: *The Conditions of Learning* (New York and London, Holt, Rinehart, and Winston, 1965).

GARRY, R.: *The Psychology of Learning* (Washington, Centre for Applied Research, 1963; London, Prentice-Hall, 1964).

HARRIS, T. L., and W. E. SCHWAHN (eds.): *Selected Readings on the Learning Process* (Oxford University Press, 1961).

HILGARD, E. R.: *Theories of Learning* (New York, Appleton-Century-Crofts, 1956; London, Methuen, 1959).

HILL, W. F.: *Learning* (San Francisco, Chandler, 1963; London, Methuen, 1964).

HUDGINS, B. B.: *Problem Solving in the Classroom* (New York, Macmillan, 1966; London, Collier-Macmillan, 1966).

JONES, J. C.: *Learning* (New York, Harcourt, Brace, and World, 1967).

MEDNICK, S. A.: *Learning* (New Jersey and London, Prentice-Hall, 1964).

MEREDITH, P.: *Learning, Remembering, and Knowing* (London, English Universities Press, 1961).

*SKINNER, B. F.: *Cumulative Record* (London and New York, Methuen, 1962).

*— *Science and Human Behaviour* (New York and London, Macmillan, 1953).

STEPHENS, J. M.: *The Psychology of Classroom Learning* (New York and London, Holt, Rinehart, and Winston, 1965).

TILTON, J. W.: *An Educational Psychology of Learning* (New York, Macmillan, 1951).

TOWNSEND, E. A., and P. J. BURKE: *Learning for Teachers* (New York and London, Macmillan, 1962).

LEARNING: SPECIAL TOPICS

Classical Experiments
*KÖHLER, W. (trs. E. Winter): *The Mentality of Apes* (London, Routledge and Kegan Paul, 1925; Penguin, 1957).

*THORNDIKE, E. L.: *Animal Intelligence* (London, Macmillan, 1911).

Verbal Learning
*AUSUBEL, D. P.: *The Psychology of Meaningful Verbal Learning* (New York, Grune and Stratton, 1963).

SKINNER, B. F.: *Verbal Behaviour* (London, Methuen, 1959).

Techniques of Study
MACE, C. A.: *The Psychology of Study* (London, Penguin, 1962).

MADDOX, H.: *How to Study* (London, Pan, 1963).

*ROBINSON, F. P.: *Effective Study* (New York and London, Harper and Row, 1961).

Remembering
*BARTLETT, Sir F. C.: *Remembering* (Cambridge University Press, 1932).
HUNTER, I. M. L.: *Memory: Facts and Fallacies* (London, Penguin, 1957).

Trial and Error
*THORNDIKE, E. L.: *The Psychology of Arithmetic* (New York, Macmillan, 1922).

Programmed Learning
CRAM, D.: *Explaining "Teaching Machines" and Programmes* (San Francisco, Fearon, 1961).
DETERLINE, W. A.: *An Introduction to Programmed Instruction* (New Jersey and London, Prentice-Hall, 1962).
LEEDHAM, J., and D. UNWIN: *Programmed Learning in Schools* (London, Longmans, 1965).
MONTAGNON, F., and R. BENNETT (eds.): *What is Programmed Learning?* (London, B.B.C. Publications, 1965).
TABER, J. I., R. GLASER and H. SCHAEFER: *Learning and Programmed Instruction* (Massachusetts and London, Addison-Wesley, 1965).

Aversion Therapy
*KESSEL, N., and H. WALTON: *Alcoholism* (London, Penguin, 1965).

DEVELOPMENT: GENERAL

BALDWIN, A. L.: *Theories of Child Development* (New York and Chichester, Wiley, 1967).
BOWLEY, A. H.: *The Natural Development of the Child* (Edinburgh, E. and S. Livingstone, 1957).
BRECKENRIDGE, M. E., and E. L. VINCENT: *Child Development: Physical and Psychological Growth through Adolescence* (London, Saunders, 1965).
*GESELL, A., and F. L. ILG: *The Child from Five to Ten* (London, Hamish Hamilton, 1946).
HAIMOWITZ, M. L., and N. R. HAIMOWITZ (eds.): *Human Development* (Readings) (New York, Cromwell, 1966).
HAWKES, G. R., and D. PEASE: *Behaviour and Development from Five to Twelve* (New York and London, Harper and Row, 1962).
KUHLEN, R. G., and G. G. THOMPSON: *Psychological Studies of Human Development* (New York, Appleton-Century-Crofts, 1963).
MAIER, H. W.: *Three Theories of Child Development* (New York and London, Harper and Row, 1966).
MILLARD, C. V.: *Child Growth and Development in the Elementary School Years* (Boston, Heath, 1951; London, Harrap, 1951).
MUSSEN, P. H.: *The Psychological Development of the Child* (New Jersey and London, Prentice-Hall, 1963).
—, J. J. CONGER and J. KAGAN (eds.): *Readings in Child Development and Personality* (New York and London, Harper and Row, 1965).

SANDSTRÖM, C. I.: *The Psychology of Childhood and Adolescence* (London, Methuen, 1966).
STRANG, R. M.: *An Introduction to Child Study* (New York and London, Macmillan, 1959).
*TERMAN, L. M., and M. A. MERRILL: *Measuring Intelligence* (London, Harrap, 1937).
THOMPSON, G. G.: *Child Psychology* (Boston, Houghton Mifflin, 1962; London, Lewis, 1962).

DEVELOPMENT: SPECIAL TOPICS

Physical Development

NISBET, J. D., and N. J. ENTWHISTLE: *The Age of Transfer to Secondary Education*, Scottish Council for Research in Education (University of London Press, 1966).
TANNER, J. M.: *Education and Physical Growth* (University of London Press, 1961).

Children's Thinking

BREARLEY, M., and E. HITCHFIELD: *A Teacher's Guide to Reading Piaget* (London, Routledge and Kegan Paul, 1966).
DONALDSON, M.: *A Study of Children's Thinking* (London, Tavistock, 1963).
*FLAVELL, J. H.: *The Developmental Psychology of Jean Piaget* (Princeton and London, Van Nostrand, 1963).
HOLLOWAY, G. E. T.: *An Introduction to the Child's Conception of Geometry* (London, Routledge and Kegan Paul, 1967).
— *An Introduction to the Child's Conception of Space* (London, Routledge and Kegan Paul, 1967).
LOVELL, K.: *The Growth of Basic Mathematical and Scientific Concepts in Children* (University of London Press, 1961).
PEEL, E. A.: *The Pupil's Thinking* (London, Oldbourne, 1960).
Some Aspects of Piaget's Work (various authors) (London, National Froebel Foundation, 1955).

Children's Drawings

HARRIS, D. B.: *Children' Drawings as Measures of Intellectual Maturity* (New York, Harcourt, Brace, and World, 1963; London, Harrap, 1964).

Twin Studies

*NEWMAN, H. H., F. N. FREEMAN and K. J. HOLZINGER: *Twins: A Study of Heredity and Environment* (Chicago University Press, 1937).
SHIELDS, J.: *Monozygotic Twins, Brought up Apart and Brought up Together* (Oxford University Press, 1962).

COGNITION: GENERAL

ANDERSON, R. C., and D. P. AUSUBEL (eds.): *Readings in the Psychology of Cognition* (New York and London, Holt, Rinehart, and Winston, 1965).

BROADBENT, D. E.: *Perception and Communication* (Oxford and New York, Pergamon, 1958).
GEORGE, F. H.: *Cognition* (London, Methuen, 1962).

COGNITION: SPECIAL TOPICS

Thinking
BARTLETT, SIR F. C.: *Thinking* (London, Allen and Unwin, 1958).
*BRUNER, J. S., J. J. GOODNOW and G. A. AUSTIN: *A Study of Thinking* (New York, Wiley, 1956; London, Chapman and Hall, 1956).
HARLOW, H. F.: "Learning to Think", *Scientific American* offprint 415 (London, Freeman, 1949).
HUMPHREY, G.: *Thinking* (London, Methuen, 1951).
MCKELLAR, P.: *Imagination and Thinking* (London, Cohen and West, 1957).
*MILLER, G. A., E. GALANTER and K. H. PRIBAM: *Plans and the Structure of Behaviour* (New York, Holt, Rinehart, and Winston, 1960).
REEVES, J. W.: *Thinking about Thinking* (London, Secker and Warburg, 1965).
SLUCKIN, W.: *Minds and Machines* (London, Penguin, 1954).
THOMSON, R.: *The Psychology of Thinking* (London, Penguin, 1959).

Language and Thinking
CARROLL, J. B.: *Language and Thought* (New Jersey and London, Prentice-Hall, 1964).
LURIA, A. R.: *The Role of Speech in the Regulation of Normal and Abnormal Behaviour* (London, Pergamon, 1961).
—, and F. I. YUDOVITCH: *Speech and the Development of Mental Processes in the Child* (London, Staples, 1959).
*VYGOTSKY, L. S.: *Thought and Language* (Massachusetts Institute of Technology Press, 1962).

ASSESSMENT: GENERAL

AHMANN, J. S.: *Testing Student Achievements and Aptitudes* (Washington D.C., Centre for Applied Research, 1962; London, Prentice-Hall, 1964).
BALLARD, P. B.: *The New Examiner* (University of London Press, 1923).
DAVIS, F. B.: *Educational Measurements and their Interpretation* (California, Wadsworth, 1964; London, Prentice-Hall, 1965).
HULL, C. L.: *Aptitude Testing* (New York, World Book Co., 1928; London, Harrap, 1929).
KARMEL, L. J.: *Testing in our Schools* (New York, Macmillan, 1966; London, Collier-Macmillan, 1966).
NUNNALLY, J. C.: *Educational Measurement and Evaluation* (New York and Maidenhead, McGraw-Hill, 1964).

ASSESSMENT: SPECIAL TOPICS

Elementary Statistics
DOWNIE, N. H., and R. W. HEATH: *Basic Statistical Methods* (New York and London, Harper and Row, 1966).

HUFF, D.: *How to Lie with Statistics* (New York, Norton, 1954; London, Gollancz, 1954)

MCINTOSH, D. M.: *Statistics for the Teacher* (London, Pergamon, 1963).

MANUEL, H. T.: *Elementary Statistics for Teachers* (New York, American Book Co., 1962).

SUMNER, W. L.: *Statistics in School* (Oxford, Blackwell, 1948).

WALKER, H. M.: *Mathematics Essential for Elementary Statistics* (New York, Holt, 1951).

Psychological Testing

ANASTASI, A.: *Psychological Testing* (New York and London, Macmillan, 1968).

CRONBACH, L. J.: *Essentials of Psychological Testing* (New York and London, Harper and Row, 1961).

Examination Construction

BROWN, J.: *Objective Tests: Their Construction and Analysis* (London, Longmans, 1966).

GERBERICH, J. R.: *Specimen Objective Test Items* (London, Longmans, 1956).

GOROW, F. F.: *Better Classroom Testing* (San Francisco, Chandler, 1966).

JACKSON, S.: *A Teacher's Guide to Tests* (London, Longmans, 1968).

Schools Council Examinations Bulletins (1–16) (London, H.M.S.O., 1963–67):
  No. 1: *General* 1963
  No. 3: *Examining Techniques* 1964
  No. 4: *Objective-type Examinations* 1964
  No. 5: *School-based Examinations* 1965
  No. 12: *English Composition* 1966
  No. 16: *Written English* 1967

INTELLIGENCE: GENERAL

ANASTASI, A.: *Differential Psychology* (New York and London, Macmillan, 1958).

BUTCHER, H. J.: *Human Intelligence* (London, Methuen, 1968).

*HEBB, D. O.: *The Organization of Behaviour* (chapter 11) (New York, Wiley, 1949; Chapman and Hall, 1950).

HUNT, J. M.: *Intelligence and Experience* (New York, Ronald Press, 1961).

MATHER, K.: *Human Diversity* (Edinburgh, Oliver and Boyd, 1964).

MAXWELL, J.: *The Level and Trend of National Intelligence*, Scottish Council for Research in Education (University of London Press, 1961).

*SPEARMAN, C.: *The Abilities of Man* (London, Macmillan, 1927).

*THURSTONE, L. L.: *Primary Mental Abilities* (Chicago University Press, 1938).

*VERNON, P. E.: *The Structure of Human Abilities* (London, Methuen, 1950).

WISEMAN, S. (ed.): *Intelligence and Ability* (Readings) (London, Penguin, 1967).

INTELLIGENCE: SPECIAL TOPICS

Intelligence and Education
FLOUD, J., A. H. HALSLEY, and F. M. MARTIN: *Social Class and Educational Opportunity* (London: Heinemann, 1957).
MCINTOSH, D. M.: *Educational Guidance and the Pool of Ability* (University of London Press, 1959).
Social Implications of the 1947 Scottish Mental Survey, Scottish Council for Research in Education (University of London Press, 1953).

Creativity
GETZELS, J. W., and P. W. JACKSON: *Creativity and Intelligence* (New York and Chichester, Wiley, 1962).
HUDSON, L.: "Intelligence: Convergent and Divergent", *Penguin Science Survey* (London, Penguin, 1965).
TORRANCE, E. P.: *Guiding Creative Talent* (New York and London, Prentice-Hall, 1962).

High IQ
FRENCH, J. L. (ed.): *Educating the Gifted* (Readings) (New York and London, Holt, Rinehart, and Winston, 1959).
*STRANG, R.: *Helping your Gifted Child* (New York, Dutton, 1960).
*TERMAN, L. M., and M. H. ODEN: *The Gifted Group at Mid-life* (Stanford University Press, 1959; Oxford University Press, 1959).

Low IQ
CLARKE, A. M., and A. D. B. CLARKE: *Mental Deficiency* (London, Methuen, 1958).
CLEUGH, M. F.: *Teaching the Slow Learner:* vol. ii, "In the Primary School"; vol. iii, "In the Secondary School" (London, Methuen, 1961).
*LLOYD, F.: *Educating the Sub-normal Child* (London, Methuen, 1953).
TANSLEY, A. E., and R. GULLIFORD: *The Education of Slow-Learning Children* (London, Routledge and Kegan Paul, 1960).

Musical Ability
SHUTER, R.: *The Psychology of Musical Ability* (London, Methuen, 1968).

PERSONALITY: GENERAL

*ALLPORT, G. W.: *Pattern and Growth in Personality* (New York and London, Holt, Rinehart, and Winston, 1961).
BROWN, J. A. C.: *Freud and the Post-Freudians* (London, Cassell, 1963; Penguin, 1964).
CATTELL, R. B.: *Personality* (New York and London, McGraw-Hill, 1950).
— *The Scientific Analysis of Personality* (London, Penguin, 1965).
*ERIKSON, E. H.: *Childhood and Society* (New York, Norton, 1963; London, Hogarth, 1964).
*EYSENCK, H. J.: *The Structure of Human Personality* (London, Methuen, 1953).
— *Sense and Nonsense in Psychology* (London, Penguin, 1957).

HAMACHEK, D. E. (ed.): *The Self in Growth, Teaching, and Learning* (New Jersey, Prentice-Hall, 1965).
LAZARUS, R. S.: *Personality and Adjustment* (New Jersey and London, Prentice-Hall, 1963).
— and E. M. OPTON (eds.): *Personality* (Readings) (London, Penguin, 1967).
MUNROE, R. L.: *Schools of Psychoanalytic Thought* (New York and London, Holt, Rinehart, and Winston, 1955).
*ROGERS, C. R.: *Client–centred Therapy* (Boston, Houghton Mifflin, 1951; London, Constable, 1965).
*— *On Becoming a Person* (London, Constable, 1962).
*— and R. F. DYMOND: *Psychotherapy and Personality Change* (Chicago University Press, 1954).
*SHELDON, W. H., S. S. STEVENS, and W. B. TUCKER: *Varieties of Human Physique* (New York, Harper, 1940).
— *Varieties of Human Temperament* (New York, Harper, 1942).
— *Varieties of Delinquent Youth* (New York, Harper, 1949).

PERSONALITY: SPECIAL TOPICS

Motivation
BINDRA, D., and J. STEWART (eds.): *Motivation* (Readings) (London, Penguin, 1966).
*MASLOW, A. H.: *Motivation and Personality* (New York, and London, Harper and Row, 1954).

Personality Assessment
SEMEONOFF, B. (ed.): *Personality Assessment* (Readings) (London, Penguin, 1966).
VERNON, P. E.: *Personality Assessment* (London, Methuen, 1964.)

SOCIAL CONTEXT: GENERAL

ARGYLE, M.: *The Psychology of Interpersonal Behaviour* (London: Penguin, 1967).
— *The Scientific Study of Social Behaviour* (London, Methuen, 1957).
*BANTON, M.: *Roles* (London, Tavistock, 1965).
BANY, M. A., and L. V. JOHNSTON: *Classroom Group Behaviour* (New York, Macmillan, 1964; London, Collier-Macmillan, 1964).
BELL, N. W., and E. F. VOGEL: *A Modern Introduction to the Family* (London, Routledge and Kegan Paul, 1961).
BLYTH, W. A. L.: *English Primary Education* (London, Routledge and Kegan Paul, 1965).
GABRIEL, J.: *Children Growing Up* (University of London Press, 1964).
*MUSGROVE, F.: *The Family, Education, and Society* (London, Routledge and Kegan Paul, 1966).
SPROTT, W. J. H.: *Human Groups* (London, Penguin, 1958).

SOCIAL CONTEXT: SPECIAL TOPICS

Child Rearing
DOUGLAS, J. W. B.: *The Home and the School* (London, MacGibbon and Kee, 1964).
SEARS, R. R., E. E. MACCOBY, and H. LEVIN: *Patterns of Child Rearing* (New York and London, Harper and Row, 1957).

Social Learning
BANDURA, A., and R. H. WALTERS: *Social Learning and Personality Development* (New York and London, Holt, Rinehart, and Winston, 1963).
BERKOWITZ, L.: *The Development of Motives and Values in the Child* (New York and London, Basic Books, 1964).
JAHODA, M., and N. WARREN (eds.): *Attitudes* (Readings) (London, Penguin, 1966).

Adolescence
BLOS, P.: *On Adolescence: a Psycho-analytical Interpretation* (London, Collier-Macmillan, 1962).
*HALL, G. S.: *Adolescence* (two vols., London and New York, Appleton, 1904).
JERSILD, A. T.: *The Psychology of Adolescence* (New York, and London, Macmillan, 1957).

Teachers
GAGE, N. L. (ed.): *Handbook of Research on Teaching* (Chicago, Rand-McNally, 1963).
RYANS, D. G.: *The Characteristics of Teachers* (Washington D.C., American Council on Education, 1960).

HANDICAPPED CHILDREN: GENERAL

CHESS, S.: *Introduction to Child Psychiatry* (New York, Grune and Stratton, 1959).
CRUIKSHANK, W. (ed.): *Psychology of Exceptional Children and Youth* (London, Staples, 1956; New Jersey, Prentice-Hall, 1956).
EGG, M.: *When a Child is Different* (London, Allen and Unwin, 1967).
GARRISON, K. C., and D. G. FORCE: *The Psychology of Exceptional Children* (New York, Ronald Press, 1965).
MACLEAN, I. C.: *Child Guidance and the School* (London, Methuen, 1966).
ROSS, A. O.: *The Practice of Clinical Child Psychology* (New York, Grune and Stratton, 1959).
ROUCEK, J. (ed.): *The Unusual Child* (London, Owen, 1962).

HANDICAPPED CHILDREN: SPECIAL TOPICS

Maladjusted Children
The Ascertainment of Maladjusted Children, Scottish Education Department (London, H.M.S.O., 1964).
BETTELHEIM, B.: *Love is not Enough* (Illinois, Free Press, 1950; London, Allen and Unwin, 1952).

HOWELLS, J. G. (ed.): *Modern Perspectives in Child Psychiatry* (Edinburgh, Oliver and Boyd).

JONES, H.: *Reluctant Rebels* (London, Tavistock, 1961).

Maladjusted Children (Departmental Report, Ministry of Education) (London, H.M.S.O., 1955).

MAXWELL, S. M. (ed.): *Emotionally Disturbed Children* (London and New York, Pergamon, 1966).

REDL, F., and D. WINEMAN: *The Aggressive Child* (New York, Basic Books, 1957; London, Collier-Macmillan, 1957).

RYLE, A.: *Neurosis in the Ordinary Family* (London, Tavistock, 1967).

SHAW, O. L.: *Maladjusted Boys* (London, Allen and Unwin, 1965).

Survey into the Progress of Maladjusted Pupils (London, Greater London Council, 1965).

WEST, D.: *The Young Offender* (London, Duckworth, 1967; Penguin, 1967).

Socially Deprived Children

PRINGLE, M. L. K.: *Deprivation and Education* (London, Longmans, 1965).

RIESSMAN, F.: *The Culturally Deprived Child* (New York and London, Harper and Row, 1962).

Index

Problem Solving
Principle
Concept
Multiple Discrimination
Chaining